RETHINKING GENDER AND THERAPY

RETHINKING GENDER AND THERAPY

The changing identities of women

Edited by
Susannah Izzard
and
Nicola Barden

Open University Press
Buckingham · Philadelphia

Open University Press
Celtic Court
22 Ballmoor
Buckingham
MK18 1XW

email: enquiries@openup.co.uk
world wide web: www.openup.co.uk

and

325 Chestnut Street
Philadelphia, PA 19106, USA

First Published 2001

A catalogue record of this book is available from the British Library

ISBN   0 335 20606 9 (pb)   0 335 20607 7 (hb)

Library of Congress Cataloging-in-Publication Data
Rethinking gender and therapy : inner world, outer world, and the developing
identity of women / edited by Susannah Izzard and Nicola Barden.
    p. cm.
   Includes bibliographical references and index.
   ISBN 0–335–20607–7 (hb) – ISBN 0–335–20606–9 (pbk.)
    1. Women and psychoanalysis.   2. Women–Psychology.   3. Gender
   identity.   4. Social sciences and psychoanalysis.   I. Izzard, Susannah,
   1959–   II. Barden, Nicola.
BF173 .R449 2001
155.3'33–dc21   2001021074

Typeset by Graphicraft Limited, Hong Kong
Printed in Great Britain by Biddles Limited, Guildford and King's Lynn

Contents

Notes on contributors		vii
Acknowledgements		xi
	Introduction	1
	Susannah Izzard and Nicola Barden	
1	The development of gender identity	6
	Nicola Barden	
2	When do I know I'm a girl? The development of a sense of self as female in the early infant	30
	Susan Vas Dias	
3	Adolescence: possibilities and limitations, experience and expression	51
	Moira Walker	
4	Women's friendships: theory and therapy	78
	Chess Denman	
5	Women and work	103
	Eileen Aird	
6	Women and intimacy	118
	Marie Maguire	
7	Nine-tenths of the pleasure: sexual expression and the female body	141
	Geraldine Shipton	
8	Creating space: women without children	162
	Susannah Izzard	

9 Emotional experiences of becoming a mother   180
   Joan Raphael-Leff

10 'An awfully big adventure': ageing, identity and gender   204
   June Blythe Ellis

   Afterword   228
   Nicola Barden and Susannah Izzard

Index   231

Notes on contributors

Eileen Aird is a psychoanalytic psychotherapist working in private practice, and the Clinical Director of the Women's Therapy Centre, London. Previous posts have included staff tutor in literature, Department of Adult Education, Newcastle University; organizing tutor in women's education, Workers Education, Northern District; Assistant General Secretary, WEA and Principal of Hillcroft College for Women. She is the author of *Sylvia Plath* (1973, Oliver and Boyd), *The Business of a Woman's Life: Re-reading Jane Eyre* (1992, NEC and Virago) and several articles on literature, women's education and counselling. She was the founding editor of the literary journal *Writing Women* and on the editorial board for several WEA publications.

Nicola Barden is currently Head of Counselling Services at the University of Portsmouth, a UKCP-registered psychoanalytic psychotherapist and a BACP registered practitioner. She is editor of the *Journal of the British Association for Counselling and Psychotherapy*, chair of the BACP Registration Committee and a past member of the Standards and Ethics Committee. She worked in the voluntary sector with alcohol and drug problems before beginning to work in higher education in 1991. Her particular interests are in gender identity and sexuality.

Dr Chess Denman is Consultant Psychiatrist in Psychotherapy at Addenbrooke's Hospital, Cambridge, and has trained in Jungian analysis at the Society of Analytical Psychotherapy; she is now an associate professional member. Also, she has trained in cognitive analytic therapy, under Dr Anthony Ryle, and is the chair of Training of the Association of Cognitive Analytic Therapists. She has maintained a long-standing interest in issues of sexuality and sexual identity, and has published articles and book chapters in this area.

June Blythe Ellis is a tutor on the MA in Psychodynamic Counselling at the University of Birmingham. She has a strong interest in early development and is a seminar leader in infant observation for the West Midlands Training in Jungian psychotherapy. She has taught at universities in the USA, West Africa and the United Kingdom, and has been involved in social work education. Arising from research in Ghana, she edited *West African Children in Britain* (1978, RKP) which examined issues that arise from differences in culture. A move into residential work at the Quaker Study Centre, Woodbrooke, in Birmingham, was followed by a Jungian psychotherapy training and she is now in private practice in Herefordshire.

Susannah Izzard is a UKCP-registered psychoanalytic psychotherapist in private practice, and Lecturer in Counselling at the University of Birmingham, where she runs the MA in Psychodynamic Counselling. She has written on gay and lesbian issues in psychoanalytic work and training, and on gender identity in women. Her research interests include personal development in counselling training, and spirituality and psychotherapy.

Marie Maguire is a psychoanalytic psychotherapist in private practice in south London. She teaches at the Guild of Psychotherapists and at other training organizations. She previously worked at the Women's Therapy Centre, London. She is the co-editor of *Psychotherapy with Women* (1996, Macmillan), and wrote *Men, Women, Passion and Power* (1995, Routledge).

Joan Raphael-Leff is Professor of Psychoanalysis at the Centre for Psychoanalytic Studies at the University of Essex and chair of the International Psychoanalytic Association's Committee on Women and Psychoanalysis. Since qualification as a psychoanalyst in 1976 she has specialized in treating people with reproductive and parenting issues and has over 50 publications in this field, including several books: *Psychological Processes of Childbearing* (1991, Chapman and Hall); *Pregnancy – The Inside Story* (1993, Sheldon); *Female Experience – Three Generations of British Women Psycho-analysts on Work with Women* (co-edited with Rosine Josef Perelberg, 1997, Routledge); *Spilt Milk – Perinatal Loss and Breakdown* (ed.) (2000, British Institute of Psychoanalysis). Past and present duties include Executive Committees of the Marce Society for Prevention of Puerperal Illness; Royal Society of Medicine's Forum and the Newborn; Association of Infant Mental Health; external consultancy to the Anna Freud Centre under-5s section; Parent Infant Centre; Tavistock's Marital Studies Institute and various perinatal projects overseas.

Geraldine Shipton is the director of the Centre for Psychotherapeutic Studies at the University of Sheffield. She also runs the MA in

Psychoanalytic Psychotherapy there and is editor of the journal *Psycho-analytic Studies*. She has a private practice in Sheffield and is particularly interested in eating disorders and body-image.

Susan Vas Dias is an attachment-based psychoanalytic psychotherapist. She is a training therapist, supervisor, teacher, and chair of the Clinical Training Committee for the Centre for Attachment-based Psychoanalytic Psychotherapy in London. She trained as a child and adolescent psycho-therapist at the Hampstead Child Therapy Clinic under Anna Freud, becoming a member of staff on qualification. In 1982 she became the first child and adolescent psychotherapist at St Bartholomew's Hospital in London. She has worked in the National Health Service for 25 years. Currently she is Consultant Paediatric Psychotherapist in the Children's Services at the Royal London Hospital. She has published many articles over the years. Some of the more recent titles include: The complexity of change: developing child and family-centred care in a Russian children's hospital (1997) in *Clinical Child Psychology and Psychiatry*, 2(3): 343–52. In conjunction with the BBC Television Series *QED-Challenging Children* an article titled Baby love was published in *QED Challenging Children* (1997, London: BBC Learning Support, pp. 3–9). Inner silence: one of the impacts of emotional abuse upon the developing self was published in *Psychodynamic Perspectives on Abuse: The Cost of Fear* (2000, Una McCluskey and Carol-Ann Hooper (eds), London: Jessica Kingsley, pp. 159–72).

Moira Walker is a part-time lecturer in counselling at Birkbeck College, University of London. She is a psychotherapist, trainer and counsellor with particular interest in the issues women bring to therapy, and in working with adult survivors of childhood abuse. She writes in both these fields and has trained and supervised extensively others who work in these areas, particularly within the voluntary sector and health and social services. She previously worked for many years at Leicester University, initially as the Head of the Counselling Service and then as a Lecturer in Counselling and Psychotherapy where she co-directed both counselling and psychotherapy trainings. She now lives in Dorset and divides her life and work between there and London.

Acknowledgements

We wish to thank Michael Jacobs in particular for his editorial skill, his clear guidance in dilemmas and his encouragement at every turn. We also wish to thank the contributors to this book for what they have offered to us and to the readership.

Susannah would like to thank: Paul, whose love and support remains independent of what I achieve or do, and whose containing presence in my life makes thought and adventuring possible; Nicola – my relationship with her is a source of joy and an agent of challenge and change; my female friends, for enriching my experience of myself as a woman and as a woman-in-relationship; my patients and students, for teaching me more than I know, about the world and a person's place in it; and my father, whose interest in and capacity to learn about things outside his experience is impressive, and for reading and responding to my chapter.

Nicola is grateful to those colleagues, clients and friends who have persistently required and enabled me to think differently about gender; to Susannah, for fulfilling this and more as both friend and colleague; to my family, for never expecting less of girls; and especially to Caro, for her consistent love, generous support, and for always adding spice to life.

Introduction

Susannah Izzard and Nicola Barden

> What is most important is not whether the feminine is defined by society or endemic to the person but whether or not women themselves determine the content and the conclusions of those definitions.
>
> (Chittister 1998: 3)

Books on women abound in the libraries of sociological and psychological texts. There are books on women as client groups, as sociological phenomena, books on the specific issues that they face or represent in culture and society. There are psychoanalytic books on the female psyche, attempting to rework and resolve the tradition of women as the second sex, the 'other', the deviation from the norm which is male.

What we have set out to do in this book is to bring together the psychoanalytic and the sociological, the internal and the external, by seeking to explore the interplay between the two. How does the way a woman is regarded by society affect how she experiences herself in relation to that society, and how does that experience in turn impact on her conception of her own identity, how she regards herself? We know that we need to 'belong', to feel we 'fit' – whether we are men or women – so we wished to explore what it is that is presented to women as 'that into which they must fit' in order to feel that they are recognizably Female. We also wished to think about what happens to a woman's identity when she feels outside of that 'fit' – when she cannot see herself mirrored in the images that society presents to her of 'Woman'. How does our society constrain women into or release them from narrow definitions and what part does psychoanalytic theory and practice play in such constraining or releasing?

Our thinking about the book was to include particular stages during a woman's life and particular aspects of her life in the world, and to ask various authors to address the above questions. Each contributor to this book has done this in her own way, and the resulting diversity of approaches is something we have come to value.

The scene is set by Chapter 1, 'The development of gender identity', with a discussion by Nicola Barden of the nature of gender identity and how this develops within the growing girl. She raises the possibility that perhaps the wrong question about gender is being asked in that the question about *how* the two genders are shaped or maintained avoids a more fundamental one. This question is about whether the only way to construe gender is via the model of two opposing poles. This model, she suggests, constrains both men and women, forcing them to place themselves on either side of a divide, which is in essence restrictive and does not permit a variety of expression in either gender. Barden suggests that the different debate may be about whether the gender divisions are seen as functional only, which then opens up the possibility of a multiform distribution of gender-based potentials whereby women (and men) are given the freedom to express their gendered selves in an infinite variety of ways.

In 'When do I know I'm a girl?' Susan Vas Dias looks at the beginnings of conscious gender identity by considering the development of the baby girl. Through clearly differentiating between the infant's own experience of themselves as gendered, and the external world's assumptions about that experience, Vas Dias emphasizes the importance of questioning the assumptive base that can underlie analytic interpretations of the infant's experience of gender. She draws out the role of the attachment world in shaping gender identity and places this alongside the biological and neurological development that is taking place in the first two years of life. In calling attention to the crucial distinction between the infant's actual sense of their own gender, and the observer's expectations of this, she demonstrates the importance of leaving space for authentic gender identity to develop as part of the 'Who am I?' question that the infant brings in relation to the world.

In 'Adolescence: possibilities and limitations, experience and expression', Moira Walker explores the confusions and agonies, the excitement and adventure of the female adolescent's experience. She discusses the culture-related nature of the experience of adolescence and the prevalence of a male bias in much psychoanalytic writing about this stage of psychosocial development. In particular this bias has resulted in a separation of identity from intimacy, whereas research suggests that young women experience their capacity for intimacy as closely related to, and a determinant of, their identity. Walker describes adolescence as a time of heightened psychological risk for girls, and due to the very specific images promoted by the group, a time of marginalization for many.

In 'Women's friendships: theory and therapy', Chess Denman draws on Cognitive Analytic Therapy (CAT) and her own revised sociological analysis of relationships to explore the nature of women's friendships among lesbian and straight women. She makes use of the notion of 'reciprocal roles' offered by CAT. This suggests that as girls are socialized in ways that encourage intimacy, disclosure and trust, they will develop reciprocal role templates in friendships that feature these things, but may find that they are impoverished as regards their capacity to take up a constructive role in relation to aggression and assertion. CAT sees the establishment of these reciprocal roles as being culturally determined, and Denman suggests that much of our social behaviour is governed by large structures that limit freedom.

Eileen Aird in 'Women and work' explores the division between the private and public worlds of work, and the employed woman's conflicts over power and authority. She suggests that there is often a clash between 'feminine' modes of communication and caring, and the male dominated culture of the world of paid work, and explores the impact of this clash on the woman's psyche. She argues that the distinction between domestic and public economy creates a false division in the female psyche, leaving women with the task of managing as internal a conflict that is actually a manifestation of external gender divides.

Marie Maguire, in 'Women and intimacy', looks at the issues that face women as they seek to form or sustain intimate relationships, and argues that psychoanalytic theory is polarized between mother- and father-centred perspectives. She suggests that we need to link Object Relations' insights about mother–daughter identification with a feminist Freudian Oedipal perspective if we are to understand women's conflicts about intimacy and independence. She illustrates how traditional analytic understandings of sexual object choice have obscured more fundamental questions about the nature of women's experiences of intimacy with both men and women.

In 'Nine-tenths of the pleasure: sexual expression and the female body', Geraldine Shipton discusses women's sexual pleasure and how it is expressed against a background of shifting attitudes to the body, sexuality and gender. She highlights the fact that there is no pre-cultural female body or sexuality, but a socially constructed metaphor. The woman's sexual use of her own body is explored, and Shipton discusses how this is affected by the conscious and unconscious knowledge the girl has of her own and her mother's body. This is further influenced by the experience of being a girl in a world where the feminine body is shaped not only by anatomy but by the predominating power structures.

In 'Creating space: women without children' Susannah Izzard explores the impact on the woman's identity of not having children. Viewed by society as a 'lack', a woman without a child is seen as at best to be pitied, at worst to be judged. Izzard explores the roots of pronatalism, and suggests a way of thinking about adult female identity that is independent from the assumption that motherhood is an essential aspect of womanhood. Women without children are a challenge to the bipolar division of the sexes, and must pioneer a pathway in which they can experience themselves and be experienced as fully female while not fulfilling conventional expectations.

In Chapter 9 Joan Raphael-Leff explores the emotional experience of women who *are* mothers in the new millennium. She suggests that far from being 'normal, natural and instinctive', each woman's experience of maternity is a compromise formation between the maternal situation itself and the often conflicting facets of her own past, present and future aspirations. Raphael-Leff draws attention to the power of the mother's internal identifications and unresolved infantile experience. She also suggests that there are differing 'orientations' towards the baby that produce different styles of mothering and therefore different causes of maternal distress.

In 'An awfully big adventure: ageing, identity and gender', June Blythe Ellis suggests that the significance of ageing for women's identity has been neglected. She examines how ways of framing women biologically have resulted in the societal view of older women as invisible. Ellis argues that restrictive and prejudiced perspectives on the ageing woman can be challenged by an exploration of the diverse experience of women in mid-life and beyond, which demands the inclusion of notions of freedom and development in our understanding of this life stage. Ellis suggests that Jungian theory, cleansed of its sexist bias, may provide a basis for understanding women's identity in later life.

There are many unwritten chapters in this book: preschool children; girls in education; women and religious experience. There are analytic themes that clearly need further exploration, such as the crucial issue of Oedipal configurations in the formation of gender identity. Perhaps there is a sense in which the book can only be a beginning, as more and more aspects of women's lives come to mind that require this sort of analysis. The task of reflecting on the interrelationship of inner and outer, of psychoanalytic thought and sociological analysis belongs to each therapist, analyst or counsellor, and is the work of each unique couple in the therapeutic encounter. It is our hope that these chapters will encourage further thought, and a more fruitful discourse between the two areas of experience.

All case examples in the chapters are either from the authors' own experiences, or are fictionalized abstractions from one or more cases. In each instance they are intended to serve an illustrative rather than evidential function. Where individual clients are discussed, names and personal details have been changed.

Reference

Chittister, J. (1998) *Heart of Flesh: A Feminist Spirituality for Women and Men.* Grand Rapids, MI/Cambridge: William B. Eerdmans Publishing Company.

1   The development of gender identity

Nicola Barden

Introduction

At some point, being female becomes a core definition of the self. The definition includes an internal and an external experience, the inner and outer shaping each other, and this circular influence of inner and outer continues throughout the whole of life. The question of how gender identity is formed is an important one; at times 'male' and 'female' are the most significant descriptions that are applied to the self, and probably the most frequently used.

The more traditional concerns about gender identity have centred around aetiological debates, often crudely segmented into 'nature' versus 'nurture', hunting for a settlement as to where gender comes from and where it should belong. To this day the debate is argumentative rather than conclusive, in psychotherapy as well as in social and biological studies. This is perhaps not surprising, as the enterprise does to a degree appear to attempt to apply reductionism to an outcome in which the whole remains more than the sum of its parts – definitive statements about the origins or content of gender never seem to do it justice. Oedipal theory has been a central analytic player in this pursuit, and feminist thinking has done much to broaden the field of the debate. Yet the area remains full of contradictions.

To consider the development of gender, several areas should be addressed that are all too often left out: the actual experience of girls and women – their voices, their position in society, their self-definitions and own narratives; the context of the world in which girls are allowed to experience themselves as gendered, and the effect of this on the experiencing of gender. Equally important are the effects of this context on the development of analytic theory. In relation to the latter, theoretical concepts of gender identity have used as source material the constructs of masculinity and femininity and, allied to this, of heterosexual complementarity. Discussion in this chapter of the development of gender identity will include examination of the assembly of these constructs, with particular reference to new perspectives opened up through recent work on transgender and transsexual issues. The relationship of such constructs to the psyche of the individual woman is central to the meaning of this chapter, which must throughout pay attention to the task of developing a sense of gendered identity.

Gender identity

> Isolated from the rest of the continent, the descendants of the American aborigines preserved their way of life for thousands of years. They even appear to have kept alive their rituals. The 1930s expeditions recorded secret initiation ceremonies . . . The tribal wisdom taught to the Fueguian initiates was secret. It was only revealed to the men. The women were kept in the dark. Any speculation about it was, and still is, strictly taboo . . . What was so secret that had to be kept from the women? Some of the chiefs confiding to ethnographers, explained that there was a time in the very distant past when women ruled society. The women must never know, lest the men lose their grip on power.
>
> (BBC 1999: 17)

All accounts of the development of gender identity harbour a value system. Gender is used to define rather than simply to describe; it is used to communicate meaning, and at the same time to keep the meaning secret, in order to preserve it. Underlying the secrecy is the knowledge that the definitions are inherently unstable – otherwise, they would not need such fierce protection. The anxiety and unnamed dread that are fed by this denial can be measured in the resistance met by attempts to alter, tear down or reform the scaffolding that supports gender structures; yet such attempts persist, attesting to the inadequacy of the structures as containers for real recognition of gender issues.

The work of feminist thinkers in the twentieth century has done much to make these structures visible, and their influence has extended across social and analytic thinking. What has become familiar is the challenge to objectivity; the position from which something is viewed will influence *how* it is viewed, and this is as true for the consulting room as for anywhere else. This understanding was not so readily available to Freud, Jung and others who initiated the analytic enterprise, and of course their work reflects this. Unfortunately, some of the essence of this confusion has been transferred into the current debate over whether gender identity is essential or relative, which quickly becomes allied with the nature/nurture debate. Freud himself saw that this question was not going to lead anywhere, understanding that theoretical attempts to separate the elements out would do little to reflect the complexity of identity actually found in practice (Freud [1920] 1990a).

This 'wrong' question is one of several faultlines observable in analytic thinking, which have the effect of breaking continuity of thought while seeming to facilitate it. Other faultlines I shall consider are the conflation of gender identity with sexual identity; the assumption of heterosexual complementarity, and its consequent normalization; and the acceptance of the binary gender divide as a discrete and complete summation of gender possibilities.

The consideration of these problems will show their effects on the question of how women develop a sense of gendered identity, and how it is that an individual girl or woman must pick her way through the gender maze, where the promise of reaching a single goal is in itself a questionable formulation of the point and outcome of the journey.

Feminine and masculine

Freud opened the search for something distinctive in the categories of masculine and feminine. His Oedipal theory facilitated the understanding of the development of little boys first, with girls' development viewed in relation to this. Masculine quickly became normative, and feminine derivative. Some authors have continued to hold this view (Mitchell 1990), and enlarged the understanding of the girl's position from this prior acceptance of the prime significance of the phallus. Others have come to the question from the object relations school, looking at the primacy of the mother in the formation of identificatory relationships (Chodorow 1994; Benjamin 1998). Freud himself maintained an ambivalence around his descriptions of female development. On the one hand, he linked femininity with passivity, and masculinity with activity. On the other hand, he acknowledged that these divisions did little to further real understanding (Freud [1932] 1990b). The analogies were derived largely from anatomy, and this had its limitations in being transferred to psychological states. Nevertheless, he maintained that the libidinal drive was active and therefore essentially masculine and, famously, that the female superego would be less developed than the male because of the different resolution of the Oedipus complex. Although Freud arrived at this view through considerations of conscious and unconscious dynamics, it is a theory which already had its place in European culture. Mary Wollstonecraft had written in 1792 (1992: 100),

> To account for, and excuse the tyranny of man, many ingenious arguments have been brought forward to prove, that the two sexes, in the acquirement of virtue, ought to aim at attaining a very different character; or, to speak explicitly, women are not allowed to have sufficient strength of mind to acquire what really deserves the name of virtue.

We need to remember that Freud's thinking was developed in the context of his time.

Another division in the debate is between those who believe there is something essentially different between the sexes, and those who believe those differences to be so indefinable or so socially controlled as to be meaningless. Baker Miller (1988), writing around the same time as Mitchell (1990), emphasized the relational aspect of women's development. Baker Miller postulated that women grow up in a world that supports male values, where these values of autonomy and separation are seen as central to healthy growth into adulthood. Behaviour that is different from this is less developed, less 'adult'. Women pay more attention to relationship, not only because of society's expectation but because of the unique nature of the mother–infant bond, and the subsequent identification with the mother that encourages relationship as central to experience. Women are by definition therefore less developed than men, as according to the hegemonic paradigm they are less autonomous and so less adult. This position is reached by perceiving the valuing of autonomy as a fact rather than as a value; other equally valuable roads to adulthood exist, including the relational one, and Baker Miller argues that if these were given equal consideration then women would no longer be allocated the psychologically subordinate position.

The relational theme of women's development has been followed through by many authors, not least by Gilligan (1993), who has conducted several studies with young girls in the United States. Listening to their subjective experiences of girlhood led to understanding core themes of what could be construed as a feminine aspect, though perhaps not an inherent one. Gilligan (1993) rejects the nature/nurture debate as disturbing and disempowering; it offers a frame that puts power 'out there', whereas her emphasis is on the individual's psychological capacity to make choices and change, whatever the circumstances. Inherent in this is the need to speak, and the need to listen (Taylor *et al.* 1997). Women are taught the art of listening, men of speaking (Freud's active and passive); this makes true dialogue difficult. The divide is not only across gender; other systems involving power, including race, class and sexuality, silence voices that would make up the human wholeness.

The experience of the Understanding Adolescence Study (Taylor *et al.* 1997) was of a complex interrelationship between race, gender, culture and class. The growth of psychoanalysis in Europe took its own culture as normal and so viewed others as different. In so doing it missed the vast range of norms that impact on gender development. Taylor cites the example of the 'othermother' tradition in many black communities that gives girls access to a number of significant relationships with women in extended family groupings. These kinship bonds form a platform from which to understand and combat racism, a struggle that could not be shared in the same way with other white girls or white women. The effect of racism on gender identity is complex for black girls growing up in a white society, where images of beauty and desirability are all white, and to be acceptably feminine may conflict with important cultural identities. Conflicts become manageable through silence, at a cost of disassociation from personal identity. It is only through the inner self finding recognition in relationship with another that the core sense of self is re-established. The power dynamic between white and black has meant that until relatively recently white people have spoken, black people have listened, parallel to the gender dynamic.

> An example of this occured in a Further Education institution, which ran a vocational course with forty participants. Thirty seven were white, three were black, two men and one woman. After the second week, the three black students began to sit together. This caused comment amongst the white students, who felt the black students were being segregationist. The fact that the majority of the white students could sit together most of the time without causing comment was not considered; it was an invisible fact, because it was the norm. In this setting, the common ground of race was more significant than that of gender, although the dynamic of both was present throughout.

The point so well made by Taylor is that people do not talk to and listen to each other as a whole group; subgroups find ways to communicate, to identify, sometimes to hear across difference; but all too often this is stopped by fear of what the other has to say, of being required to change, which is always difficult, of being for a while in a place of no resolution. This is painful for those with power, for it threatens loss of power, and more painful still for those without, for the vulnerability it entails. This dynamic has resulted in women's voices that have tried to speak against the norms of gender being heard as strident, emasculating, unfeminine, and therefore being dismissed.

It remains difficult to know whether relational capacities are *inherently* more female than male; Gilligan's point (1993) is that, at the moment, it does not really matter. Yet there are some areas in which it does seem to matter, and a contemporary debate is raging fiercely over this issue. The book *Why Men Don't Iron* (Moir and Moir 1999), postulating inherent biological differences between the genders that explain gender inequalities, was televised in three parts, such was the public interest in the subject. What is interesting about the book is not so much its findings, but the use made of them. Central to its concept is an acceptance that hormonal, physical and brain functioning differences between the sexes, identifiable through scientific experimentation, have an inevitable outcome on gender identity and in fact explain most of the differences in place today. From these findings Moir and Moir completely repudiate the 'bisexual fallacy': homo- and heterosexuality are both biologically determined; there is no intermediate female side in most males. Moir and Moir also argue that vegetarianism is unhealthy for men, and the denial of 'real meat' in the male diet is tantamount to an attempt at feminization; exposure of the brain to male hormones in the womb 'masculinizes' it and this explains differences in achievements and character (for example risk taking, spatial awareness, relational capacities); difference in sexual drive is also explained by physiological events. The book seems packed with red-blooded testosterone, and certainly speaks to a generation of men – and women – who have had to experience changes that they were not in control of, and which have been unsettling and frightening.

Clare (2000) approaches the same subject from a substantially different perspective. He considers the position of men in today's society, uncertain and confused by changes in employment and relationship patterns, adapting to new expectations that feel hard or impossible to meet, failure to meet them sometimes bringing serious consequences of suicide and depression. He takes issue with the idea that biological factors are primarily responsible for male characteristics such as aggression and competetiveness, and does not agree that such characteristics are indicators of masculinity. His emphasis lies on the release of masculinity from precisely these sorts of stereotypes, recognizing that the changes women have begun can also be in men's interest – more value on relationship and community, less on power, possessions and achievement.

It is interesting that current books on the development of women do not focus with such intensity on the cause of difference. One wonders what the arguments might really be about. It is clear that Moir and Moir feel that masculinity is under attack, and they defend it with passion; they leave little room for questioning the meaning of masculinity. They certainly do not seek to place it in any relationship to the feminine, unless to the feminine of old, defined by its relationship to the masculine. What seems to concern them deeply is any confusion or alignment between male and female. Moir and Moir separate homosexuality from heterosexuality very clearly, likewise for masculinity and femininity. Clare seems less anxious about this, more interested in the possibility of movement between the two.

Now, why is this of relevance to the development of female gender identity? Perhaps the nature/nurture argument serves to further the wider purpose of maintaining the dimorphic gender position. As long as the discussion focuses on *how* two genders are shaped and maintained, there is no discussion over *whether* this is in fact the only way to construe gender, in two distinct and opposite poles. The creation of binary divides along gender and sexuality lines are so ubiquitous that there is a temptation to see them as purely 'natural', but a good look at nature quickly shows it to be so polymorphous and diverse as to make a nonsense of such a statement. And what is psychoanalysis, if not in part an examination of the natural into its component parts, revealing not a single edifice, but a potential for many natural outcomes?

The consequence of this is that individuals may be faced with apparently natural gender choices, which are in fact highly constructed. A client, Jane, told her therapist the following experience from her childhood:

> Jane, at age 7, was taken to a 'Wild West' show with a group of other children. Horse riding stunts were a part of the show – riding bareback, standing up, controlling several horses at once, and so on. At one point there was a call for any children who wanted to have a go at this to come to the front. Jane ran down, the only girl to do so, with half a dozen boys. There was a harness, fixed to a scaffold, which was to be attached to the children to enable them to 'stand up' while riding the horse. Jane marched straight up to the horse. She was lifted up, sat on the horse, walked around the ring, lifted off again, and the audience was asked to give her a round of applause. The next child was likewise sat on the horse; the harness was then attached to him, the music played, and the harness winched him to a standing position, carefully moving with the horse so he could 'stand' on its back as it trotted round the ring. At the end he was released from the harness, flushed with success; again, the crowd applauded. All the other boys were given rides with the harness. The show then continued. Jane, back in her seat, was puzzled. Something different had just happened to her, but she did not know exactly what, or why. She thought she must have done something wrong to have been denied the full ride. She felt disappointed and guilty, but she did not say anything, and nothing was said to her.

This event taught Jane something about the nature of being a girl. On one level, she received the message that girls are less adventurous and more in need of protection than boys. Slightly deeper was the communication that girls should be able to accept and hold the expectations of gender difference within themselves – no adult commented on her different treatment, which was perhaps not even seen as different, only as gender syntonic. If gender difference – whether born or made – is accepted as a basis for different treatment, Jane had to make a choice between being a girl or expressing her desires – the two things had become oppositional. To bring them together, she would have to be a girl who wanted to be like a boy.

The actual content of gender differences are not relevant to the problems with this scenario, nor is the issue of whether such differences are stereotypes or truth. The problem is that division between the genders has in itself taken on an ordering function for what is the inherently untidy process of identity; attempts to contain chaos have resulted in rigid structures that are in a relationship of opposition rather than dialogue. Foucault's view that 'identities are derived not from essences but constructed by discourse' (Benjamin 1995: 11) underlines the difficulties of developing an authentic sense of gendered identity when the choice is to be either a boy or a girl – categories that have assimilated so much meaning that they have gone far beyond any original simple reference to biological sex. Although this is eased by the distinction between sex and gender, in practice much of psychotherapy still operates as if the two are the same, and there are 'proper' masculinities and femininities to be developed. This leaves girls in a complex dilemma in terms of finding authentic expression for the self. The 'girl' category can only encompass so much of life, and it is allowed a limited amount of coterminosity with the 'boy' category. So girls who behave in stereotypically male ways are given the in-between status of 'tomboy' – both pseudo boy and pseudo girl. This allows them to be 'boys' for a while as they grow up, without renouncing girlhood, or heterosexuality. The irony is that both society and therapy can see this as an indication of cross-gender identification (hence the concern about sexuality) without seeing that such identification is one of the few choices a girl has if she wants to express parts of herself that now belong to the male domain. The other choice is to stay within the girl's domain, and either repudiate the 'masculine' wishes or disguise them in a manipulation of femininity (Kaplan 1993).

Freud acknowledged the insoluble complexities of gender definitions. Jung, certain of the place of otherness in the human psyche, described an archetypal otherness in the binary gender divide. The feminine within the man he called anima; the masculine within the woman was called animus (Jung [1951] 1986) – a part of his overall vision of a psyche based on polarities. At the time it was revolutionary for him to consider a contrasexuality in men and women, and he certainly seemed to believe in their equality. Nevertheless, the descriptions of animus and anima qualities failed to become different from the masculine and feminine stereotypes of the day. Jung held a deep sense of innate differences between men and women. Men's consciousness was more focused, and related to the principle of Logos; women's consciousness was more diffuse, and closer to the principle of Eros. In some way empowering, as it gave recognition to a female principle traditionally held in low regard, this stance was problematic because it did not acknowledge the value base out of which it grew. As often happens, the archetypal image became conflated with the archetype itself, so the imagery determined the content of feminine and masculine properties in a way that paid no attention to their origins in time and culture.

In a way the animus/anima archetype only served to further mytho-logize gender, rather than move towards fully humanizing it, as it was possible to label parts of the self as 'the animus' or 'the anima', and thereby keep the sense of something 'other'. If a woman was focused and logical, it indicated an integrated animus, rather than saying some-thing about female thinking on its own terms. Wholeness was again achieved through complementarity. This leaves the problem of gendering wholeness.

Vas Dias, in this book, remarks that girls may receive many messages about acceptable and unacceptable parts of themselves from their at-tachment world. These are unlikely to be understood as gender mes-sages in the first two years of life, but they will contribute to a sense of identity as they are taken in as reflections of the infant's self. As gender consciousness increases with age, the sense of 'fit' will start to have an attribution: 'I don't want to do that because I am a girl'. Not wanting to do something boy-like becomes an affirmation of girlhood: 'I was never interested in getting dirty'. Being female becomes an explanation for experience and behaviour. The difficulty is that experience and behaviour are always mediated through gender in the first place. The very young infant may have a gender-free internal experience, but it will not be attributed as gender-free by the attachment world. Thus the gradual accumulation of gender-specific experience is already a mix of internal and external; the girl meets what is hers and what has been given to her without differentiation. Differentiation occurs when there is discord, and this is as likely to be interpreted as discord of gender as of self. A poor fit between the self and the gender stereotype can be interpreted for example as 'too much animus', 'over-identification with the father', or an 'unresolved Oedipal complex'.

In Shakespeare's play, Lady Macbeth's ruthless determination to have her husband kill the king so that he can accede to the throne and she can become queen is portrayed as possible only through a complete denial of her femininity. Her mothering capabilities are removed – 'Come to my woman's breasts, and take my milk for gall'. She must become a man to ensure that the deed is done – 'Come, you spirits that tend on mortal thoughts, unsex me here'. Macbeth says to his wife, 'Bring forth men children only; for thy undaunted mettle should compose nothing but males', as he goes to murder at her bidding.

In Jungian terms, Lady Macbeth evokes the Great Mother image of the mother archetype. A larger than life constellation of positive and negative maternal potentials, the Great Mother contains 'maternal solicitude and sympathy . . . wisdom and spiritual exaltation . . . all that is benign, that cherishes and sustains' at one extreme, and 'the abyss, the world of the dead, anything that devours, seduces and poisons' (Samuels *et al.* 1986: 62) at the other. The image is split in the way that infants at first split their perception of mother into good and bad, and this finds echoes in the Kleinian notion of innate psychological structures and infantile phantasies. What is interesting in *Macbeth* is the method of protecting the good mother by projecting bad maternal qualities – which are the terrifying qualities, threatening destruction of the infant's fragile sense of self – into the male. This is perhaps easier to bear than the reality of the potential terrible mother.

If all goes well, the individual child and mother come to an accommodation of the good and the bad that allows for both to be experienced as part of a continuous relationship. Yet even then a split has been started along gender lines, both between and within the sexes, of certain types of good and bad. Gender becomes a regressive mechanism for retaining a primitive split position in relation to psychic polarities. It also reinforces the polarization, which becomes necessary for the defence to be effective.

Through thinking in this way, it is possible to imagine that it is the problem of dimorphism that, at least in part, underlies the 'problem' of gender. 'If sex and gender as we know them are oriented to the pull of opposing poles, then these poles are not masculinity and femininity. Rather, gender dimorphism itself represents only one pole – its other pole is the polymorphism of all individuals' (Benjamin 1995: 79).

Jung believed that tension between opposites was a creative force that could inspire transformation. The choice is not either/or – such a choice is in fact deadening, evidenced in the sterility of many gender debates. Choices need not be about opposition. Freud's assumption that identificatory love and object love do not co-exist can be questioned (Benjamin 1995). Acquiring different significance in different stages of development, it is nevertheless the case that the girl pre- and post-

Oedipally identifies with the mother, and will also experience her as a love object; she may also experience the father as a love object, and later as identificatory. All these experiences are in the girl's repertoire. How the tension between them is held, thus emphasizing their potential creativity, may be a more useful way of thinking about the construction of gender identity than a concept of how they are resolved, which labels them as problematic and disposable.

If gender divisions can be seen to be functional, then it is possible to consider gender itself, rather than its contents, and this opens a different discussion. The problem occurs when wholeness is reserved for an amalgam of the sexes, which puts them in a compulsory complementary relationship to each other. Binaryness thus becomes a principle and a contradictory constituent of wholeness. There is some thought that there is such a pervasive reliance on binary categories in human thinking that the pattern may be hardwired into our brains (Blechner 1995). Whatever the truth of this, there is no doubt that bipolar thinking as a solution to the problem of chaos promotes reliance on defensive manoeuvres of projection and splitting, to the point where an unhealthy split can be read to signify healthy integration. Jane, sitting quietly with her disappointment and frustration, was being a 'good girl'.

This points to a perversion at the centre of gender in which stereotypical femininity acts as a disguise for the forbidden 'masculine' strivings underneath (Kaplan 1993). Jane as an adult may, in order to be female, project her active desires into her boyfriend, or son, while not acknowledging them as her own. Disappointment in their achievements carries the weight of disappointment in her own, but acknowledgement of her own is not made visible. Thus her femininity is a vehicle for the indirect expression of an apparently unfeminine desire and, in this sense, is perverse.

Should Jane choose to own her desire, she is subject to the accusation of being a boy, through having male desires. A boy would similarly stand accused of being a girl in a reversal of fortune. In adolescence, these accusations are equivalent to being called gay or lesbian, and it is to the area of the conflation of gender identity and sexual identity that we turn next.

Gender identity: sexual identity

Psychoanalysis has generally treated 'the homosexual' as an identity, a state of being. This is congruent with society's current view of it, but this is itself a fairly recent western concept, invented in the last two centuries and now being challenged as any sort of psychological category (O'Connor and Ryan 1993). Urbanization was a part of the change (Houlbrook 2001) as it gave a place for men to gather with other men (women did not have independent access to city life) and form some identity as a group. Secularization also played its part, as the medical professions – including psychoanalysis – gained ascendancy, at some cost to the established church. The medicalization of sexuality emphasized normal and abnormal as well as right and wrong, and as heterosexuality – an equally new concept – was normal, other sexualities took up the only position left to them in what had already become a binary divide.

It is not that homosexuality had a particularly favourable relationship with society prior to the nineteenth century; rather, it was a concept of doing rather than being. Even in the somewhat romanticized days of ancient Greece, with its acceptance of sexual relationships between certain groups of men, these same men would be married, or planning to marry, and there was no need to coin the word 'bisexual' because there was no contradiction to be solved. Sex divided along many lines, and it is a modern choice that we so emphasize gender as the significant category, as opposed to class, or race, or age, which are just as significant in terms of object choice. Ancient Greek culture may not have been prescriptive about same-sex coupling, but it was very specific for example about the protocol of penetration, whatever the sex of the participants – masters penetrated slaves, older men penetrated younger ones, and men, of course, penetrated women, which made it as much a political as a sexual act.

Nevertheless, medical research continued – and does to this day – to search for a cause of this new category of homosexuality, in order to demarcate it from normal heterosexuality. The parallels between this and the search to prove distinct racial characteristics that would clearly separate one race from another are interesting and horrifying. The methodology used by nineteenth-century sexologists reproduced earlier studies done on the comparative anatomy of races (Somerville 1997). The white, heterosexual body was taken as the norm, and deviations were sought. The use of words like abnormal, irregular and poorly developed were common in the studies of both African people and gay men and lesbians. The struggle to define precise racial differences that related solely to the body served the white political purpose of segregation through the 'separate but equal' ideology, which could not be anything but a nonsense when constructed in an embeddedly racist society. Inter-racial marriage and same-sex sexuality were both markers of perversion. Clear differences between racial groups had to be marked, in order to be held apart, and for a mythical and dangerous purity to be maintained. In a similar way the hunt is now on for an ultimate cause of gender differences, as if that will provide an answer.

There is a history of physical evidence being sought in order to justify or give explanation to inequity and discrimination. For this reason it is sometimes enlisted even by those who are discriminated against, as it means that whatever exists is involuntary, therefore beyond blame. An example would be the so-called discovery in 1994, using research done amongst a male prison population in the USA, of a 'gay gene'. In 1993 a different study posited the site of sexual orientation to be the hypothalamus. A more recent one found connection between sexual orientation and the length of the index finger. However flawed, contradictory or bizarre the studies, people were excited by the possibility of such concrete location, willingly blurring correlation and causality. Perhaps it answered an unanswerable question, and left the door open for tolerance. However, as comparative anatomy has been updated into gene technology both have continued to operate in the service of a search for definition that contains a wish for separation; to identify 'them' as different from 'us' means no consideration of the 'them' that is in, and a part of, 'us' and it means there is no further need for thought. Perhaps a more useful question to return to is why it is important to search for distinctive markers between one thing and another. Gender identity may be better thought of as a process rather than an event.

Another strand of the appeal made for a normative category of heterosexuality is to 'nature' as an evolutionary, reproductive force. Homosexuality raises concerns about the survival of the species. Yet these concerns are so palpably unnecessary in real terms – the current problem is with over rather than under population; recent evolutionary theory points to the survival of the gene rather than the species as nature's driving force; conception and childrearing patterns are culturally versatile and do not rest on a 50:50 male/female heterosexual ratio – that the real purpose of the concern merits questioning. Nature has recently been 'outed' (Bagemihl 1999) as containing an infinite diversity of sexual practice, with same-sex sexual behaviour observable across the board from crustaceans to mammals. The behaviour may or may not be referenced with cross-gender identification; it does not relate to a shortage of one sex in the population; it includes the rearing of young, and long term partnerships as well as fleeting sexual contacts. There was no evidence for hormonal or other physiological explanations of same-sex sexual behaviour. In the richness of this extraordinary work cataloguing the 'biological exuberance' of nature, Bagemihl comments on how the information – always available, seldom published – was often withheld by scientists afraid of being disbelieved or ridiculed. The animal behaviours were labelled abnormal – perhaps statistically, but hardly biologically, correct. The influence of the subjective position of the observer on the observation can hardly be made clearer.

Human and animal studies resist all efforts to impose a binary divide on sexuality. Blechner (1995) suggests that the concentration of analytic thought on the anatomical sex of the love object amounts to a fetish: it is single minded; it separates the individual from their sex; an enormous weight of sexual significance is placed on this one aspect of the object. It is certainly worth considering that the analytic insistence on a clear sexual identity may be, in its current form, more part of the problem than the solution, because it cannot be separated from dichotomous thinking.

The conflation of gender identity and sexual identity has served to support a dimorphic gender structure. To retain heterosexual complementarity, and the subsequent maintenance of the binary gender divide, the problem of homosexuality is resolved if lesbians are really women wishing to be men, and gay men are identified with the female. The problem then is of confused gender identity in the individual rather than confusion in the thinking about gender identity. When the Kinsey reports into human sexuality were published (Wardell *et al.* 1948; Pomeroy *et al.* 1953), the findings on the unexpected frequency of same-sex sexual contact brought with them the new idea of a spectrum of sexual orientation, rather than two distant and separate points. Now a further flexibility is needed that allows for different positions to be taken at different times, and for each position to carry with it an element of identification that is both true and transitory. Real lives portray infinite variety. Women have same-sex relationships after years of happy marriage; from time to time, with or without a concurrent male partner; from as early as they can remember; without ever having had a male partner. They may penetrate, be penetrated or never use penetration. They may fantasize about sex with men or women or both. The divide between inner and outer is fluid. If a woman has sex with a woman while fantasizing that she is having sex with a man, does that make her object choice heterosexual? If she makes love to her female partner while fantasizing herself to be a man, is it any less a lesbian act? Two 'feminine' women fall in love – must one of them have a hidden male identification for it to be a proper lesbian relationship? To have identifications with the other gender is part of being female (and so with men too), not to be equated with gender confusion. It is the equation itself that is confusing.

If gender has been highly constructed, then radical deconstruction is a necessary part of finding any core. While the construct may remain a useful way of expressing something about the contemporary shaping of gender, gender itself should not be confused with that expression. If there is a wholeness to human sexuality, it lies in the complete range of potential that exists for sexual expression. This must also be true for the complete range of experience that is available to gender. To move beyond binary strategies, it is necessary to think about these potentials being distributed between women and men in a way that is responsive to and shaped by culture, custom, individual need and personality, alterable over generations or within one particular lifetime. Kinsey's spectrum, revolutionary at the time, allowed the polarities to be connected to each other but still operated within the binary divide. For women to have access to an authentic experiencing of the self, it must be possible to take up a position that is near the current 'masculine' constellation, and still be no less of a woman. Circularity may be a more helpful image than the spectrum. Complementarity has become functional, yet of course each gender, each man and woman, is fully human. Fear of chaos and loss, primitive, individual and collective, has restricted recognition of the plural psyche (Samuels 1989).

Ethnographic studies (Brettell and Sargent 1997) consistently show the existence of different gender roles; however, the content of the roles is not fixed. One can predict the fact but not the shape of difference. The studies show that the interpretation of difference is affected by the position of the observer; the real significance of women's work is not seen precisely because it is women's work, and therefore already of secondary significance.

Most studies of gender and sexuality have suffered from this inevitable perspective. As a result, expectations of proper feminine gender and sexual development have been limiting and even cruel. To be herself a woman may have to identify as masculine; to retain identity as a woman she may have to repudiate parts of herself – an activity that Kaplan (1993) refers to as soul murder.

Perhaps psychoanalysis has yet to move on from the assumption that sexual relationships that do not include the opposite sex are narcissistic or regressive. Negotiation of otherness is prioritized as a part of healthy development, but otherness is literalized into gender, which becomes the major difference, rather than a major signifier of difference. Projective use of the other means that difference can be avoided in heterosexual as well as same-sex relationships; projection of split-off parts of the self into the other, which is a ritualized part of established patterns of hetero-sexuality, does not necessarily herald a move towards integration. Dif-ference can be signified in many ways in intimate relationships – class, ethnicity, culture, age, disability, personal qualities such as extroversion and introversion. The capacity to engage with difference is the point. The emphasis on this point has occluded the other important act of engaging with similarity while maintaining a self-identity. The capacity to do this may be particularly important for women, for whom feminine qualities of empathic caring have been encouraged at the expense of ruthlessness and autonomy. It could be that homosexuality has become the object of projections about loss of autonomy, narcissism, incorporation. The emphasis on difference has come about because of unresolved anxieties which, in a heterosexual construct, are split off onto the 'other' of homosexuality. Homosexual lifestyles are referred to as ultimately sterile as they do not include the generative capacity to bear children. Yet it is perhaps another mark of anxiety that creativity is literalized into childbirth (Izzard, in this volume), whereas it is the symbolic content that is key, with actual generativity coming in many forms. Homosexuality is a two-person relationship, not a single uroboric unit.

Psychic health should encourage the taking back and owning of these projections, facing the early fears of incorporation and assimilation that belong to the pre-Oedipal era. Post-Oedipal life moves on from but does not in itself resolve them (Benjamin 1998). In Freud's construct, the Oedipal position requires a moment of opposition between identification and object love – the girl cannot be like *and* have the mother, and so the being must be separated from the having. The domination of this moment in analytic theory both stemmed from and reinforced the link between gender identity and sexual identity; if opposite sex object love was not achieved, it implied a failure in same-sex identification, and the failure in same-sex identification was responsible for the same-sex choice of object love.

A client, Agnes, was in therapy for the second time. The first time had been when she was coming to terms with her sexuality, and the sessions had included much guilt, anger and disappointment towards her parents, particularly her father, who had been completely unable to discuss the issue of her lesbianism. The rift never healed, and family contact declined to routine Christmas and birthday visits. She would sometimes meet her mother to go shopping, and this single contact was easier.

Some years later the father died. Here started the second occasion of therapy, with a different therapist, the first one having moved away. Agnes found herself flooded with longing for her father, full of grief for the missed years of contact. All the things she had loved about him came to the fore, and she spent some time just sharing this with the therapist, relieved and glad that there was someone to hear it.

Later in the therapy, the therapist mentioned to Agnes that perhaps it was not surprising she was lesbian, as clearly there would never be a man who could match up to her father.

This last remark to the client is an example of the link made between object love and gender identification. If Agnes had been in a heterosexual relationship and the mother had died, the same material would have been heard, but no link would have been made between the idealized love of the mother and sexual object choice. Viewing homosexuality as the deviation from the norm means an inevitable, inappropriate and often clumsy search for causation, in analysis just as in biology or genetics.

Once homosexuality is understood as normal, it ceases to be a part of gender confusion. For boys, the worst playground taunt is to be a sissy, a girl, and this feminization is equated with being gay. Male and female stereotypes point to the gender role expectations, and are stepped over only at peril. Gay men who confound the stereotypes through behaving in feminine ways ironically serve to reinforce them, as they are conferred with a not-real-man status. Similarly, girls who do not conform to their gender stereotypes are called butch, which is a short step from lesbian. Lesbians who then continue to confound the stereotypes are accused of not being real women, or of wanting to be men. This acts as a defence against the fear of maternal abandonment that can be aroused by women's independence from men (Jukes 1993).

The mixing of sex roles is not new. There is evidence in many cultures (Williams 1997) of this existing in a formal way – children being 'allocated' sex and gender roles according to the needs of the family, for example; women taking on warrior roles and being accepted as if they were men; men being allowed to become sexually indeterminate, literally or metaphorically castrated, and thereafter take on quasi-feminine, or certainly non-masculine, roles. There is also a long history of women who chose to go about the world disguised as men in order to live the life they wanted, Pope Joan being one famous example. The problem of the relationship of gender identity to sexual identity was resolved in various ways – through women-as-men having female partners, or maintaining a sexual ambivalence, or refraining from intimate engagement. The records appear not to show many having sexual relationships with men, but this may be a failure in documentation, or a tribute to the taboo against male homosexuality, as much as any reflection of the individual's personal orientation.

What is new is the psychiatric definition of 'gender identity disorder' (Morrison 1995: 381) and the medical capacity to facilitate sex reassignment surgery. The siting of this identity issue within a psychiatric category is still ambivalently received. Legitimacy is bestowed at the expense of normality. Insurance companies will not pay for reassignment surgery, as they will for treatment of other labelled psychiatric disorders. Analytic thought also tends to have approached transsexualism from the assumption of a disorder, and this has restricted the development of analytic thinking on the issue. If approached openly, 'gender confusion' leaves room for consideration of the difference between the restrictions of gender stereotyping – Kaplan's (1993) 'soul murders' – and an actual sense of gender. Samuels (1989) refers to gender confusion, rather than gender certainty, as a psychically healthy place to be.

Samantha consulted a therapist after a year at university because of confusion over her identity. The middle child of a large family, she had grown up in a rural area, surrounded by loving but robust siblings. She had learnt early to stand up for herself, to take part in rough and tumble play, and also to look after the younger children. There was a sense in which her sex had not been particularly relevant in the mix of the family group; gender roles were fairly fluid, and Samantha was just Samantha. As a 19-year-old woman, she found herself comfortable in jeans and sweaters, treated men her own age like brothers, and had a number of good male friends 'for laughs', but found it hard to be close to women, who made her feel nervous and inadequate. She had little sense of where her sexual attraction lay. Sometimes she thought she was nervous of girls because she never felt that she was one of them, and was afraid this might mean that she really wanted to be a man, and that this would mean that she was a lesbian. She had only started to think about these things since leaving home and coming to university, although there had been times at sixth form college when she felt uncomfortable and unsure of where she belonged.

What was important for her in therapy was to separate out her identity as a woman from her sexual identity. Not being able to identify with a stereotypical femininity together with the possibility of being attracted to other women had both become confused with whether or not she was really a woman herself. The first thing was to open up a place to think about what sort of a woman she might be, and to separate this out from pressure she suddenly felt to conform. Second, it was important to recognize the difference between wanting to be a man, and not knowing if she felt comfortable as a woman. Third, sexual feelings needed to grow out of an awareness of herself, without prescription as to their object, so that they could be enjoyed as well as understood. The therapist had to be careful to allow all these things room in his own mind, and to carefully think through any countertransference feelings that might have a neurotic aspect as Samantha started to work out her own sense of being female. His work with the past focused on the sense of her individuality being lost, and sometimes pleasurably so, in the large family, and how it was hard for her to bear the feelings of one to one intimacy that were engendered in the therapy room. In the end this proved more important than any pronouncements Samantha made over whether she felt male or female, heterosexual or gay.

Gender/transgender/transsexual

Consideration of transsexual and transgender issues, touched on by Samantha, can actually help to clarify the sexual identity/gender identity conflation and something of the nature of gender identity itself.

It is important for this discussion not to focus on the gender reassignment surgery itself. Questions about mutilation and artificiality are complex, and should be considered in conjunction with the history of routine manipulation of female bodies – corsets, stiletto heels, breast enlargement, liposuction, collagen implants, body waxing, electrolysis – which is called enhancement and is considered unexceptional, despite pain and long term health risks.

If transsexual is a psychological identification with the sex other than the one assigned at birth, transgender is a wish to identify with other gender norms, without necessarily changing sex identification. Transgender challenges the very basis of ideas of gender. In a physical sense, individuals 'play', albeit intently, with sex – learning the art of being a drag king, going partway down the road of sex reassignment and stopping at a point that contains physical elements of both male or female. In the body it challenges the dependence of the masculine subject on the female 'other', and vice versa. It queries the assumption of a binary sexual divide as normal by asking what defines that divide; is it natural, anatomical, chromosomal, hormonal? In contrast, transsexualism can be conservative in its intent, wishing to become woman rather than question what woman is. Yet at the same time it is radical in its belief that such a becoming is possible – indeed has already happened in the psyche.

Several personal accounts have now been written about the experience of transsexual identity. They attempt to portray what it is that is missing, or sought, or already felt to be there, as yet inexpressible to the outside world. Sometimes the accounts seem banal, gender transition seeming to centre on wearing the right clothes (Spry 1997), or learning the right mannerisms (McCloskey 1999). The inadequacy of these things to express what is female can be mistaken for an inadequacy in the transsexual case. Yet what other ways are there for giving shape or form to the female? Male definition seems to come down to the phallus; female definition comes down to the absence of the male. In the absence of a positive presence, stereotypes are the resort left to describe the female. Their ridiculousness is as acute whether they are part of a transsexual or any other agenda. Yet there appears nothing better to be done. The attempt to perform gender (Butler 1990) is 'deeply superficial' (McCloskey 1999: 8) only because attempts to grapple with gender have been afraid of confusion, preferring to enforce binary constructions on experience.

Clothing, facial hair, voice, posture all matter because they are the ways in which gender can be legitimately expressed and defined. In this sense transsexualism exposes the 'persistent impersonation' (Butler 1990: viii) of gender at the same time as reinforcing its reality. In the end the body is the only way of turning something around, of making it fit. Freud ([1923] 1995) acknowledged the bodily foundations of the ego; conceptions of the self are intimately bound up with the body. A case reported by Sacks (1986: Ch. 3) refers to a woman who, through an acute and particular polyneuritis, lost sensation and with it perception of her body. The effect was an urgent loss of self-identity, even though she could see and use her limbs. Sacks described it as 'operating' rather than 'being'. Prosser (1998) highlights the distinction that can be found here between the felt and the seen body, and the need for congruence between sensory and internal perception in order for there to be an experience of personal integrity. If the internal identity is female, it is impossible to feel at ease until the body can concord with that. Thinking on this level is closer to Morris's (1997: 30) description of gender:

> To me, gender is not physical at all, but is altogether insubstantial. It is soul, perhaps, it is talent, it is taste, it is environment, it is how one feels, it is light and shade, it is inner music, it is a spring in one's step or an exchange of glances . . . It became fashionable later to talk of my condition as 'gender confusion', but I think it a philistine misnomer . . . Nothing in the world would make me abandon my gender, concealed from everyone though it remained; but my body, my organs, my paraphernalia, seemed to me much less sacrosanct, and far less interesting too.

Transsexuality paradoxically points towards gender essentialism, while questioning the essentials of gender. It also confirms the separation of gender identity from sexual identity. To undergo gender reassignment is not necessarily to undergo sexual reorientation. Orientation may remain the same in terms of the object choice, so that a heterosexual man may come to identify as a lesbian woman, or a man more at ease with same-sex relationships may remain attracted to men and so identify post-operatively as a heterosexual woman. Identification and object choice need not be exclusive categories. There is often an assumption that one of the reasons for wanting to change sex is because of a same-sex attraction that is desired within a heterosexual construct. In reality, this is only one of a range of possibilities, and seems to be irrelevant as a reason for sex reassignment.

Gender identity is seen by some as fixed by 2 to 3 years old (Stoller 1968). Transsexual accounts to date indicate a sense of not fitting from a very early age, sometimes as far back as can be remembered. In contrast, work by Money from the 1960s onwards indicated the opposite: that if a child was offered gender reassignment while very young they could successfully be raised with a different gender identity. This treatment was given to babies born with, or developing, 'intersex' sexual characteristics. It was also given to adolescents who, due to a number of recognized medical conditions, developed secondary sexual characteristics at variance with the primary ones. Money's work is currently being heavily challenged (Colapinto 2000) and therefore remains inconclusive, but for years these extreme treatments were seen as preferable to living with indeterminate sexual characteristics. Better to be made a boy or a girl than to be confusing. Anxiety about stepping over the clarity of imposed binary states, so well represented by reactions to transsexualism, was also found in early race laws in America: miscegenation was forbidden through intermarriage, although it happened often enough through sexual violence towards black women. In modern times this can be recognized as racist, stemming from white assumptions of racial purity and racial superiority. So too do gender divisions rest on assumptions of purity and superiority. As long as they do, it is impossible to know what gender identity really consists of, because security and safety are tied up with preserving the current perspective.

The most powerful single influence on gender and sexuality in psychoanalysis has undoubtedly been the Oedipal theory of development. Izzard (1999) gives a succinct account of three approaches that can be taken in relation to the Oedipal complex. First, that it is a useful and crucial organizing concept, capable of expansion to more accurately take account of different sexualities. Second, that sexuality is constitutional and so requires no fundamental explanation; the work is in understanding the variety of its expressions in human nature. Third, that a complete rethinking of developmental theory and the concept of identity in the light of current understanding and critique might lead to a radical move away from the Oedipal complex altogether. There is no doubt that an enormous amount of creative work has gone into developing Oedipal theory, to the point of recognizing that it really does not explain heterosexuality at all (Benjamin 1998). Perhaps it is now more hopeful than it was that analytic theory can embrace change, even when that means shaking its foundations.

Conclusion

This chapter has concentrated on outlining the hazards of developing a gender identity. None of this negates the importance of having a gendered 'home' (Prosser 1998). The earliest experiences of self and other are mediated through the body (McDougall 2000), and transsexual auto-biographies highlight the importance of somatic and psychic congruence to the sense of a gendered self. As the ego grows beyond the body, the importance of gender extends to all aspects of the self.

The home offered to gender in analytic and social discourse has not often been where the heart is. Heterosexual and gender conventions have been superimposed on experience; the creation of order has taken the place of the joy of diversity, which has been misunderstood as representing chaos. To some extent home is a myth, an archetypal image of belonging that reflects the longing for the early infant–other bond. It is also necessary, just as the need from time to time to experience blissful intimacy is necessary. As a clear view of gender development has always been obstructed by preformed expectations, it is realistic at the moment to observe the journey rather than the destination. Perhaps this will always, and healthily, be the case; the experience of being female will continually unfold in relation to the attachment world it encounters. If the encounter can be free of binary gender and sexual rigidity, a much more authentic experience and understanding of gender might emerge, and girls can, without loss of self, grow up to be women.

References

Bagemihl, B. (1999) *Biological Exuberance: Animal Homosexuality and Natural Diversity*. London: Profile Books.

Baker Miller, J. (1988) *Towards a New Psychology of Women*. London: Pelican.

Benjamin, J. (1995) *Like Subjects, Love Objects: Essays on Recognition and Sexual Difference*. New Haven, CT: Yale University Press.

Benjamin, J. (1998) *Shadow of the Other: Intersubjectivity and Gender in Psychoanalysis*. London: Routledge.

Blechner, M. (1995) The shaping of psychoanalytic theory and practice by cultural and personal biases about sexuality, in T. Domenici and R. Lesser (eds) *Disorienting Sexuality: Psychoanalytic Reappraisals of Sexual Identities*. London: Routledge.

Brettell, C. and Sargent, C. (eds) (1997) *Gender in Cross Cultural Perspective*. Upper Saddle River, NJ: Prentice Hall.

British Broadcasting Corporation (BBC) (1999) *The Hunt for the First Americans*. Manchester: BSS.

Butler, J. (1990) *Gender Trouble: Feminism and the Subversion of Identity*. London: Routledge.

Chodorow, N. (1994) *Femininities Masculinities Sexualities: Freud and Beyond*. London: Free Association Books.

Clare, A. (2000) *On Men: Masculinity in Crisis*. London: Chatto and Windus.

Colapinto, J. (2000) *As Nature Made Him: The Boy who was Raised as a Girl*. London: Quartet.

Freud, S. ([1920] 1990a) The psychogenesis of a case of homosexuality in a woman, in E. Young-Bruehl (ed.) *Freud on Women*. London: Hogarth Press.

Freud, S. ([1932] 1990b) Femininity, in E. Young-Bruehl (ed.) *Freud on Women*. London: Hogarth Press.

Freud, S. ([1923] 1995) The ego and the id, in P. Gay (ed.) (1995) *The Freud Reader*. London: Vintage.

Gilligan, C. (1993) *In A Different Voice: Psychological Theory and Women's Development*. Cambridge, MA: Harvard University Press.

Houlbrook, M. (2001) For whose convenience? Gay guides, cognitive maps and the construction of homosexual London: 1917–c.67, in B. Morris and S. Gunn (eds) *Identities in Space: Contested Terrains in the Western City Since 1850*. Aldershot: Ashgate.

Izzard, S. (1999) Oedipus – baby or bathwater? A review of psychoanalytic theories of homosexual development, *British Journal of Psychotherapy*, 16(1): 43–55.

Jukes, A. (1993) *Why Men Hate Women*. London: Free Association Books.

Jung, C.J. ([1951] 1986) The syzygy: anima and animus, in A. Storr (ed.) *Jung: Selected Writings*. London: Fontana.

Kaplan, L. (1993) *Female Perversions*. London: Penguin.

McCloskey, D. (1999) *Crossing: A Memoir*. Chicago, IL: The University of Chicago Press.

McDougall, J. (2000) Sexualities and neosexualities. Paper given to the European Federation for Psychoanalytic Psychotherapy, Oxford, April.

Mitchell, J. (1990) *Psychoanalysis and Feminism*. London: Penguin.

Moir, A. and Moir, B. (1999) *Why Men Don't Iron: The New Reality of Gender Differences*. London: Harper Collins.

Morris, J. (1997) *Conundrum*. London: Penguin.

Morrison, J. (1995) *DSM IV Made Easy: The Clinician's Guide to Diagnosis*. London: Guilford Press.

O'Connor, N. and Ryan, J. (1993) *Wild Desires and Mistaken Identities: Lesbianism and Psychoanalysis*. London: Virago.

Pomeroy, W., Martin, C.E. and Gebhard, P.H. (1953) *Sexual Behaviour in the Human Female*. Philadelphia, PA: Saunders.

Prosser, J. (1998) *Second Skins: The Body Narratives of Transsexuality*. New York: Columbia University Press.

Sacks, O. (1986) *The Man Who Mistook his Wife for a Hat*. London: Picador.

Samuels, A. (1989) *The Plural Psyche: Personality, Morality and the Father*. London: Routledge.

Samuels, A., Shorter, B. and Plaut, F. (1986) *A Critical Dictionary of Jungian Analysis*. London: Routledge and Kegan Paul.

Shakespeare, W. *Macbeth*, in P. Alexander (ed.) (1951) *Complete Works of Shakespeare*. London: Collins.

Somerville, S. (1997) Scientific racism and the invention of the homosexual body, in R. Lancaster and M. di Leonardo (eds) *The Gender Sexuality Reader*. London: Routledge.

Spry, J. (1997) *Orlando's Sleep: An Autobiography of Gender*. Norwich, VT: New Victoria Publishers Inc.

Stoller, R. (1968) *Sex and Gender: The Development of Masculinity and Femininity.* London: Karnac.

Taylor, J.M., Gilligan, C. and Sullivan, A. (1997) *Between Voice and Silence: Women and Girls, Race and Relationship.* Cambridge, MA: Harvard University Press.

Wardell, W., Pomeroy, B. and Martin, C.E. (1948) *Sexual Behaviour in the Human Male.* Philadelphia, PA: Saunders.

Williams, W. (1997) Amazons of America: female gender variance, in C. Brettell and C. Sargent (eds) *Gender in Cross Cultural Perspective.* Upper Saddle River, NJ: Prentice Hall.

Wollstonecraft, M. ([1792] 1992) *A Vindication of the Rights of Woman.* London: Penguin.

2 When do I know I'm a girl? The development of a sense of self as female in the early infant

Susan Vas Dias

Introduction

To write about specifically female development in the early infant (0–2 years) is challenging in several respects. This period in life is one in which the greatest and most profound developmental growth takes place in the lifetime of a human being.

Physically, areas of the brain and nervous system not yet completed at birth continue to evolve, upright motility takes place, language and its capacity for symbolic thinking and communication develops, and the completion of eye and hand coordination necessary for using tools occurs.

Psychologically 0–2 years is the period during which the infant becomes aware of and consolidates their sense of their own individuality, their self, which will then become a core part of their identity. It is the time when the continual interaction between the external environment, the attachment world, and the infant's internal world, his or her subjective experience, lays down the foundation for the developing capacity to become an autonomous human being.

The interplay between the biological baby and the psychological baby is constant and facilitates each new stage of development in the 0–2-year-old infant. This dynamic process happens irrespective of whether the infant is male or female.

Therefore, to describe that which is only female development at this age is fraught with difficulty. Clearly, in discussing female psychological development it would be tempting to concentrate predominantly on the cultural and social expectations for sex and gender, and to explore the many ways in which the female infant's attachment world fantasizes about and experiences the baby's sex and how this impacts upon her development. Although crucially important this concentration on what the environment conveys runs the risk of overlooking what the infant might be experiencing in favour of the adult's experience. This creates the danger of superimposing speculation and conjecture on the infant's development.

Until relatively recently the understanding of infant emotional development has been derived primarily from psychoanalytic thinking stemming from reconstruction in adult psychoanalytic treatment. This method of understanding infant development, in combination with the fact that most of the founders of psychoanalysis had little or no experience of working with or observing infant development, is open to the dangers of taking speculation, fantasy, and conjecture to be the same as observation.

The great danger in this approach is that what is actually going on in the infant's development may well not be observed or acknowledged. This could mean the individual infant's experience might be bypassed and overlooked. Instead a 'theory' of development may be superimposed and the infant seen only through that lens. This could have lasting repercussions on the infant's perception of themselves and consequent development.

The pioneers of direct observational research on infants (Freud and Burlingham 1944; Winnicott 1958; Robertson 1971; Mahler *et al.* 1975; Bowlby 1979; Emde 1983; Stern 1985) prepared the way for our current understanding of the importance of an infant's psychological development, especially his or her experience, or sense, of their own unique individuality to the rest of their development. The internal feeling state that, 'I am an autonomous person in my own right who feels welcome in the world and of value for being me' is central to the development of a sense of self and identity that is confident and comfortable in relation to the world.

The development of this sense of self, the 'I am me', is the primary developmental task of the infant from 0–2 years irrespective of sex and gender and is accomplished with little or no awareness of them. By 18 months to 2 years enough psychological, neurological, motor, and verbal development has occurred for the infant to begin to have a hazy idea that they are a girl or boy.

In cultural and sociological terms the understanding and sense of themselves as being female or male (their sex) with feminine or masculine behavioural traits (gender) will become more central to the development of the over 2-year-old. However, this understanding is built upon the established foundation of the sense that 'I am me!' irrespective of gender. It is the internal psychological experience of this that is the bedrock upon which all else is built.

The widening field of direct observational research into infant development and the rapidly growing body of neuroscientific knowledge and how it applies to infants and their experience of themselves is opening up an era full of possibilities for shifting our understanding of infant experience without resorting to fantasy and speculation. This is likely to have a far-reaching impact upon the ways in which we parent, work with infants and children, and eventually on how we approach clinical therapeutic work with adults.

How is this relevant to understanding female development from 0–2 years? As most of the research currently indicates that infants of this age have only a dim awareness of sex and gender it seems an opportunity to try and explore the various factors which might contribute to an infant girl's growing sense of herself as female. One of the areas that research suggests is a factor is that a sense of sex and gender are 'hardwired' in the brain. How and when does this create a sense of being a girl? Many of the answers to the questions that the research elicits seem to lie in how we continue to develop further ways in which to understand an infant's subjective experience without superimposing our adult experience. Until then perhaps all that can be done in this chapter is to try and delineate the aspects we do know that might facilitate the developing awareness of a sense of self as female.

In the beginning

Infants are conceived and born within the context of their own specific environment. Conception begins the complex set of genetic, physiological, neurological, psychological, social, and cultural interactions that facilitate the baby's development as an individual with a sense of unique identity. This dynamic process is a lengthy one progressing in overlapping and interconnected pathways from conception to early adulthood. The quality of interaction of the environment, the attachment world, with the developing infant plays a key role in the development of a healthy sense of self and the evolution of a personal identity which eventually incorporates gender.

What is a sense of self? What is identity? Perhaps a sense of self could be thought of as an awareness of selfhood, that is, 'existence as a person' (Chambers Dictionary 1993) and identity as 'who or what a person is' (Chambers Dictionary 1993). The infant from 0–2 years is first and foremost developing a sense of existence as an autonomous person. The toddler (2–3 years) extends this process into an awareness that there is an 'I am' who knows s/he is a girl or boy who is part of a family system, and an even wider world. Most toddlers have mastered motility and the use of language. They have also incorporated an awareness of sex as part of their identity which facilitates the establishment of their core gender identity (Stoller 1968). This has become part of who they are. The toddler knows that part of being an 'I' is their name but also includes being a boy or girl.

Self and identity are the words used to symbolize the existence of a person's subjective experience of him or herself. Part of the challenge of exploring the early infant's development of gender identity is the difficulty in discerning the subjective experience of a very young baby.

Psychoanalysts and psychotherapists beginning with Freud have attempted to understand infant experience through the reconstruction of the early lives of their adult patients, a process fraught with bias. Anna Freud and Dorothy Burlingham led the way in using their observational skills in direct work with infants and children (1944). This work helped pave the way for future studies of young infants and their emotional development (Winnicott 1958; Robertson 1971; Mahler *et al.* 1975; Bowlby 1979; Emde 1983; Stern 1985). Klein (1921) postulated an infant subjective experience based on her theories of a baby's and child's inner world. The fact remains that we really do not know what an infant subjectively feels.

This makes it difficult to assess with any certainty precisely when a little girl or boy really 'knows' they are female or male and when this knowledge becomes an integral part of their identity with a developed sense of masculinity and femininity, that is, gender identity. Perhaps the best we can do is explore what is known about infant development from 0–2 years with a particular emphasis on the impact of the attachment world upon the infant's developing sense of self and eventual experience of their individual identity. During this exploration some of the factors that contribute to the formation of specific gender identity will be explored.

Behind the scenes of an infant's birth

An infant begins his or her journey to individuality when sperm fertilizes an egg. The twentieth century introduced technology that once upon a time would have been considered the province of science fiction. It no longer takes 80 days to go around the world, humans have stood on the surface of the moon, developed the theory of relativity, eradicated killer diseases, discovered DNA, and transplanted hearts. Babies born at 24 weeks can be helped to live, sheep have been cloned, and gene and stem therapies are developing as new treatments. The twentieth century has also brought global warming, the melt-down of the icecap, ethnic cleansing on an unimaginable scale, and the development of nuclear energy. Throughout much of the world slavery has been abolished, education and health care for all is emerging, women have been given the vote, entered the job market, and different solutions to the problems of infertility are being developed. It is possible for a woman to abort a child of an unwanted gender as well as conceive without ever knowing the donor of the sperm which fertilized her egg. However, it is still impossible for a baby to be conceived solely by one person.

At even the most basic and primitive level the infant begins his or her development out of and in relation to others. The attachment world, the environment into which the baby will be delivered, is one of the central influences upon an infant's development (Bowlby 1969, 1973; Brazleton and Cramer 1991; Wright 1991; Karen 1994). The experience of the quality of repeated interactions between the baby and his or her primary attachment world gradually becomes an integral part of the baby's perception of the external world (Stern 1985). This helps foster an internal perception of oneself as an autonomous sentient being as well as affecting the quality of the sense of self which develops to be, for example, secure or insecure (Spitz 1965; Bowlby 1969; Mahler *et al.* 1975).

The way in which parents and caregivers greet the conception, pregnancy, and birth of their infant will be affected by a whole variety of things. Predominant among these will be the individual past histories that are brought to the experience of becoming a parent. We each carry with us the impact of our own development upon our sense of ourselves. As Fraiberg (1987) observes there are always ghosts in the nursery. These 'ghosts' can profoundly affect ideas of how a baby and child should be parented as well as the fantasies about oneself as mother, father, grandparent, aunt, uncle, and sibling etc. These ideas and fantasies become part of the attachment world's interactions with the developing infant.

Other general factors that influence the quality of relationship with the baby are economic, social, cultural, nutritional, health, and family system circumstances. The specific experience of pregnancy and birth can also have a considerable effect upon the developing relationship between parent and infant. A significant influence in the quality of relationship and style of care of the infant is undoubtedly the gender of the baby. Money and Ehrhardt (1973: 179) state:

> In human beings, so strong is the stereotype and the expectancy of sexual dimorphism of infant behavior that, in our antinudist society, a newborn's sex is publicly declared by the colour coding of blue for boys and pink for girls, long before an infant has enough hair for a boy's or a girl's haircut, or enough excretion control to make different styles of pants functional. Even strangers are left in no doubt as to what gender-dimorphic vocabulary, or stereotypes of gender-identity behaviour to employ. From earliest infancy onward, a baby's social experiences are inevitably gender-dichotomized.

In everyday language once we conceive a baby all our cultural, social, and emotional relationships to gender start to interact with the developing infant even if most of it is out of consciousness. A neonatal unit is an excellent place in which to observe many of these factors at work. Although it is a place in which the babies all have difficulties of one kind or another this very fact intensifies the expression of how past histories can colour so vividly the quality of the primary care relationship which will become so important in the infant's progress towards selfhood.

Sitting around an incubator looking at her newborn son Mrs X stared fixedly at him. She was a woman in her early 40s, of Middle Eastern heritage, who had suffered several prior miscarriages. The baby was her first live birth. Mrs X had been traumatized by the loss of her previous children, unable to grieve for them and feeling very much alone and a failure as a woman. Her husband was immensely pleased that he had a son but was angry with his wife for producing one who had arrived prematurely and was in an incubator. Neither parent would touch or speak with the baby or give him a name. It emerged that they wouldn't do this until they knew the boy was 'viable', that is, would live and be healthy. He was not an individual in their eyes as yet and therefore no relationship could be allowed to develop between them and their son.

Ms D was a highly anxious single mum of a baby girl. She too would not hold, touch, or feed her baby. Her mother had been at the birth and from then on took on the role of primary caretaker. It became clear that Grandma needed to keep both her own daughter and her granddaughter under her control.

Eventually, in the therapeutic work offered to facilitate Ms D's capacity to relate with her baby it emerged that the grandmother's own mother had died in childbirth and she had always kept Ms D strictly under her thumb and close to her.

In each family the gender of the infant was an important factor. Mrs X felt that it was essential to produce a strong healthy baby boy to satisfy her culture's definition of a good woman and therefore her own self-esteem. Ms D had desperately wanted a baby girl to 'buy pretty dresses for'. In her internal reality she wanted a girl who would become her 'friend' and help her get away from her controlling mother.

It was also in the neonatal unit that the cultural stereotypes of expectations according to gender were made crystal clear. The sicker the baby the more toys were put in their incubator or cot. The boys had small, wheeled vehicles, trains and soft footballs, as well as teddies. The girls were surrounded by plush pink bunnies, dolls and soft picture books.

Despite these stereotypical cultural communications the newborn infant cannot subjectively know that she or he is a girl or boy. It is the attachment world into which they come that knows. This is clearly very important in the development of gender identity. Schore (1994: 264) states, 'The critical variable in determining gender identity is known to be postnatal learning experience, specifically the sex in which the infant is raised in the first two years.'

The baby's gender and the social and cultural expectations of it will heavily influence a family's interaction with their newborn infant. When observing 'newborn' parents it is noticeable that a little girl will be handled more gently than boys. There seems to be an expectation that boys require more energetic, excited handling. Whether this difference in handling is the result of the parent attuning to the infant's physical cues or predominantly the result of social and cultural expectations is unclear. It may well be a mixture of both.

It is interesting to note when observing nurses, parents, and grandparents in the neonatal unit that the voice tones they use to speak with the different genders is quite striking. Little girls are most often spoken to in softer, more modulated tones than the boys. It is also the boys who are jocularly labelled 'naughty', 'mischievous', 'greedy', 'sly', 'lazy'. Girls are labelled 'a little angel', 'so well-behaved', 'waits her turn so nicely', 'a real flirt, look at her eyelashes . . . She'll have them lining up!' It is always amazing to hear these things said of infants who are only hours old. How any infant can possibly suffer the trauma of birth and then spend their first hours in the outside world gaining these attributes remains a mystery! Clearly, these are cultural expectations already being assigned according to gender. Often in the neonatal unit it is clear boys are expected to be cheeky, full of energy and naughtiness while girls are patient, caring, good, and/or flirtatious.

In addition to conveying cultural expectations according to gender, each family member will bring to the interaction with their baby aspects of their own past history. These may also contribute to the girl's or boy's sense of themselves as female or male. Whatever various individual parental styles contribute to gender identity it is clear that across most cultures socialization processes result in girls being more nurturing, making more intimate (that is, not rough and tumble) physical contact while boys are more aggressive, dominant, and rough and tumble in their play (Whiting and Edwards 1973).

It is intriguing to wonder whether the female's caregiving, nurturing capacities are also responsible for her ability to handle several different tasks all at once. It seems likely that girls from early on build upon their innate stamina and develop more constructive mechanisms than boys for dealing with the experiences of feeling vulnerable and/or anxious. From observation of infants, children and parents in many different settings it appears that girl infants and children are given greater 'permission' from birth to speak the language of feeling, to be more comfortable than boys with their affective self and as a consequence are better able to cope with stressful situations. It is interesting also to note that in clinical settings it appears that there are many more boys referred for emotional and conduct disorders than girls. Is this primarily due to environmental or biological and genetic factors? This leads to the question of the role played by biology in the early infant girl's or boy's understanding of themselves as feminine or masculine.

Biological baby

We know that all human life begins with female organ development. However, each individual has a genetic makeup that drives the biological development through the endocrine system towards male or female structure. Towards the second month of life testosterone in the potentially male baby begins to circulate and cause the testicles to form, which might otherwise have developed as ovaries. Without the production of the male hormone the embryo would retain female genital structures. This raises questions about the role of the endocrine system, its interface with the developing brain, and the possibility that there is an inborn unconscious knowledge of gender at birth.

There is no doubt that the interaction with the world into which a baby is born plays one of the central roles in development. However the importance of understanding the infant from the moment of conception as a biological as well as a social and psychological being cannot be underestimated. Freud (1937, 1953) throughout his work never lost his belief that biological makeup was an essential part of the development of both sexuality and gender identity, that is masculinity and femininity. During his lifetime it was not possible to measure precisely the roles of biology and social determinants in infant development.

Stoller (1968: 65–6) felt that there is a 'biological force' defined as 'energy from biological sources (such as endocrine or CNS systems), which influences gender identity formation and behaviour'. Over the years neuropsychologists, biologists, endocrinologists, and psychiatrists have developed and are developing research which gives evidence that gender identity is an integral part of brain development from conception (Diamond 1965; Diamond and Sigmundson 1997). In what way might this affect the development of the early infant's subjective experience of gender identity? Before speculating about this it might be helpful to outline briefly the early infant's emotional development.

The development of 'I am!': primary caretaking and emerging domains of self

The newborn infant comes into the world biologically programmed to send out signals that will elicit caregiving from his or her environment (Fairbairn 1952; Bowlby 1979; Parkes *et al.* 1991; Heard and Lake 1997). The first two months of life are spent sending out cues to the primary attachment world. They are designed to get basic survival needs met. The cues, or attachment behaviours, usually arise from sensations in the body such as hunger, cold, heat, wet, the feel of air on skin, smell, touch, sound etc. The baby whimpers, develops a repertoire of cries, sucks vigorously, or not as the case may be, wriggles, startles, or turns bright purple from wind. She or he becomes able to track moving objects, turn to look at a sound, or stare fixedly at a shaft of light. From birth babies can recognize their mother's face, smell, and voice. Smiles are elicited from wind, social interplay, and finally a special person, usually the mother or primary caretaker, is given the wonderful specific smile.

Through this whole interactive process with the outside world the infant begins gradually to build up an internal perception that there is a 'me' and a 'not me'. In other words there is an external world that is different and separate from the infant. From 0–6 months a slow unfolding occurs. Stern (1985) suggests that the infant's 'emergent' self develops into a 'core self' which at 2–6 months has four self-experiences: self-agency, self-coherence, self-affectivity, and self-history.

Each of these 'stages' describe different aspects of the core self such as the infant's experience of his or her own actions as being their own, separate from others, having intention, and the control to be self-generated (self-agency). Self-coherence is the experience of being a whole, non-fragmented being with their own boundaries who has the capacity for integrated action both in behaviour and being still. The experience of emotional, that is, affective response as being part of oneself (self-affectivity) contributes to that part of the core self which has a sense that it will endure, maintain continuity with its own past and 'go on being', remaining the same while still capable of change (self-history).

Do 'I' know 'I' am a girl yet?

Although it is speculative, it is quite likely that part of the infant's sense of their body boundaries, its dimensions, and the sensory experiences it evokes that develop from 0–6 months is accompanied by the gradual internalization of the primary caretakers' conviction of the baby's gender. The tiny girl of 6 months will have made huge developmental strides and will be well practised in scrutinizing the world around her. She will have experienced myriad interactions between herself and her caretakers which will have been accompanied by their awareness of her being female. The bathing and dressing – 'Look at the pretty flowers on your dress!' – the excited cooing about being a beautiful little girl – 'Oh! Who's a pretty girl, then?' 'Oh! what dainty feet you have?' She will have seen her mother, grandmother, aunties, older sisters and/or nanny caring for the household, either real or imaginary, for example, her sister with dollhouse and dollies.

An internal, unconscious template of what it is to be female within her culture and social setting will be developing throughout a girl infant's earliest years. The types of toys and activities she chooses may be encouraged or discouraged by her attachment world as appropriate or not for girls. For example, when they can walk girls are still more likely to be given toy prams to push as opposed to army tanks. Boys often learn by their environment's somewhat anxious or ambivalent reaction to their wish to push a pram that this activity is mainly 'for girls'. Equally, the little girl who wants to carry around toy work tools and play with a hammer is made to feel she is 'being boyish'.

All of these interactions will be stored and will become part of what Stern (1985: 97) calls RIGS or 'representations of interactions which have become generalized'. These will help lay the foundation for the girl's developing awareness that she is 'a me!' and that the rest of her world is a 'not me'. In time part of 'me' will also be perceived as 'she'.

Stoller (1968: 58) maintains it is this cumulative internalization alongside the infant's exploration and awareness of their body that develops into an unquestioning sense of being female or male. He also says the 'sense of gender is fixed in the first years of life and is a piece of identity so firm that almost no vicissitudes of living can destroy it'.

The question is if it were possible to map out accurately an infant girl's subjective experience of herself what would we see? Leinbach and Fagot (1993) have shown that infants as young as 5 months have some clear categorical knowledge of female and male voices and faces. But does this mean that the little girl exploring her body alone in her cot has an awareness that her body is in some way related to her ability to distinguish a female voice and or face? It is almost impossible to know.

We do know that by 9 months the infant has developed awareness that she or he has a mind and that other people also have minds. Stern (1985) terms this the intersubjective self. Its development creates the potential for sharing individual inner, subjective experiences with another. Therefore, perhaps by 9 months the cognitive understanding of difference between female and male voices and faces takes on added depth. The increased awareness of another's experience of themselves, including gender, is internalized and becomes a core part of the infant's subjective experience of self as female or male.

However, most likely this remains unconceptualized. A 12-month-old baby if asked if they were a girl or a boy would not be able to understand what was being asked. They can certainly point to their nose, eyes, mouth etc. and distinguish them from mummy's and daddy's. They could probably delight in the 'other's' pleasure in asking, 'Well, who's a gentle girl, now?' but the delight would be in the affective experience of shared pleasure rather than in any understanding that they were a girl who was gentle.

The role of brain and affect in becoming 'I am me'

Schore (1994: 7) states:

> Development essentially represents a number of sequential mutually driven infant caregiver processes that occur in a continuing dialectic between the maturing organism and the changing environment. It now appears that affect is what is actually transacted within the mother–infant dyad, and this highly efficient system of emotional communication is essentially nonverbal. Human development, including its internal neurochemical and neurobiological mechanisms, cannot be understood apart from this affect-transacting relationship.

The cumulative effect of this interchange of affect can aid or inhibit the development of a solid sense of self in the early infant, a sense that it is 'all right to be me in the world' separate from mother or primary attachment figure. The concept of 'me' is a highly complex one. It comprises many different developmental processes converging into the whole picture of 'I am me', one of which is the evolving sense of 'me' as a girl or boy.

Animal research into developmental neuroanatomy and neurochemistry has revealed the biological and chemical changes that are part of internal processes which underpin the complex affective and cognitive capacities of the human being. Schore (1994: 6) states:

> It is now very clear that well before the advent of language the baby's capacities to interact with the social and physical environments, functions supported by these internal processes, are extremely complex and sophisticated. The fast acting, psychobiological mechanisms that mature in early and late infancy continue to operate throughout life. Indeed they serve as the keystone of all future human intra-organismic, intrapsychic, and interpersonal functioning, as the manifestation of all later developing capacities is contingent upon their initiatory expression.

One particularly interesting aspect of the developing awareness of the existence of 'I am me' in the early infant is the relationship between the experience of the affect-transacting relationship of the infant/caregiver dyad and the development of the parts of the brain which eventually allow the infant to function as a feeling, autonomous, social being, who is aware of their own gender.

The human brain weighs only 400g at birth. By 12 months it weighs 1000g. Its growth spurt continues until approximately 18–24 months (Dobbing and Smart 1974). Complex functional brain systems 'are formed in the process of social contact and objective activity by the child' (Luria 1980). These systems, among many other functions, are responsible for the process of imprinting the attachment world's response to the infant's gender. By 18 months they have also interacted with sex and gonadal steroids resulting in permanent feminized or masculinized brain circuitry which then produces gender differences in affect regulation (Schore 1994).

Two of the central systems of the brain are the cortical and limbic systems. The limbic system has several structures within it, two of which are thought to play a central role in emotional experiences and reactions (the amygdala) and memory (hippocampus). In general the limbic system is concerned with visceral processes, especially those of emotional response. The cerebral cortex is the outer layer of the brain. It too has different parts. One of them, the prefrontal cortex, has the highest level of organizational complexity and serves an inhibitory function. It helps to inhibit drives and impulses, and regulates arousal and activity states and generally sees to it that we are not completely overwhelmed. The development of this part of the brain happens after birth and is especially influenced by the infant's interaction with her or his environment. The subcortical limbic region of the brain is the site of spontaneous emotional expression while the cortical area is the inhibitory control centre.

At birth, the human organism is remarkably ill-equipped to cope with the various excitations of its new environment. It is a subcortical creature that is in danger of going into shock through overreacting to powerful or unexpected stimuli because it lacks the means for modulation of behaviour, which is made possible by the development of cortical control. The role of the higher structures is played by the mother; she is the child's auxiliary cortex (Diamond *et al.* 1963: 305).

Within the prefrontal lobe of the cortex lies the orbital frontal cortex. This part of the brain has extensive connections with the limbic system. It acts as an association cortex for the limbic forebrain (Pribram 1981; Martin 1989). The orbitofrontal cortex is particularly instrumental in processing social and emotional behaviour. It is crucially involved in attachment processes (Steklis and Kling 1985).

Another function of the orbitofrontal cortex is modulating the auto-nomic nervous system. In this role it influences the stimulation of hormonal and neurohormonal changes. The orbitofrontal cortex's capacity to process the imprinting of the infant's attachment world's response to her or his gender plays a crucial part in the evolving awareness of being a girl or boy. Equally important in the evolution of this awareness is its role in stimulating the hormones that produce feminine or masculine brain wiring.

The period of 7–18 months is a critical time for the maturation of rapidly developing areas in the brain, especially the orbitofrontal cortex. Schore (1994) notes that this coincides with Bowlby's period when attachment patterns are established as well as with Margaret Mahler's practising and rapprochment periods of separation–individuation, three key aspects of early infant development. Meyersburg and Post (1979) have shown that there is a general correspondence in time between postnatal neurodevelopmental cycles, Mahler's stages of infant development, and critical periods of psychosocial maturation.

The developing central nervous system of infants drives them towards understanding and mastery of their world. As they arrive at a certain level of achievement the nervous system according to Brazleton and Cramer (1991) urges them on to the next stage. This naturally impacts upon their interaction with their attachment world and their developing perception of their sense of self as a unique individual.

How does the interaction with the attachment world affect the develop-ment of the nervous system and vice versa? According to Schore (1994) the primary caretaker, by providing attuned affective and social inter-action, facilitates the growth of connections between the cortical and subcortical limbic structures of the brain. These connections neuro-biologically mediate self-regulatory functions.

The attachment world's holding environment and its capacity for attuning, validating, soothing, appropriately stimulating, challenging, and encouraging the early infant is finely integrated with postnatal neural anatomic and neurochemical development. The various interventions of the primary caretaker appear to be essential for neural development to occur. The dynamic interaction between the attachment world's rela-tionship with the infant and his or her developing brain is the foundation of the infant's emotional development (Grotstein 1994).

Schore (1994) places particular emphasis on the importance of the development of the neural anatomy of the affect regulatory centres of the brain, especially the right hemispheric orbitofrontal cortex. This is the area of the brain that controls the regulation and mediation of affect, social relations, and emotional balance amongst other things. Grotstein (1994: xxi) says that it is responsible even for 'development of the humanness of the infant!'

'I am', individuation, and dawning gender awareness

To 'know' in every pore of one's being that 'I' am a unique individual with my own name, my own body, my own gender, takes at least three to four years. It is interesting to note that the period of infant development during which consolidation of perception of individuality, greater control over body, and the establishment of rudimentary gender identity takes place when the baby is increasingly able to move away from the primary attachment/caregiver figure. This ushers in the practising and rapprochement phases, significant for all aspects of an infant's development.

Margaret Mahler *et al.* (1975) proposed that there were specific phases of social and emotional development. In this they are in agreement with the concept of sequential stages of early development put forth by other disciplines such as neurobiology, neurochemistry, ethology, embryology, psychology and biology.

Mahler *et al.* developed a program of developmental psychoanalytic research which concentrated on observing what they termed the 'separation–individuation process' (1975: 41) of infants and toddlers from 0–3 years. This process starting at birth was divided into several subphases, each of which facilitated the next phase of development, culminating in 'the psychological birth of the human infant' (Mahler *et al.* 1975: 3) towards the end of the second year. By this time the internal world of the infant is structured enough that she or he can experience themselves as autonomous beings capable of knowing and self-regulating their emotional world. During this process they described two particular subphases, the practising phase, and the 'rapprochment' subphase, which have particular relevance to the infant developing a sense of themselves as an individual person.

During the practising phase of the separation–individuation process the infant of about 7–15 months begins to be able to sit up, crawl away, stand, move upright while holding on and eventually walk alone. The advent of motility brings with it an enormous joy, increase in curiosity and an exploration of the world 'other than mother'. However, each foray away from mother requires 'checking back to mother' in order to assure the infant that the secure base is still there. In primitive attachment terms the young mobile infant needs to be assured that protection is still there and a 'tiger' won't eat them! The repeated coming and going continues the lengthy process begun at birth of the baby learning about and consolidating 'me' from 'not me'.

The way in which the caregivers react to the infant's increased motility and desire to explore further afield contributes to the consolidation of a sense of self as secure as a separate individual within their environment.

It also plays an important role in the infant's perception of actions that the attachment world considers appropriate gender behaviour.

The infant's exuberant love affair with the world leads her or him to climb, run, jump, experiment with toys, make a mess, put things inside things and then dump them out, and so on. Boys may well be encouraged to wander further than girls, be praised for their athletic prowess in climbing, and treated with chuckles and pride when they get into a tussle over a toy or begin to explore the video machine by putting things in it. The general message conveyed would be 'Go for it! Aren't you brave and adventurous!' The girl on the other hand might more often be told to 'Be careful! You might hurt yourself.' 'Don't go too far. Why don't you make Mummy some tea . . .' She might also be warned not to make a mess and get her 'pretty shirt dirty'.

Girls will gradually learn that they are meant to satisfy their wish to explore nearer to homebase and concentrate on quieter activities which are considered more 'feminine' such as playing with soft toys, doll houses etc. A girl may learn that her wish to pretend to be a fire engine making a loud noise is frowned upon as tomboyish. Equally, a little boy who wants to carry around a handbag full of tiny dolls and their hairbrushes will be made to feel he is playing with girl's stuff.

The ongoing internalization of the caregiving of the primary caretaker includes the caretaker both as emotional secure base and conveyor of perception of gender. As the infant moves away s/he refers both to the 'internal' mother and to the one talking on the telephone. Both continue to facilitate the separation–individuation process and the development of a sense of self as a secure individual girl or boy.

Around 15–18 months the baby goes through a period of low-keyedness and becomes alternately clingy and whiny, and demanding and aggressive. This is a period that Mahler *et al.* (1975) called the 'rapprochement crisis'. During this time the infant experiences an increased awareness that she or he is truly separate from mother and is an autonomous person in their own right. There is a heightened sense of being independent but also alone and unsafe and in considerable need of refuelling at mother's knee or on her lap.

The rapprochement crisis can be a time in which gender expectations can impede the process of resolution. For example, the exploring, independent little boy may have his needs for being dependent and refuelling denied under the guise of 'big boys don't cry and sit on Mummy's lap.' They may be left to 'get on with it'. Girls on the other hand may have their refuelling prolonged and be kept on mother's lap and not encouraged to get on with their independent exploration.

Once the balance of independence and refuelling is achieved and internalized the infant can begin to trust that she or he is really safe in the world as an individual. They are well on the way to the developed solid sense of themselves necessary for future healthy development.

Part of this sense of themselves is a rudimentary awareness of gender identity, an understanding that they are a girl or a boy. This awareness becomes increasingly conscious although not fully conceptualized between the ages of 18 months to 3 years. The 2-year-olds in Mahler *et al.* (1975) know their name, that they are separate and autonomous individuals, and that they are called boys or girls.

Two-year-old thinking about gender

The separation–individuation process facilitates the internalization of the 2-year-olds' attachment world to which they can refer as they test their independence and autonomy. This knowledge is emotionally 'known' and acted upon in the contrariness of the 'terrible 2s'. The toddler of this age will refuse a favourite meal of fish fingers when especially hungry in order to state his or her autonomy, but they cannot conceptualize that this is what they are doing. The subjective experience of the toddler is very impulse driven, guided by the overriding need to act upon the feeling of 'I am I! And me wants what I want *now*!'

In the same way a 2-year-old may have both a primitive, biological–in-the-brain understanding of being masculine or feminine, of gender identity, which through the years since birth has been reinforced by their attachment world. They still would be unable to conceptualize this, however, so that it became part of their conscious subjective experience. They could answer the question, 'Are you a girl or a boy?' by first looking at what they were wearing and then answering according to the style of clothes they had on. Ben, a 2-year-old in the hospital playroom, knew he was a boy because 'big boys get badges' (from the doctors). Lucy, another 2-year-old, knew she was a girl because, 'Have ribbons in hair . . . Barbie [a doll] ribbons too'. It was interesting to note that these children, even though they were in hospital and more than usually exposed to their own and other children's bodies, still predominately seemed to identify their gender by what were clearly socially and cultur-ally learned experiences.

The increased motility, autonomy, and social interaction with peers that the 18-month–2-year-old infant experiences make them increasingly aware of their own and others' bodies. They note genital differences. Even though they have an imperfect grasp of them the developing capacity for language may help in understanding how each sex is different. If their attachment world has been able to discuss with them the difference in genital structure between girls and boys they stand a much better chance of knowing that they are a girl because they have 'a front bottom with a hole inside it. . . . boys don't have front bottoms' and a boy if they have a 'willy which does pee-pee standing up . . . not like girls who have to sit down!'

Bern (1989) argues that those children who have adults in their environment who can discuss the difference between male and female genitals will be less likely to suffer confusion between gender identity and gender constancy. In other words, they will be able to understand that their awareness of themselves as female or male (gender identity) cannot change (gender constancy).

However the ability to conceptualize gender identity and gender constancy will be vastly different according to age as well as to past experience. An 18-month-old baby's understanding of gender identity will be considerably different from the 3-year-old and 5-year-old. Toby was an 18-month-old boy who loved dancing with his sister, Gina. She was 2.5 years old. They had an older brother, Tom, who was 4.5 years old. When Toby was asked, 'Where's a girl?' he looked blank and then began bouncing in time to the music that was playing. Gina when asked the same question smiled bashfully and pointed to her skirt. Tom said to Gina, 'You're a girl 'cause you can't beat Action Man and I can!!'

The outside world tells me how to be a girl or boy. My brain also tells me.

Girls and boys by the time they enter nursery school towards the end of their second year and beginning of their third year are well aware that boys are meant be more active and play with things like trucks, and pretend to be Spiderman or Batman and girls are supposed to play with dolls, pretend to play house, and cook, and dress up like mummies and nurses. Even in the eternally fascinating game of 'let's play doctors!' it is usually the boy who is the doctor and the girl the nurse. It is the boy who flies the spacecraft to the moon and the girl who brings him his dinner and sees to it that the rest of the spacecraft is running properly.

Despite the changing social and cultural scene of the twentieth century most of these stereotypes still hold true. Even the most 'liberated' female 3-year-old will feel free to ride a bike, play Superwoman, and pretend to fly a plane but will then spend hours dressing her collection of teddies and 'sorting out' what they are supposed to do and not do.

Girls still have more 'permission' to express their feelings while boys even today are expected to 'be brave' and not express their emotions. Babies are not born with these expectations. They learn them from their attachment world. Their parents, grandparents, siblings, aunties, uncles, teachers, TV, computer games and so on all have a role to play in 'telling' the infant how to be a boy or girl.

It is also true that the brain 'tells' the infant they are a girl or boy. Sex steroids directly influence the maturation of the cerebral cortex, the organization of brain circuits, and the developing orbitofrontal region of the brain. This results in this structure developing a permanent feminized or masculinized circuitry (Schore 1994). In other words from early post-natal life the wiring of those parts of the brain particularly responsible for the regulation and mediation of feeling, social interactions, and emotional balance is chemically influenced by genetically driven sex steroids. This then produces feminine and masculine wiring patterns in the brain which then create gender differences in how feeling is expressed and contained.

In addition, the masculine or feminine maturing orbitofrontal cortex is 'responsible for observed sex differences in structure (cerebral lateralization, hemispheric asymmetry) and function (cognition, spatial perception)' (Schore 1994: 268). This in combination with the input from the infant's environment would account for many of the differences in the ways girls approach thinking and doing and the ways in which boys do.

The toddler in their second year also begins to experience an increase in genital excitement which is caused by a sensual-sexual system that is motivated within in the brain (Schore 1994). It is this that triggers the beginning of infantile sexuality. The late 2 to 3-year-old is thoroughly delighted with their body and the pleasure it gives them. How their attachment world responds to this delight is imprinted into the orbitofrontal cortex that eventually comes to function in the regulation of sexual drive. Little girls may learn from their environment that it is shameful to display their pleasure in sensuality and retreat into demure, non-competitive behaviour.

I know I'm a girl and I'm 3!

The attachment world's interaction with the little girl from conception onwards, her brain's wiring and development, and the process of her own gradual discovery of herself as a unique autonomous individual all contribute to the little girl's subjective understanding at the ripe old age of 3 that part of her 'being me' is being a girl.

The 'subcortical' infant girl was born programmed to interact with her environment. The myriad interactions of her first 2.5–3 years helped her along the road towards selfhood. She became able to exist as a person in her own right separate from but still part of her attachment world. Once a separate sense of self was established she began to extend this into her own specific identity. She began to know who and what she was. She knew her name, her family and social world and she became conscious of the fact that she was female. Her gender identity became an integral part of her whole identity.

Questions 2.5–3-year-olds can't ask but are still there

The early infant from 0–2 or 3 years of age does not yet have the full capacity for abstract thinking and conceptualization that develops in later childhood. The nascent capacity for symbolic thinking begins towards the end of the first year of life as the 'domain of the verbal relatedness' (Stern 1985: 163) becomes active. Infants even before their first half-formed word is uttered have begun the use of sound and language as communication, the start of symbolic thinking. If we are exploring female (or male) development from 0–2 years the question arises, 'What is the subjective experience of developing gender identity of a 2-year-old?' The self-narrative of a toddler, her inner dialogue with herself, is still really unknown. We as psychotherapists, psychoanalysts, cognitive therapists, developmental psychologists, parents, and teachers etc. can really only speculate and extrapolate from outward behaviour – or we can superimpose on toddlers our own ideas and purported hypotheses gained from work with older children, adolescents, and adults, often including our own fantasy world. Working with a 2-year-old in psychotherapy is a privilege and great fun, but it is also a tremendous challenge just to listen to the various communications of the toddler and understand what they mean to her or him rather than what they mean to and for us.

The mystery of a 2-year-old's internal conversation with herself still remains. We can only guess about which part of that conversation includes an understanding of gender identity. Perhaps it's just as well, as the infant works towards becoming an autonomous self, that we cannot yet intrude upon their private world.

References

Bern, S.L. (1989) Genital knowledge and gender constancy in preschool children, *Child Development*, 60: 649–62.
Bowlby, J. (1969) *Attachment and Loss*. London: Pimlico.

Bowlby, J. (1973) *Separation*. London: Pimlico.

Bowlby, J. (1979) *Making and Breaking of Affectional Bonds*. London: Tavistock Publications.

Brazleton, B. and Cramer, B.G. (1991) *The Earliest Relationship*. London: Karnac Books.

Chambers Dictionary (1993) Edinburgh: Chambers Harrap Publishers Ltd.

Diamond, M. (1965) A critical evaluation of the ontogeny of human sexual behaviour. *The Quarterly Review of Biology*, 40: 147–75.

Diamond, M. and Sigmundson, H.K. (1997) Management of intersexuality. Guidelines for dealing with persons with ambiguous genitalia. *Archives of Pediatric and Adolescent Medicine*, 151(10): 1046–50.

Diamond, S., Balvin, R. and Diamond, F. (1963) *Inhibition and Choice*. New York: Harper & Row.

Dobbing, J. and Smart, J.L. (1974) Vulnerability of developing brain and behaviour, *British Medical Bulletin*, 30: 164–8.

Emde, R. (1983) The affective core. Paper presented at the Second World Congress of Infant Psychiatry, Cannes, France, March.

Fraiberg, S. (1987) *Selected Writing of Selma Fraiberg*. Columbus, OH: Ohio State University Press.

Freud, A. and Burlingham, D. (1944) Infants without families: the case for and against residential nurseries, in *Infants Without Families and Reports on the Hampstead Nurseries 1939–1945*. London: Hogarth Press.

Freud, S. ([1905] 1953) Three essays on the theory of sexuality, in J. Strachey (ed. and trans.) *The Standard Edition of the Complete Psychological Works of Sigmund Freud* (24 vols). London: Hogarth Press.

Freud, S. ([1937] 1964) Analysis terminable and interminable, in J. Strachey (ed.) *The Standard Edition of the Complete Psychological Works of Sigmund Freud* (24 vols), Vol. 23. London: The Hogarth Press.

Grotstein, J.S. (1994) Foreword, in A. Schore, *Affect Regulation and the Origin of the Self*. Hillsdale, NJ: Lawrence Erlbaum Associates Inc.

Heard, D. and Lake, B. (1997) *The Challenge for Caregiving*. London: Routledge.

Karen, R. (1994) *Becoming Attached*. New York: Warner Books.

Klein, M. ([1921] 1981) The development of a child, in *The Writings of Melanie Klein*. London: Hogarth Press.

Leinbach, M.D. and Fagot, B.I. (1993) Categorical habituation to male and female faces: gender schematic processing in infancy, *Infant Behaviour and Development*, 16: 317–31.

Mahler, M.S., Pine, F. and Bergman, A. (1975) *The Psychological Birth of the Human Infant*. London: Hutchinson and Co. Ltd.

Martin, J.H. (1989) *Neuroanatomy: Text and Atlas*. New York: Elsevier.

Meyersburg, H.A. and Post, R.M. (1979) An holistic developmental view of neural and psychological processes: a neurobiological and psychoanalytic integration. *British Journal of Psychology*, 135: 139–55.

Money, J. and Ehrhardt, A.A. (1973) *Man, Woman, Boy and Girl*. Northvale, NJ: Jason Aronson Inc.

Parkes, C.M., Stevenson-Hinde, J. and Marris, P. (eds) (1991) *Attachment Across the Life-Cycle*. London: Routledge.

Pribram, K.H. (1981) Emotions, in S.B. Filskov and T.J. Boll (eds) *Handbook of Clinical Neuropsychology*. New York: Wiley, pp. 102–34.

Robertson, J. (1971) Young children in brief separation: a fresh look, *Psychoanalytic Study of the Child*, 26: 264–315.

Schore, A. (1994) *Affect Regulation and the Origin of the Self*. Hillsdale, NJ: Lawrence Erlbaum Associates.

Spitz, R. (1965) *The First Year of Life: A Psychoanalytic Study of Normal and Deviant Development of Object Relations*. New York: International Universities Press.

Steklis, H.D. and Kling, A. (1985) Neurobiology of affiliative behavior in non-human primates, in R.M. Reite and T. Field (eds) *The Psychobiology of Attachment and Separation*. Orlando, FL: Academic Press.

Stern, D. (1985) *The Interpersonal World of the Human Infant*. New York: Basic Books.

Stoller, R.J. (1968) *Sex and Gender, the Development of Masculinity and Femininity*. London: Karnac Books Ltd.

Whiting, B.B. and Edwards, C.P. (1973) A cross-cultural analysis of sex differences in the behavior of children aged 3–11, *Journal of Social Psychology*, 91: 171–88.

Winnicott, D.W. (1958) *Collected Papers*. London: Tavistock Publications.

Wright, K. (1991) *Vision and Separation: Between Mother and Baby*. Northvale, NJ: Jason Aronson.

3 Adolescence: possibilities and limitations, experience and expression

Moira Walker

I wasn't good
At adolescence. There was a dance,
A catchy rhythm: I was out of step.
My body capered, nudging me
With hair, fleshy growths and monthly outbursts,
To join the party. I tried to annul
The future, pretending I knew it already,
Was caught bloody thighed, a criminal
Guilty of puberty.
Not a nice girl,
No.

(Fanthorpe 1989: 6)

These brief lines vividly express the agonies, uncertainties, and discomfort often experienced by female adolescents: the 'pretending' to know – that false confidence of the 'you don't tell me what to do, *I know*' variety that can simultaneously infuriate, frustrate and alarm adults; the unpredictability of a newly changed body; the feeling that everyone else is somehow mysteriously 'in step' and you should be too; the lack of 'fit' combined with a huge need to be acceptable to your peers. For some, there is an underlying sense of a deep lack of ease with self, and for others, sadly, a real feeling of shame at their changing body, often reflecting major life difficulties experienced during childhood. What is not captured here is the converse – and adolescence is perhaps epitomized by these alternating phases – is the excitement, exploration, experimentation and discoveries that can also be experienced by adolescent girls. As they build the bridge between childhood and adulthood, particularly in the early years of adolescence, they vacillate – often with remarkable speed between these two states – again to the perplexity of adults around them. At this point in their lives activities, friends and relationships outside of the family become increasingly significant in their search for love, attention, new experiences and excitement. No wonder then that it is a chance to rework earlier issues (Blos 1962). The essential fluidity that marks adolescence, the rapidity of changes during this time physiologically, psychologically and hormonally, all lead to the possibility of earlier issues being revisited. It is a time when past, present and future are extraordinarily intermingled and overlapping. This is recognized by parents as well as professionals; one mother of a 13-year-old girl who had battled to be independent as a toddler and now fought the same battle with renewed energy, commented wistfully that it was like living through the terrible 2s all over again except that at 13 her daughter could do it so much better, for so much longer and brought to it so many new-found skills.

Adolescence then is commonly marked by growing separation from the family, both socially and psychologically. There is greater independence in all aspects of being: in thought, word and action. In this major transition, this bid for separation, this striving to be herself, her parents can become scorned and rejected. Mothers in particular describe how at adolescence they metamorphose from being their little girl's 'best mummy in the world', to being a mother who just does not understand, who is treated with withering glances and contemptuous words, and find that their previously companionable child has become a young person who walks 10 paces behind them. Even this is not constant, however; mothers will also describe how quickly this face of independence can shift under pressure; how the little girl can re-emerge playfully or needily, or how the apparently independent young girl's need for mother can be expressed as an immediate and desperate demand for reassurance, comfort, solutions or for the projection of blame or uncertainty ('I can't stay at that party all night – my mum won't let me – you know what she's like'). It can feel for the parent as if they too have to metamorphose into the equivalent of the genie from the lamp, to appear instantly on demand when needed and to back off when not required. In the midst of this, of course, there can be moments of pure delight both from and to this newly emerging young woman. No wonder it can be such a demanding and confusing time for all involved.

Adolescence: a universal experience?

This process, which is essentially not static within the individual, is not static in external terms either. The descriptions above are placed in a UK context but a girl's adolescence is influenced and affected by socio-economic class status, sexual orientation and subculture (Ponton 1993). Even the term adolescence has no neat definition in terms of time span and no attempt to create one will be made here. However it can be helpful to think of adolescence as falling into broadly three periods – early, middle and late (Blos 1962; Laufer 1974). It is clear to those who work or live with adolescent girls that they present and behave very differently at, say, 13 and 17.

The examples given throughout of adolescent behaviour are inevitably culture related. For many girls and young women around the world self-expression would be impossible. Inness (1998) explores how the realities of girls' experience drastically differs between countries and cultures. She describes the bleakness experienced by many in their current day-to-day living and in terms of their future prospects. A stark example is the number of girl prostitutes in Thailand, Brazil and the Philippines (Kurz and Prather 1995). It is too easy to see these countries as unrelated to the UK, but of course many of their 'customers' are visiting business-men. We need only to look at the numbers of young women homeless on our streets to realize that within the UK culture exist many subcultures. There is not one adolescent experience. Being female and adolescent has entirely different meanings in say the UK from Japan, and within different subcultures in the UK. Inness points out how in many cultures girls are still 'ghostless voices'. The expression of 'withering glances and contemptuous words' referred to above is an unknown luxury to many girls; some cultures do not allow any expression of their views; they are forced into silent compliance – as indeed can be girls in the UK who are victims of violence within the family. So while 'girl power' has become a popular term and ideology in this country in many others it could not exist. It would have no place and no fit with the emotional or political vocabulary.

It is also important to explode the myth that exploitation of adolescent girls is exclusively a Third World phenomenon. In recent years in the US a famous and well-publicized case (US Department of Labor 1995) was taken to court by trade unions against a clothing manufacturer that netted $9 million annually and was using child labour:

> To support their claims they bought in fifteen year old Wendy Diaz who worked in the Honduran sweatshop Global Fashion. Diaz described having started work in the sweatshop at the age of thirteen. Her days often consisted of working anywhere from thirteen to twenty-four hours to meet deadlines, and she often received only thirty-one American cents per day. She and her three brothers are orphans and she is the family's main source of income.
>
> (Ige 1998: 48)

This young woman's experience is a powerful reminder of the diversity of adolescent experience. Her world bears little relationship to that of the majority of those in the UK, who have the space and permission to be involved primarily and egocentrically with the task of growing up. For children and young women like Wendy Diaz adulthood is thrust upon them; the transition between child and adulthood is eroded – it is a luxury that cannot be afforded. The need to survive financially is paramount. Economic necessity fills the transitional space. It is evident that there is no one concept of adolescence; rather it is in part a social, economic and political invention, re-created by every society and age. That is, the period labelled youth is historically and socially variable – youth and adolescence are social constructs. In Victorian times children and adolescents had not been 'invented'; although girls in wealthy homes may have been protected, nurtured and cherished, it was an entirely different scenario for those from the working class. Many worked in factories or domestic service from an early age, and although developing legislation relating both to employment and education gave some protection, life was hard, and earning a living essential:

> Domestic service also involved long hours and little independence, but in 1905 it was Rose Ashton's only hope of work. Then aged thirteen, she was sent by her parents to the local hiring fair at Ulveston. Rose remembers the local farmers inspecting the girls rather like cattle at a market. If they liked what they saw, they made an offer . . . For six months she was virtually a slave in her employer's house, working even on Christmas Day.
>
> (Holdsworth 1988: 63)

A far cry perhaps from the experience of a 13-year-old living in the UK today, although horribly reminiscent of the story of Wendy Diaz 90 years on.

An overview of developmental theory

As noted, it is crucial to recognize that adolescence is not clear cut, either in terms of its time span, or its content and meaning. It is influenced by many factors, notably cultural, social and historical. However, the focus of this chapter is primarily to examine the current world of adolescent girls within the UK. To put this into context what follows is a brief overview of aspects of developmental theory that has influenced thinking and practice, focusing on how it pertains specifically to the development of girls.

Much has been written about adolescence from both sociological and psychological perspectives – as a term it was first used by Stanley Hall (1904). Around the same time that Hall was writing, Freud was recognizing childhood as a distinct psychological and developmental state worthy of study and inextricably linked to, and exerting a powerful influence on, adult life (1905). Freud describes adolescence as a time when young people begin to separate from parents and begin the process of seeking sexual partnership. He argues that girls are less able to separate, remaining in 'childish love far beyond puberty' (1905: 150) and later argues that puberty brings a new awareness of 'the wound to her narcissism, resulting in a scar, a sense of inferiority' (1925: 253). He did acknowledge the influence of the sexual double standard that existed; simply put, young men were free to enjoy their sexuality and sexual relationships, young women were not. He himself recognized that his understanding of girls and women had its limitations (1923: 309). This however does have the flavour of hedging his bets; he writes at length and authoritatively on female development and his views were and are extremely influential. He was at times extremely derogatory towards women; 'it seems that women have made few contributions to the discoveries and inventions in the history of civilization' (1933: 166). When Karen Horney questioned the phallocentricity of Freud's theories, arguing that his theories were value laden and representing the interests of men, his response was similarly dismissive and belittling: 'We shall not be so very greatly surprised if a woman analyst who has not been sufficiently convinced of the intensity of her own desire for a penis also fails to assign an adequate importance to that factor in patients' (quoted in Kelman 1967: 26). Statements such as these render questionable Freud's apparent uncertainty and modesty regarding female development. Horney's considered and careful challenges met with attack from Freud; he appeared personally affronted and Horney's career certainly suffered as a result of her continued challenges to his theories. It is interesting to note that the ideas being developed by Horney during the 1920s and 1930s were to lie dormant until the advent of feminist psychotherapy in the 1960s.

Since these early formulations female adolescence has created a problem for developmental theorists that reflects the confusions and questions arising from these times. Erikson (1965), influenced by Freud, identified eight stages of psychosocial development – the 'Eight Ages of Man'. The gender specificity is pertinent although it must also be acknowledged that such specificity was typical and accepted writing practice of the time. However, as with Freud, there is a male bias in his work, and this is highlighted in his work on adolescence. Adolescence is Erikson's fifth stage when identity comes through a growing autonomy. Identity precedes intimacy as the sixth stage. Herein lies the problem in respect of adolescent girls. For women identity and intimacy cannot be so easily separated; they seem to be one and the same thing. Gilligan (1982: 10) notes that Piaget and Lever, also both influential in the field of child development, similarly equate male development with child development overall without any gender differentiation. She argues that attachment and connectedness are intrinsic to the development of girls and women. They value these aspects; they are not impediments but central and core to the self.

A study of college students in the US (Hodgson and Fischer 1979) backs up Gilligan's (1992) argument. It found that young men focused on intrapersonal aspects of identity whereas young women focused on interpersonal aspects. For young women achieving intimacy was more closely related to their identity than in the young men – further supporting the view that Eriksonian theory is better at explaining male development. Similar results came from a study by Jossleson (1973) who also noted that identity in young women differed from male identity and was marked by the greater emphasis on the importance of intimacy. To Erikson separation is both the model and the measure for growth and although he acknowledges that intimacy has a special significance to women this acknowledgement does not translate into a place in his developmental chart. By this measure girls then are almost by definition unable to fully grow up, reminiscent of Freud's words. This is also reflected in the Broverman *et al.* study (1970) which found that mental health practioners were less likely to attribute traits characterizing healthy adults to women than to men. In other words, what is seen as normal for a woman does not match up with what is seen as normal for an adult. Gilligan (1982: 6) comments that:

> Implicitly adopting the male life as the norm, they have tried to fashion women out of a masculine cloth. It all goes back of course to Adam and Eve – a story which shows, among other things, that if you make a woman out of a man, you are bound to get into trouble. In the life cycle, as in the Garden of Eden, the woman has been the deviant.

Chodorow has also explored the masculine bias of psychoanalytic thinking and in tune with Gilligan argues that girls experience themselves as being essentially connected with others. Therefore the development of their identity does not rest on separation and individuation as it does for boys:

> Feminine personality comes to define itself in relation to connection to other people more than masculine personality does . . . Moreover issues of dependency are handled and experienced differently by men

and women. For boys and men, both individuation and dependency issues become tied up with the sense of masculinity, or masculine identity. For girls and women, by contrast, issues of femininity or feminine identity, are not problematic in the same way.

(Chodorow 1989: 47)

To summarize, the theories of Freud and Erikson argue that it is the successful completion of specific developmental tasks that differentiate the adult from the child and adolescent, and marks a mature person. The work of Gilligan, Chodorow and others into the development of girls and young women indicate that by taking these tasks as indicators then by definition girls and women are not going to achieve that status. Their work shows that the male experience has been generalized to women and that this was biased, inaccurate and failed to capture the essence of female experience. The importance of their work in offering another perspective that is relevant to understanding girls in their transition to womanhood should not be underestimated.

The experience of adolescent girls

For over a century adolescence has been identified as a time of heightened psychological risk for girls – from Freud and Breuer (1895) suggesting that girls lose their vitality, to Seligman (1991) who felt that they lose their capacity to resist depression, and to Herman (1981) who notes the increased risk of being abused sexually. Certainly the twentieth century has seen enormous changes from a world where the establishment of adult identities was relatively straightforward, where the occupational world was more stable and social norms well established and gender definitions very clear. Routes available to girls were clearly defined, albeit restrictive, and frames of reference well established and stable:

At the beginning of the [twentieth] century, only 29 per cent of the work force were women and only 10 per cent of married women worked. Men lost face if they could not support their wives. Middle-class women did not work and respectable working-class women tried hard to do the same. Their unmarried daughters expected to stay at home, kept by father, until their wedding day.

(Holdsworth 1988: 62)

Nowadays, the range of social and cultural influences are complex, and possibilities previously denied are available to girls and young women. Cote and Allahar (1996) suggest that this range of influence and opportunity create a particular vulnerability to adult profiteers. This vulnerability is also a consequence of the dramatic changes in girls' bodies that occur during early adolescence. This disconnects them from their childhood world before they are able to join an adult world and the transition between the two is not comfortable. This is neatly summed up by one 13-year-old who, as she swung around to show off a new outfit, managed to leave a trail of debris behind her as she swept objects off a shelf. Looking quite astonished and perplexed she commented that 'the problem is I don't know where I am any more – I don't know where I start or where I end'. At one level she was referring to having grown five inches in a year but taken as a metaphor this captures the bodily and psychical disconnection, and the complexity of relating, both to their own self, and between self and others. As Brown and Gilligan (1992: 184) point out, this is a difficult process:

> Here at this watershed in girls' development . . . each will struggle with a central relational quandary: how to stay with herself and be with others, how to keep her voice in connection with her inner psychic world of thoughts and feelings and also to bring her voice into her relationships with other people.

This conflict all has profound consequences; there is a paradox that as girls find it more difficult to know and communicate what they feel, where they are, who they are and what they think they become more dependent on others to place their identity for them. On the one hand they want to become and develop their individual selves, on the other they look for a world that offers clarity and purpose. This makes them particularly vulnerable to a mass media culture that makes millions out of selling the necessity of a particular image.

The menarche and becoming accustomed to ongoing menstruation is a key aspect of adolescence. Land (1997) notes that responses to the menarche vary between cultures and within cultures between families. Some cultures celebrate and have rituals to mark this beginning of womanhood. Working with women in the UK it is evident that in the past many girls were not told about the onset of periods, or if they were, only in terms that left them confused or mystified. One woman recalls this being the subject of a biology lesson:

> We had to write notes that the teacher dictated and then we copied diagrams from the board. To this day they don't bear any relationship to any part of any anatomy – either male or female – that I've ever seen. The teacher was much happier when she got onto the reproduction of frogs. And my mother never told me anything.

Nowadays generally more openness prevails but the onset of menstruation can still be a shock and not necessarily understood even when full explanations are given. One mother of a 13-year-old described how she had always been open with her daughter. She had explained every-thing clearly and answered all her daughter's questions. Yet one day her daughter came home from school and burst into tears saying, 'You never told me periods go on for ever. I don't want them all the time'. This mother had explained (and to an adolescent the menopause must in-deed seem like another planet) but clear information does not overcome ambivalence, fears and anxieties.

Another girl the same age, who had been talked through all the various aspects of the menarche, cried bitterly when her periods started and when soothed by her mother that it was just another step in growing up, responded that she didn't want to grow up yet – she wanted to be a child still. These 13-year-olds all had good relationships with their mothers. They also all had the ability to express the confusions they felt and trust that they would be heard and responded to. However they also give a clue to some of the difficulties that can arise in adolescence for girls when they are not well supported and contained, or when earlier difficulties come to the fore. Some girls are excited by the onset of periods – one 18-year-old, the youngest of four girls, described that when her periods started at 14 she felt that at last she would again be part of her older sisters' world. However others, as the girl quoted above, can experience the onset of menstruation as the loss of childhood and need to grieve this. This theme of loss and mourning is discussed by Anna Freud (1958) who notes that it is difficult to analyse adolescents because they are mourning and there is not yet sufficient distance to enable them to view this process and its effects.

Dealing with loss can also be a difficulty for mothers – the young woman who was the youngest of four recalled that this was so for her mother: 'I was so excited and she hugged me and then cried that now she didn't have a baby any more. It didn't worry me, I just said, "Don't be daft mum, I haven't been a baby for years." Now [at 18] I think I could have been a bit nicer to her.' However the individual experiences the menarche, and this is very various, it is undoubtedly always significant; it is the start of being a woman whether or not she is ready for it and 'even nowadays, for most girls menarche puts an end to dreams of adventure at sea or as an explorer, of a career as a racing driver or an oil-rig fire-fighter' (Land 1997: 61).

Concerns with her body extend beyond the changes brought about by the menarche. Typically girls are characterized by preoccupation with appearance, weight and image, and the spontaneity that can characterize childhood tends to go underground: 'they lose their resiliency and optim-ism and become less curious and inclined to take risks . . . they become more deferential, self critical and depressed. They report great unhappi-ness with their own bodies' (Pipher 1995: 19). While most young women do not suffer from eating disorders (although a proportion do and this will be discussed later) many young women are anxious to control their weight and this is central to their image and identity: 'normative discontent with weight is now part of the day to day psychological life of most young women, accompanied, at least temporarily, by some alteration in their behaviour' (Fombonne 1995: 647). There are many explanations for this concern over weight and appearance; preoccupation with self can be seen as a normal part of adolescence and because bodily changes are so rapid it is not surprising if the body becomes a focus for this preoccupation. It can be a defence against the muddles and uncertainties of the inner world, combined with a desire to control identity at a stage in life where full autonomy is denied. In other circumstances it can be a denial of femininity, particularly when a girl has experienced sexual abuse. Neither should the power and influence of advertising and the media be dismissed in its portrayal of ideal women as thin – many models are in fact prepubescent girls made up to look older.

Adolescent girls spend much time with their friends. They are often to be found deep in intense conversations on the phone, or huddled together talking in their bedrooms with the door firmly shut, conversations which cease when parents appear, with the very strong message that it is none of their business. This has both a containing and a comforting function; girls are remarkably good at mothering one another. Many parents comment on how their own words of wisdom, apparently rejected by their daughters, will be repeated by the daughter to a distressed friend in a most comforting and containing way. Parents learn not to comment on this for to suggest that she has in fact taken notice of the parent is not popular, especially with younger adolescents. However May (1994) comments on this tendency still being present in older adolescents. He notes that students are still in the throes of separating from their parents and can be critical or dismissive towards them and 'are likely to become quite alarmed by any emotional experience of still being tied to parents or, horror of horrors, coming to realize one's similarities to a despised parent' (1994: 14).

Adolescents tend to learn by doing and the defences of splitting and projection are strongly in evidence. They can take up extreme positions on many things, and their feelings too can be extreme. 'Identification with the mother, angry repudiation of her concern, strong feelings of love and hate towards the father, swings of wild emotion, are perfectly normal and strain relations in the most temperate of families' (Land 1997: 65). The depressive position is once again being negotiated and good and bad views of their parents, their selves, their teachers and their peers can alternate rapidly. Certainly girls in their struggle to be their selves, to find their own way, to stay connected while finding their own distinct identity, do commonly become dismissive of parental involvement while also desperately needing it. Rather like a toddler they need space to explore but then, though with more ambivalence than their younger self, return for parental support. Also like the toddler the space they explore needs to be contained safely. It is vital that containment and boundaries are in place. These will be challenged but she needs to know they will not collapse and neither will her parents. Winnicott suggests that 'if the child is to become an adult, then this move is achieved over the dead body of an adult' (1971: 145). This is meant metaphorically and Winnicott adds that the parent must survive. Indeed adolescent girls with seriously ill parents where death is a possibility or a reality suffer greatly.

When boundaries are not held safely the adolescent girl can find herself floundering or worse.

A 15-year-old girl was raped following an argument she 'won' about staying out at an all night party. At 18 she could see how she had really needed her parents to have stayed firm and not allowed her to go. The party was a distance from home; she was the youngest there; having arrived she wanted to go home but had no way of extricating herself. She was raped by an older man who offered to drive her home when she became distressed. Her mother was so upset by the rape that in the girl's eyes she became seriously depressed as a direct result and was hospitalized for a time. Her fears of her own potency in terms of her apparent uncontainability by her parents, her mother's breakdown, reinforced by what the rapist said to her was enormous. Her anger was also so fearful to her that it became deeply internalized and then expressed against herself – at 18 she regularly self harmed by cutting. For this young woman her parents did not contain her aggression, her challenges, or her need for firm containment and clear boundaries, and a tragic situation with very long lasting consequences were the result.

Growing up female includes sorting out and facing delicate sexual dilemmas. 'Claiming her sexuality and her status as a sexual woman is a vital task for the adolescent girl but a very complex one' (Land 1997). Settlage and Galenson (1976) discuss the impact of earlier sexual intimacy for girls, suggesting that this gives less space and time for resolution of other conflicts and issues. In addition, adolescent girls have to balance the desire to be attractive and feminine without making themselves sexually vulnerable. Rape and sexual assaults are awful realities for far more girls and young women than is generally recognized. In my clinical experience few report these crimes, feeling they will simply suffer all over again. Coward (1992: 174) points out that rape victims

often feel not only invaded, degraded and made dirty, but also intensely self doubting, questioning how far their own behaviour could have contributed to what happened. It is a feeling which has been compounded by the convention of defence lawyers trying to pin the blame on women and accusing them of ambiguous sexual messages.

The problem is wider than this; Coward quotes a teacher (1992: 167) who felt that on average 7 out of 10 girls she had taught had been frightened and upset by sexual incidents. Larkin (1997: 116) supports this finding in another context: 'I have found that street harassment is such an inevitable part of girls' passage into womanhood that many young women are emotionally worn down long before they enter the workplace or academia.' Lees (1986) focuses on how definitions of sexuality contribute to continuing inequalities. She discovered that sexual double standards still exist whereby sexual experimentation by boys is regarded positively and that by girls negatively. She notes that a body of language supports this difference with negative vocabulary being attached to girls who experiment sexually – for example, the highly derogatory term 'slag'.

Of course young women now take up more public space than in prior generations; they are both more visible than previously, and are more likely to walk and to use public transport than older women. Young black women receive a particular form of harassment based on sexual stereotyping and encounter comments such as 'I hear black girls are easy' (Larkin 1997: 120). Budgeon in her study takes up the issue of race and racism as perceived and experienced by young black women and concludes that:

> One might expect ethnic identity to be experienced as a limiting factor via the experience of racism but the women in this study did not speak of their ethnicity in this way. When ethnicity was construed as a limiting factor, it was expressed as a restriction originating from within a racist dominant culture, because these women drew upon their experiences of being treated differently compared to the treatment men received within their ethnic community.
>
> (Budgeon 1998: 133)

This does not mean they did not suffer racism elsewhere but that this was not their perception. Their experience of their gender combined with their ethnicity was experienced as imposing limitations. This is validated by my own experience of counselling young Asian women. Budgeon argues that the issues they presented that related to ethnicity are most commonly related to feeling that their choices of career, partner, where they choose to live, who they live with, leisure activities, clothes and image are severely restricted and cause great unhappiness and conflict. It may of course be that these young women have become so used to their treatment in the wider culture that they fail to identify racism or see it as unusual or concerning.

In the same way girls do not always identify certain forms of male behaviour as harassing. This may be a defence against their potential distress or powerlessness but it is noticeable. For example, a group of young male football supporters were swaggering down the street, shouting at passing girls, 'Get your tits out, let's see them then', and occasionally lunging at any young woman who failed to get out of the way quickly enough. Some girls looked embarrassed or scared but most just seemed to shrug it off as typical lads' behaviour. Yet it raises the question of the effects on these girls of 'typical laddish behaviour' in terms of their perceptions about self, sexuality and safety.

Potentially gender raises other areas of difficulty and conflict. Schaffer (1998) identifies four ways that girls' responses to difficulties become identified and responded to from a perspective of gender bias. First, girls can be punished and rejected if they use bad language, act out sexually or are angry or confrontational. Second, girls may develop relationships with older men. Schaffer sees this as a response to living in families where the members are emotionally and sometimes economically exhausted. In this context girls may find a sexual solution in an attempt to meet their needs. Third, lesbian girls can experience marginalization and rejection and fourth, the sexual abuse of girls takes its toll in many ways often unrecognized, and therefore interpreted incorrectly, including labelling a girl as difficult, manipulative or attention seeking.

Being 'out of step': marginalized girls

It has already been noted that the desire to belong, to be identified with, and attached to a peer group, to be both be the same as others while somehow establishing an individual identity, are all characteristic of adolescence and the adolescent struggle. However this raises the question of the experience of girls whose struggle for identity extends beyond these parameters.

Although they are not alone in this, lesbian girls, as noted above, are one group who can experience marginalization. Sexuality and sexual identity are complex areas of identity to negotiate for heterosexual girls and for lesbians the homophobia of society can cause enormous unhappiness, alienation, and can lead to bullying and victimization (Schur 1984).

'Coming out' as a lesbian is difficult for many who fear both parental and a wider rejection. One 17-year-old who sought counselling was terrified that her parents would throw her out if she told them that she was lesbian. Another, brought up in an apparently liberal home where there was staunch support, theoretically, for the right to choose and own one's sexual identity, felt betrayed by her parents' reaction to her lesbianism. They were initially shocked and distressed, moving into denial and a reframing of her sexuality into a 'normal phase of experimenting that she would grow out of'.

A student who was actively involved in gay politics found her room in her student hall of residence daubed with anti-gay graffiti by male students who also urinated over her window. The warden of this hall responded that it was just lads being lads, adding that she invited this response by her involvement in gay rights campaigns. He suggested that she 'lay low' and keep her opinions to herself. Unlike, of course, the young men who were apparently given free reign to express theirs in this most obnoxious and unacceptable fashion.

Another young woman of 22 referred herself to counselling with panic attacks. The source of these was her extreme anxiety that her parents would discover that she was living in a lesbian relationship. Consequently, the subterfuges undertaken were enormous. Their flat was arranged so that in the event of parental visits it would appear that they were two friends sharing, and visits to her parents were inevitably based on deceit. Her partner became increasingly resistant to these tactics and offended by them, and the relationship began to suffer. These examples give some indication of the agonies, conflict and isolation experienced by many lesbian girls. To own their identity they face actual and potential losses and victimization that are considerable and often deeply distressing.

Girls are marginalized for other reasons too. Some just do not fit the prevailing image of how girls in this day and age should look and act. They may be overweight, dress unacceptably, be of a different class or with a different accent from the predominant one, have different interests from the mainstream, or their life at home may make them estranged both from their self and from others. The latter particularly applies to the consequences of sexual abuse and this will be explored later.

A counsellor described her work with an 18-year-old student who presented as not settling and not fitting in. The counsellor described how as soon as she saw her she understood why this was. She described her as wearing her hair in a long plait, wearing ankle socks, a hand knitted jumper, no make-up, and also described how this girl told her she thought it was wrong to drink, that she had only come to university to work and that she thought the other students were 'decadent'. At the same time she was miserable and unhappy, and was very hurt that her attempts to make friends with the girl next door had been rebuffed. Her neighbour had clearly not wanted to be friends and had rushed off at the first opportunity to find others who, presumably, matched the prevailing style. In addition, she was expected to ring home every night and return to her parents at weekends. In contrast to the freedom loving, fashion conscious, pub visiting students who surrounded her she stood out as different and they avoided her, generally not unkindly but occasionally so, especially when she expressed her disapproval of drink and sex.

For other girls their marginalization comes from different sources. Girls who are the primary carers in families because of the disability or illness of their mother are another group. Their central concern from an early age is the welfare of others, and the process of separation from mother and the development of a distinct identity becomes highly problematic.

An 18-year-old described how from the age of 11 she looked after her mother disabled with multiple sclerosis. Her father had left and there were two younger siblings. She would rush home from school to care for her and although her younger siblings, thanks to her, had a childhood and adolescence, hers was curtailed at age 11. At 18 she described how she felt both very old and very young, and how she felt on a different planet to her peer group. Her anxieties about the future were vast; her mother's condition had deteriorated and the prognosis was poor.

Similarly, for those girls who themselves are stricken with illness or disability, the usual developmental pathways are unavoidably altered, and are strewn with obstacles not present for other young people.

The changing world: the impact on the position of girls and young women

Historically young women have underachieved in the UK. Indeed in the 1970s and 80s concern was rife about the underachieving of girls after primary school age. In school they always achieved higher standards than boys at primary level but fell behind at secondary school. However this has turned around dramatically in recent years; they now consistently do better than boys at secondary level, are more likely to enter higher education and are moving into traditionally male subjects at an impressive pace never seen before (Roberts 1995). Throughout the 1970s and 80s female participation in higher education increased rapidly. By 1992, 47 per cent of full-time undergraduates were female and more women than men are currently in medical schools training to be doctors.

However impressive these figures, and they are indeed deeply encouraging in terms of access to education for young women, inequalities do still exist. In 1993 a quarter of working-class men and a third of working-class women had no educational qualifications. Among the Pakistani and Bangladesh communities over half of men and three-fifths of women lacked qualifications (Central Statistical Office 1994). However in the African-Caribbean population girls also outperform boys (Cross *et al.* 1990). Although in educational terms girls are now doing well, inequalities do not stop there. At age 18–19 women earn less than men and wage inequalities increase with age (Lee *et al.* 1990). However, women graduates have better chances of finding employment quicker than their male counterparts. Unemployment is higher amongst young men than young women and young men are more likely to be unemployed for longer periods of time (*Sunday Times* 1995).

Life for young people has changed dramatically in the last two decades of the twentieth century (Furlong and Cartmel 1999), profoundly affecting the lives of young women and young men. Changes in the labour market, social policy and further educational funding has meant that many young people remain dependent on their families for much longer. In 1987 students were prevented from claiming supplementary benefit in short vacations; in 1990 they lost entitlement to housing benefit and in 1991 they lost the right to claim income support during long vacations. Grants to students are now severely restricted, having been replaced by a system of loans that makes working life begin with debt (Roberts 1995). However although they share the same social context, girls tend to leave home earlier than boys; more move away to study and they enter partnerships earlier. They are also treated differently; they are likely be subject to greater scrutiny in terms of their movements and they are expected to help more in the house (White 1994). This may be a factor in encouraging them towards greater independence younger. It may also be that because more has been expected of them they have greater skills for autonomous living.

Certainly the journey into adulthood has taken on new routes that are less predictable than those taken by previous generations and are accompanied by more unpredictable outcomes. Giddens (1991) suggests that young women today experience a situation of both greater opportunity, accompanied by greater risk and uncertainty. A somewhat mixed picture begins to emerge. Sue Sharpe has undertaken two studies of girls and young women – the first in the 1970s (1976) and the second in the 1990s (1994). In her second study (Sharpe 1994) she concluded that the attitudes and perceptions of girls had changed in many ways. They expected and wanted more equality with men, valued education more, wanted to stay in it longer, and placed a greater value on independence and self-sufficiency. However Sharpe (1994) argues that there is a mismatch between reality and expectations, that the constraints she had identified 20 years earlier had not changed as much as these young women felt. What is very evident from her second study is that 20 years has seen a major shift in how young women feel about themselves and their world. The world may not always match this but expectations are certainly higher.

McRobbie (1991) also explores changes in how girls identify themselves as feminine. She examined and analysed the content of magazines aimed at teenage girls and shows how the prevailing image has shifted from one of girls as focusing on romance and dependence on a male, towards one of independence and self-satisfaction. She argues that a greater range of personal identity is now available. Budgeon (1998: 121) argues similarly:

> Young women are not cultural dupes. With the advent of girl power in Britain, it would seem that the current moment is ripe for conditions of self determination. If identity is contingent upon the discursive positions made available to the individual, the emergence of new subject positions, consolidated in the assertive and self-determined subject of girl power, may well bring the potential for young women to exercise choice and define themselves in new and positive ways . . . The range of subject positions available to young women has widened considerably since the mid 1970s and the path young women will take in the transition to adulthood cannot be assumed to be a homogenous route.

In Budgeon's study of young women a central theme was their recognition of themselves as able to make their own individual decisions and choices from a range of available options. They recognized that both traditional and modern versions of womanhood were available to them. Some young women did eventually want marriage and children, but not in the traditional sense of being a stay at home partner and mother. Rather they recognized that they would need to negotiate the tension between motherhood and careers. They felt they had more choice than their mothers and were aware of their increased opportunities. Their focus was on equality in relationships and parenthood. She concludes that:

these young women have been able to actively seek out and create a space in which they are able to construct a 'self' that does not simply reproduce traditional femininity. Therefore, the ways in which structures were said to limit and determine the lives of young women in the 1970s and 1980s no longer appear to be straightforward.

(Budgeon 1998: 135)

The work of McRobbie, Sharpe and Budgeon all point to girls nowadays having a central concern with sexual equality, valuing individualism, having the right to feel good about oneself, and wanting independence even if they are in relationships. However contradictions and resistance exists: the double sexual standard that still exists and is explored by Lees (1986) is one good example. The relationship between sex and power remains complex and was recognized as such by these girls. The formation of their self-identity is therefore not simple even in the context of greater choices unheard of for earlier generations of women. The question that is posed by Sharpe (1994) about the mismatch between actual possibilities and false perceptions of these is central. The wage differentials that still exist is just one very crucial example of where the reality is harsher for young women than young men.

Particular issues for girls and young women

A number of issues could be considered in relation to girls and young women. Although in childhood girls are healthier than boys, in adolescence this reverses and they are more likely to suffer from illness and psychological disturbances (Sweeting 1995). Levels of depression and stress-related illnesses seem to have increased, as have depression, eating disorders, and suicidal behaviour. Girls are more likely to consider suicide although they are less successful in carrying this out than boys, partly because of the gender differential in methods chosen (Smith and Rutter 1995). As practioners know adolescence is a risky time. Dependence on alcohol and heavy drinking is not the norm for girls and young women although most do drink. This is likely to reflect a changing culture. They feel comfortable in pubs; it is a social venue they feel they have a right to, unlike previous generations of women. For most drinking is associated with socializing and sociability and is a problem for a minority only. However drinking alcohol starts young for many girls (Fossey *et al.* 1996). Similarly, drug use is increasingly a normal part of adolescent experience and drug experimentation is on the increase (Measham *et al.* 1994). Sexual abuse and eating disorders affect the lives of many young women in especially powerful ways. These are explored in more detail in the following sections.

Sexual abuse

Although boys as well as girls suffer sexual abuse it still appears that more girls are at risk than boys and that their abusers are more likely to be men. One pattern is survivors who have been sexually abused by the father or other close male relative, and physically abused or neglected by the mother. Some have been abused in many ways by many people. Commonly abusers are family members or someone known and trusted by the child and the family; for instance, abuse occurs in children's homes, schools, churches, nurseries, hospitals and with child minders. Abusers and their victims come from all walks and classes of life. Abuse is frequently meticulously planned, especially where this is part of an organized ring.

Girls and young women who have been abused carry with them the legacy of a spoilt childhood in which their belief in the trustworthiness of others has been demolished. For some abuse starts young and carries on into their teenage years and sometimes well beyond. Others are groomed for abuse from a very early age by the abuser who waits until they reach puberty to begin abusing them. The age 10–12 is a very risky time for children in terms of the likelihood of sexual abuse (Finkelhor 1986). Eating disorders in girls and young women have been linked to childhood abuse (Oppenheimer *et al.* 1985) although research varies in estimating the degree of significance. The effects of abuse on the young woman are extensive; sexual and relationship difficulties, extreme feelings of low self-esteem, lack of self-confidence, a sense of shame and badness, self-loathing, and a deep sense of lack of trust are all symptomatic of the effects of abuse in childhood. For some young women their childhood is a blank, as if it had not existed. They have little recall – only a sense of depression, anxiety and loss that cannot be attached to specific events.

It has already been noted that adolescence for girls is a fluid and normally volatile process. Sexuality is explored; boundaries are challenged; conflict is normal; relationships with peers are crucial and there is an enormous need for adults to provide a safe and containing environment. A girl has to learn to safely accommodate within herself strong and often contradictory feelings and to know that those around her can contain theirs and hers. For the transition to be made successfully from childhood to adulthood young women need sufficient ego strength, good internalized boundaries, sufficient maturity in their adult carers, privacy that is respected, parents who will allow and recognize the need to separate and challenge, and sufficient hope and trust in the world. For the sexually abused girl, especially where the abuser is a close family relative, the converse of this situation exists. Sexual abuse kills off trust and damages hope (Walker 1992). It turns the world into a dangerous place and attacks the ability to allow safe dependency. This renders real independence extremely difficult although a false self (Winnicott 1965) may emerge. A sexually abused girl's experience of difficult feelings is that they are not safely contained; the abuser has in the most extreme way been unable to do just that. Her boundaries of her self and her body have been continually attacked by the abuse and her privacy disregarded in the most appalling way. She has been forced to keep secrets, and this will often have been accompanied by the perpetrator threatening those close to her, and by blaming her for the abuse. In addition, abused children are often isolated, depressed, are revictimized and experience themselves as essentially different. Abuse damages self-esteem and often schooling and peer relationships are limited (Walker 1992).

The developmental damage of abuse is huge and is seen particularly vividly at adolescence. Self-harm (Cairns 1988) is a common manifestation; it frequently involves cutting the body and it can be a comfort, a self-punishment, a communication of pain and hurt, a way of speaking the pain when words cannot be said or do not suffice, a dissociative technique, an expression of self-loathing, an attempt to avoid further abuse, or an expression of loathing or ambivalence towards the abuser. This list is not complete – self-harm is complex and multifaceted. Abuse also affects the ability to form close relationships; close relationships may be simply impossible or abuse can lead to attempts to create very close relationships inappropriately, including sexually. Other effects are poor performance at school and being absent from school, drug and alcohol misuse, running away from home, depression and anxiety. For many abused girls there is no safe place to turn and no one to trust. After all, if the abuser is someone deemed by society to be trustworthy, as is usually the case, then who does this leave to trust?

Separating and leaving home can be a nightmare. One described it as follows:

> After I'd left home [at 17] it was really hard. There was no respite if you needed a break: nowhere to run back to; no retreat. It was like camping in an open plain without even a cave to go back to. And it's canvas, so you've got nothing firm. And I was still suffering under the delusion that it was all my fault. I carried that one for ages and ages; like, 'What do you expect? It's you.' And the sense of difference that I had all through my childhood, that just carried on and coloured lots of other things all the way through.
>
> (Walker 1992: 66)

One of the tragic consequences for young women when they try to leave the abusive environment is this experience described above. They often hope that physically leaving will mean the abuse ends but even if it does literally stop they discover that consequences remain and that they are ill-prepared for the difficulties of the adult world. Many young women cannot even leave the abusive home; they have no money, no job, no place to live, no sense of self and self-value. In other words they lack both the internal and external resources that they need for the next step to independence.

> An 18-year-old, physically abused by her mother throughout childhood and sexually abused by her father from the age of 11, managed somehow to succeed academically and move away to university. She was confident that now all would be well. It was not. She could not cope with such a free environment, her boundaries had been so invaded that she could not put these in place for herself; she began to suffer flashbacks of the abuse so she could not study; and her relationships with her peers were extremely difficult. She formed extreme and intense attachments very rapidly and could not understand why her new 'friends' then abandoned her. She had many sexual encounters, including some which put her at considerable risk, and became very depressed as she began to recognize the full impact of her childhood abuse. She became suicidal before vacations when she had to return to the abusive home. She also began to clearly recognize what she had missed and what damage had been done. Her father had kept her away from other families but now she saw parents visiting their children, and she had a glimpse of a different world. She described her extreme pain and distress when friends were visited and brought cakes and food parcels, were taken out for meals and generally cherished.

I have noted earlier how adolescents need to mourn their childhood as they become adult, but in the event of abuse this process is distorted and sometimes dangerous. For the adolescent girl who has been abused the process of growing up is indeed a treacherous journey.

Eating disorders

Anorexia nearly always has its onset during adolescence and as such is an important and concerning developmental issue. It mainly affects those from the white middle classes. It peaks at ages 14 and 18 while bulimia is more likely to start at age 19 or 20. Although more boys are now developing eating disorders the proportion of boys to girls who develop these difficulties is about one to ten (Smith and Rutter 1995). However it is now increasing more rapidly amongst working-class girls than middle-class girls, and it has been argued that slimness becomes taken on as the ideal once a social class literally acquires the financial means to indulge its appetite (Mennell *et al.* 1992). Bruch (1973) points out that eating difficulties frequently appear when adolescent assertion of independence and rebelliousness could be expected, suggesting that not eating is another way of expressing control over self and to some extent those around her. As stated above, there is a link between abuse in childhood and the later development of eating disorders. This does not mean that all those with eating disorders have been abused, but studies indicate that this is the case for about 40 per cent of cases (Oppenheimer *et al.* 1985; Palmer *et al.* 1990). It is a significant factor.

Unravelling the causes of eating disorders is controversial and complex. One set of theories views them as a reflection of disturbed and disturbing family dynamics. Food becomes a means of expressing emotions, of conveying messages and making statements. In this way the anorexic becomes the spokesperson, through their actions, for what cannot be said or acknowledged directly or in any other way. It may be easier for the family to focus on the individual's difficulty with food than to look at what is occurring elsewhere. Secrets are common in these families – as I have noted above, sexual abuse can be one such secret. Commonly families of an anorexic or bulimic tend to contain a confusing mixture of passivity, control, distance and apparent closeness that is invasive rather than supportive. There is often a pattern of a passive, powerless mother and a distant but powerful father. Issues of power and control are very intensely present without being thought through, talked over or fought over. There is little ability to acknowledge or resolve conflict and the anorexic is rendered powerless and out of control. She can, however, control eating or not eating, and so gain some of the power that is denied her elsewhere.

However family dynamics alone cannot explain the preponderance of girls and women with these disorders. It is here that understanding the social and political context is vital. Feminist clinicians and writers (MacLeod 1981; Orbach 1987) understand eating disorders as a way of protesting in a world in which it remains difficult for a woman to have a place in her own right. Women are seen as being caught in a myriad of conflicting expectations and demands, with little room for manoeuvre or legitimate protest. As discussed previously there is a pressure to be attractive and sexually desirable, which is nowadays equated with being thin. Food is no longer functional. It is highly symbolic and as such is the focus for the conflict, confusion and unhappiness experienced by many young women who struggle to find a place in the world, within themselves and in a relationship.

Anorexia can also be understood as a rejection of adult female sexuality. This understanding links with both the family and societal aspects discussed above. If a girl comes from a family where she is not validated and valued, in a society in which she struggles for a place, the adult world may not seem too attractive. Childhood may seem the lesser of the two evils. The very thin body of an anorexic does appear asexual and prepubertal, and menstruation is likely to cease. This desire to feel and appear non-sexual can be seen as an extreme rejection of, and rebellion against, the stereotypical portrayal of a woman. In other instances it can ensure that the girl or adolescent is not able to leave home. This may reflect an anxiety to watch over and protect a parent.

> For example, an anorexic girl was the youngest in a family where her father was very violent to her mother. Her anorexia meant she could not leave home as her older siblings had done. If she left, no one would be left to care for her mother, and she feared for her life. Developing anorexia was an unconscious move on her part to exert some control over her own destiny, to protest – albeit silently – and to ensure she stayed with her mother.

Another young woman of 20, Marie, recalls the power of stopping eating when she was 14. Hers had been a difficult family to live in. Her older and more volatile sister had always been in very direct conflict with her father. Her father used to hit her sister, on several occasions hurting her quite badly. Marie had grown up in terror of her father, with a deep concern for her sister, with her mother adopting an extremely passive and emotionally absent presence. Marie never dared get angry or be assertive, appeals to her mother were unheard and she missed her sister terribly when she left home at 18. At the age of 20 Marie was becoming able to recognize the complexity of emotions that led her to stop eating when her sister left home. She began to identify that direct expression of any feeling had been impossible for her. Refusing food gave her a sense of power and control in the absence of any real influence over her life and events in the family. It worried both her parents and then this was deeply satisfying to her. She felt rage towards them, was also very distressed at what she had witnessed, was fearful of growing up like her mother and worried that all men would be violent like her father. The adult world did not seem a very attractive place. In addition, her self-esteem was low and she found the world of her experimental and rebellious peers terrifying. Not eating seemed, unconsciously at that time, an effective option for resolving these issues. At 20 this unconscious struggle was becoming more consciously accessible to her. But the battle was not easily won. Anorexia had in her words 'become my friend and my supporter'; it had served her well and was not easily abandoned.

Eating disorders arise from intense and complex dynamics, and produce symptoms that are powerful and anxiety provoking. Eating disorders are tenacious and are not easily given up. The responses of the caring professions to eating disorders vary greatly. Very judgemental language is frequently heard: anorexics are called 'difficult', 'manipulative', 'secretive' and 'devious' without apparently any awareness that this behaviour may reflect the circumstances that created the problem. Others try to understand the meaning of anorexia and bulimia, and recognize that tracking down the feelings and experiences that triggered this particular response is a difficult task, but an essential one if this concerning feature of female adolescent development is to be given the serious attention it deserves.

Adolescence is not just for adolescents

Adolescence is a process and not an event and is one that can be revisited throughout life. We all have the capacity for rediscovering our adolescent selves, sometimes enjoyably (one only has to think about how 'grown-ups' can behave at parties and conferences to be aware of this) and sometimes not so happily. Indeed, adolescents themselves have a particular skill at triggering this aspect of the adult. Many mothers of adolescent girls will recognize the scenario, especially common when, tired after a heavy day at work, they enter the type of argument with their daughter that their adult side strongly advises against. However another part comes into play more powerfully, to the chagrin of mother, who can feel herself rapidly become more adolescent than her daughter. Anyone who has ever witnessed, or been part of, couples arguing will know that the adult self can be a very thin veneer, as slamming doors and threats to walk out are rapidly invoked by the apparently emotionally sophisticated. So adolescent girls are not the only ones to have fun, take risks, be rebellious, feel misunderstood, be volatile, want to be independent *and* dependent, and not care what others think *and* want to be accepted. These are part of the human experience and of the human condition. These aspects of the self are particularly intense and significant at this exciting and difficult transition of adolescence, especially in these rapidly changing times, but they are universal. Hopefully as a girl grows into a woman these parts become better integrated; the fit becomes more comfortable, and self-doubt and questioning settles into a growing confidence and ease with self that allows her to take up her rightful place in the world. The picture, on balance, is one where this is becoming more possible and young women are entering worlds never dreamed of 50 years ago.

References

Blos, P. (1962) *On Adolescence*. New York: Free Press.

Broverman, I., Broverman, D., Clarkson, F., Rosenncrantz, P. and Vogel, S. (1970) Sex role stereotypes and clinical judgments of mental health, *Journal of Consulting and Clinical Psychology*, 34(1): 1–7.

Brown, L.M. and Gilligan, C. (1992) *Meeting at the Crossroads: Women's Psychology and Girls' Development*. Cambridge, MA: Harvard University Press.

Bruch, H. (1973) *Eating Disorders*. New York: Basic Books.

Budgeon, S. (1998) 'I'll tell you what I really, really want', in S.A. Inness (ed.) *Millennium Girls. Today's Girls Around the World*. Lanham, MD: Rowman and Littlefield Publishers.

Cairns, C. (1998) Deliberate self-harm and sexual abuse in adolescence, *European Journal of Counselling Psychotherapy and Health*, 1(3): 353–64.

Central Statistical Office (1994) *Social Trends*, 24. London: HMSO.

Chodorow, N. (1989) *Feminism and Psychoanalytic Theory*. New Haven, CT: Yale University Press.

Cote, J.E. and Allahar, A.L. (1996) *Generation on Hold. Coming of Age in the Late Twentieth Century*. New York: New York University Press.

Coward, R. (1992) *Our Treacherous Hearts: Why Women Let Men Get Their Own Way*. London: Faber and Faber.

Cross, M., Wrench, J. and Barnett, S. (1990) *Ethnic Minorities and the Career Service. An Investigation into Processes of Assessment and Placement*. London: Department of Employment.

Erikson, E.H. (1965) *Childhood and Society*. London: Penguin Books.

Fanthorpe, U.A. (1989) Ain't I a woman, in I. Linthwaite (ed.) *Poems by Black and White Women*. London: Virago.

Finkelhor, D. (1986) *A Sourcebook on Child Sexual Abuse*. London: Sage.

Fombonne, E. (1995) Eating disorders. Time trends and possible exploratory mechanisms, in M. Rutter and D.J. Smith (eds) *Psychological Disorders in Young People. Time Trends and Their Causes*. Chichester: Wiley.

Fossey, E., Loretto, W. and Plant, M. (1996) Alcohol and youth, in L. Harrison (ed.) *Alcohol Problems in the Community*. London: Routledge.

Freud, A. (1958) Adolescence, *Psychoanalytic Studies of the Child*, 13: 255–78.

Freud, S. (1905) *Three Essays on the Theory of Sexuality*, Penguin Freud Library, Vol. 7. London: Penguin.

Freud, S. (1923) *The Infantile Genital Organisation*, Penguin Freud Library, Vol. 7. London: Penguin.

Freud, S. (1925) *Some Psychical Consequences of the Anatomical Distinction between the Sexes*, Penguin Freud Library, Vol. 7. London: Penguin.

Freud, S. (1933) *New Introductory Lectures on Psychoanalysis*, Penguin Freud Library, Vol. 2. London: Penguin.

Freud, S. and Breuer, J. (1895) *Studies in Hysteria*, Standard Edition, Vol. 2. London: Hogarth Press.

Furlong, A. and Cartmel, F. (1999) *Young People and Social Change*. Buckingham: Open University Press.

Giddens, A. (1991) *Modernity and Self Identity*. Cambridge: Polity.

Gilligan, C. (1982) *In a Different Voice: Psychological Theory and Women's Development*. Cambridge, MA: Harvard University Press.

Hall, G.S. (1904) *Adolescence. Its Psychology and its Relations to Physiology, Anthropology, Sociology, Sex, Crime, Religion and Education*. New York: Appleton.

Herman, J. (1981) *Father–Daughter Incest*. Cambridge, MA: Harvard University Press.

Hodgson, J. and Fischer, J. (1979) Sex differences in identity and intimacy development in college youth, *Journal of Youth and Adolescence*, 8: 37–50.

Holdsworth, A. (1988*) Out of the Doll's House. The Story of Women in the Twentieth Century*. London: BBC Books.

Ige, B.K. (1998) For sale: a girl's life in the global economy, in S.A. Inness (ed.) *Millennium Girls. Today's Girls Around the World*. Lanham, MD: Rowman and Littlefield Publishers.

Inness, S.A. (ed.) (1998) Introduction, *Millennium Girls – Today's Girls Around the World*. Lanham, MD: Rowman and Littlefield Publishers.

Josselson, R. (1973) Psychodynamic aspects of identity formation in college women, *Journal of Youth and Adolescence*, 2: 3–52.

Kelman, H. (1967) *Feminine Psychology*. New York: Norton.

Kurz, K. and Prather, C. (1995) *Improving the Quality of Girls' Life*. New York: Unicef.

Land, P. (1997) Women's relationships with their bodies, in M. Lawrence and M. Maguire (eds) *Psychotherapy with Women, Feminist Perspectives*. Basingstoke: Macmillan Press.

Larkin, J. (1997) Sexual terrorism on the street: the moulding of young women into subordination, in A. Thomas and C. Kitzinger (eds) *Sexual Harassment – Contemporary Feminist Perspectives*. Buckingham: Open University Press.

Laufer, M. (1974) *Adolescent Disturbance and Breakdown*. London: Penguin Books.

Lee, D., Marsden, D., Rickman, P. and Duncombe, J. (1990) *Scheming for Youth. A Study of YTS in the Enterprise Culture*. Milton Keynes: Open University Press.

Lees, S. (1986) *Losing Out: Sexuality and Adolescent Girls*. London: Hutchinson.

MacLeod, S. (1981) *The Art of Starvation*. London: Virago.

McRobbie, A. (1991) *Feminism and Youth Culture*. London: Macmillan Education.

May, R. (1994) The centre cannot hold: challenges in working psychodynamically in a college or university, *Psychodynamic Counselling*, 1(1): 5–20.

Measham, F., Newcombe, R. and Parker, H. (1994) The normalisation of recreational drug use amongst young people in north-west England, *British Journal of Sociology*, 45: 287–312.

Mennell, S., Murcott, A. and Van Otterloo, A.H. (1992) *The Sociology of Food, Eating, Diet and Culture*. London: Sage.

Oppenheimer, R., Howells, K., Palmer, R.L. and Chaloner, D.A. (1985) Adverse sexual experiences in childhood and clinical eating disorders: a preliminary description, *Journal of Psychiatric Research*, 9: 357–61.

Orbach, S. (1987) *Hunger Strike*. London: Faber and Faber.

Palmer, R.L., Oppenheimer, R., Chaloner, D.A. and Howells, K. (1990) Childhood sexual experiences with adults reported by women with eating disorders: an extended series. *British Journal of Psychiatry*, 156: 699–703.

Pipher, M. (1995) *Reviving Ophelia: Saving the Selves of Adolescent Girls*. New York: Ballantine Books.

Ponton, L. (1993) Issues unique to psychotherapy with adolescent girls, *American Journal of Psychotherapy*, 47(3): 353–72.

Roberts, K. (1995) *Youth and Employment in Modern Britain*. Oxford: Oxford University Press.

Schaffer, L. (1998) Do bad girls get a bum rap? sexual solutions and state interventions, in S. Inness (ed.) *Millennium Girls. Today's Girls Around the World.* Lanham, MD: Rowman and Littlefield.

Schur, E. (1984) *Labeling Women Deviant: Gender, Stigma and Social Control*. New York: McGraw-Hill.

Seligman, M. (1991) *Learned Optimism*. New York: Random House.

Settlage, C. and Galenson, E. (1976) Psychology of women: late adolescence and early adulthood, *Journal of the American Psychoanalytic Association*, 24: 631–45.

Sharpe, S. (1976) *Just Like a Girl: How Young Girls Learn to be Women*. London: Penguin Books.

Sharpe, S. (1994) *Just Like a Girl: How Young Girls Learn to be Women*. London: Penguin Books.

Smith, D.J. and Rutter, M. (1995) Time trends in psychosocial disorders of youth, in M. Rutter and D.J. Smith (eds) *Psychological Disorders in Young People. Time Trends and Their Causes.* Chichester: Wiley.

Sunday Times (1995) Angry young men, 2 April.

Sweeting, H. (1995) Reversals of fortune? sex differences in health and childhood and adolescence, *Social Science Medicine*, 40: 77–90.

United States Department of Labor, Bureau of International Labor Affairs (1995) *By the Sweat and Toil of Children in US. Agricultural Imports and Forced and Bonded Labor.* Washington DC: Government Printing Office.

Walker, M. (1992) *Surviving Secrets: The Experience of the Child, the Adult and the Helper.* Buckingham: Open University Press.

White, L. (1994) Co residence and leaving home. Young adults and their parents, *Annual Review of Sociology*, 20: 81–102.

Winnicott, D.W. (1965) *The Maturational Process and the Facilitating Environment*. London: Tavistock Publications.

Winnicott, D.W. (1971) *Playing and Reality*. London: Routledge.

4 Women's friendships: theory and therapy

Chess Denman

The aims and scope of the chapter

Although almost all works in the field of friendship begin by noting the paucity of research in the field there is now a considerable literature on the subject, enough to make a comprehensive review difficult to achieve in the space of a chapter. Major reference works in the sociological field include Blieszner and Adams (1992) and Fehr (1996) on the general topic of friendship and O'Connor (1992) specifically on women's friendships. In contrast with this, at least average coverage, a literature search on the subject of friends and peers amongst the main line psychoanalytic journals and publications is highly instructive. No papers of any kind on friendship relations can be identified. There were mentions of peer transferences in the group literature but no work on friendships in groups. However the word 'friend' did bring up a significant proportion of the historical papers published in these journals. Thus one could read about friendships between Freud and Firenczi or with Guntrip but search in vain for any psychoanalytic theorization of friendship. Two writers have contributed a major book (Orbach and Eichenbaum 1987) on women's friendships and there are other scattered contributions (for example Buhrmester and Furman 1986). However the importance of friendship to mental health is well-recognized and therapeutic interventions aimed at improving friendships have been introduced within the cognitive behavioural tradition (Young 1986).

This chapter begins by looking at difficulties in defining the term friendship. It then considers and critiques some of the current sociological work on women's friendships chiefly for lacking a sufficiently psychological perspective. Psychological views on women's friendships from a range of therapeutic traditions are expounded and here the tendency to make universalizing assumptions and in consequence to impoverish the resulting analysis of women's friendships is noticed. In order to deal with some of the difficulties outlined in the first part of the chapter a new therapeutic approach, Cognitive Analytic Therapy (CAT) (Ryle 1990, 1998) is introduced along with a revised sociological analysis of relationships developed by the author drawing on the work of O'Connor (1992). Current theories of women's friendships have a universalizing tendency and as a result have problems accounting for difference between friendships. In this chapter aspects of women's friendships in general and lesbian friendships in particular are analysed using CAT and the revised sociological analysis of relationships. It is shown that such an analysis can account for difference in ways which other theories found difficult to achieve.

What is friendship?

Considerable sociological effort has been directed towards obtaining some kind of definition of friendship. This effort has had two broad strands: first, attempts by sociologists at definitions of friendship which combine descriptive and functional elements. Examples of these include seeing friendship as voluntary (Wright 1984; Hays 1988; Rawlins 1992), intimate (Donelson and Gullahorn 1977; Hays 1988; Fehr 1996), altruistic (Reisman 1979; Davis and Todd 1985) and authentic or individual (Wright 1984). There are problems with all these definitions. One obvious one is their range. Faced with competing definitions it is difficult to find reasons for preferring one over another other than the extent to which they mark out friendship as distinct from all other relationships. However in this respect they all they tend to break down at the various boundaries friendship has with other relationships. Sexual relationships for example are also voluntary and it is simply arbitrary to say that sacrifice in kin relationships is not altruistic.

A second strategy which combats the accusation that functional definitions are arbitrary attempts to describe what friendship is by determining what respondents mean by the use of the term. Responses to this kind of questioning change through the lifecycle. However when adults were asked to complete the sentence 'A friend is someone . . .' responses were things like 'with whom you are intimate', 'you can trust', 'you can depend on', 'with whom you share things', 'who accepts you' and so forth (Sapadin 1988). There are gender differences in these responses. In this study, for example, on the whole, women generated responses to do with trust, keeping confidences and intimate self-disclosure more than men.

This second strategy might at first appear free of the theoretical burden of the first approach; however quite apart from issues raised by the representativeness and inclusiveness of the sample of respondents chosen (far too much work on friendships uses American college students) there are profound difficulties embedded in this methodology. Notice how the question put to the participants varies from the ecologically natural question 'Why did you make friends with X?' Instead asking people to complete the sentence 'A friend is someone who . . .' determines the form of the answers given and prespecifies the kind of response required. It asks the respondent to abstract and generalize. In so doing it may result in a distortion of the answers in a 'sociological' direction, that is to say drawing the eye away from the idea that there might be something intrinsic to friendship not best captured by a functionalist analysis.

While friendships may serve functions it is not self-evident that they are best defined or accounted for as being entered into on that account. Indeed asking an individual 'Why did you make friends with X?' will not produce the reply 'in order to meet my needs for intimacy'. Instead 'liking' is the general response combined with some defining attribute – 'because I liked her, she's good fun'. Yet the sociological literature on friendship contains little on the idea of liking. Arguably considering friendship rather than friends has drawn the eye away from exactly those elements of friendship which are idiosyncratic, such as liking. It might be hoped that a more psychological approach would be able to step in and inform sociological perspectives in this area. Sadly while some aspects of sociology have drawn on psychoanalytic and other psychological theories such considerations have not infused the friendship literature. This is quite understandable when the absence of friendship from most of the psychological literature (other than social psychology) is so marked.

Sociological perspectives on women's friendships

Women have long been defined in contrast to men, often in ways that are deeply regrettable. Even so, outlining the ways in which women's and men's friendships differ offers the most practical way of giving an account of the distinctive nature and importance of women's friendships.

The literature on the amount of time women and men spend with friends is equivocal with a slight bias in favour of women spending greater amounts of time largely due to telephone contacts (Fehr 1996). However a large number of studies have shown that men's and women's same-sex friendship activities differ markedly. Talk is the hallmark of female friendships whereas men prefer activity (see for example Rubin 1986). This has led Wright (1982) to characterize men's friendships as 'side by side' and women's friendships as 'face to face'. The gendered pattern of activity in same-sex friendships starts in childhood. Boys play largely in groups whereas girls interact in dyads (Maccoby 1990). Gendered patterns continue in adolescence when girls spend more time talking with friends than boys (Raffaelli and Duckett 1989). Recently this characterization of male and female same-sex friendships has been sharply challenged and contrary findings (such as Walker 1994) have been produced. While the issue has yet to be settled the balance of evidence is still probably on the side of distinctive differences between activity patterns in male and female same-sex friendships.

Consistent with the pattern of activity in their friendships men and women also differ in their topics of conversation, with men discussing activity related topics and women personal relationships (Fehr 1996). Unsurprisingly women rate talk in friendship as one of its chief benefits, setting it above help and shared activities (Lewittes 1989). The idea that women 'do' friendship 'face to face' while men do it 'side by side' became for quite a while a common-place of friendship research. However, more recently there have been a number of studies that re-evaluate men's friendship style and aspirations and the idea that men shun intimacy has been challenged in favour of the notion that men would like deeper intimacy but are not able to achieve it. For example, while men do not talk as much about intimate topics there is evidence that they would like to (Reisman 1990).

There is evidence that women depend strongly on friendship for social support. Rubin (1986) showed that women were readily able to name a person, very frequently a friend, to whom they would turn in an acute crisis whereas men were most often lost for a person to name or named a female relative. Equally differences in demonstrations of physical love and affection appear between male and female friendships during early primary school age. Girls soon show much more physical affection than boys (Thorne and Luria 1986) and this continues into adult life.

Fehr (1996) from whom this summary of gender differences in men's and women's same-sex friendships is drawn, devotes considerable space to considering why the pervasive pattern of differences described occurs. She reviews a number of options. For example Feher wonders whether men and women define the term 'intimacy' differently and as a result respond differently at interview. She also considers if men and women have differing ways of achieving similar degrees of intimacy that are not appropriately taken into account by studies that seem to show differences. Fehr shows how these and other potential explanations are not true. Nor is it the case that men like not being intimate, rather she decides that men simply chose not to exercise the capacity for intimacy with other men. Indeed men's rating of meaningfulness in same-sex interactions are lower than both women's ratings of same-sex interactions and their own ratings of cross-sex interactions (Reiss 1988). This suggests that men perceive that their lower levels of intimacy, talk, meaningfulness and touch in same-sex relationships can be corrected by cross-sex relationships.

Women also have cross-sex friendships but these are much more troubled relationships. Particularly among older women socialization pressures result in difficulty distinguishing between friendship and romance (Adams 1985). Men and women rate their cross-sex friendships' intimacy levels differently. Men rate cross-sex friendships as more intimate than same-sex ones while women give exactly converse answers (Buhrke and Fuqua 1987). Cross-sex friendships must negotiate issues of sexuality, public identity and gender inequality (Fehr 1996). For these reasons it is not surprising that although women describe important close friendships with men they are vastly outnumbered by female friendships. An important exception in some circles are friendships between gay men and women. These friendships, which are often described as highly enriching, offer all the potentially enriching advantages of cross-sex friendship without any sexual challenge. Additionally the oppressed status of gay men and sometimes their public visibility may help to deal with difficulties involving the public identity of the friendship and with gender based power relations. Thus gossip about potential sexual involvement is quelled to the extent that the gay friend is 'out'. Also ubiquitous experiences of male hegemony take on a new piquant ambiguity, when for example a waiter in a stuffy restaurant tries to decide who should have the menu with the prices on it.

A major difficulty with the literature on gender differences in same-sex friendships is the absence of any discussion of difficulty, conflict, or bitterness in same-sex male and female friendships. This lack mirrors a more general failure to consider negative aspects of female friendships. As with many of the defects in the sociological literature a more psychological approach might have helped to point up this lack.

A similar problem with this cornucopia of sociological information is that while it gives a detailed account of the value of female friendships and shows that they are more important to women than to men, it is as yet unable adequately to theorize the reason for this difference. However one reason for the importance of friendship to women may be that they sense that friendships are important to their mental health.

Why is friendship important to women?

When Brown and Harris wanted to study the social origins of depression they chose women in Camberwell as their sample group. Out of their studies grew a complex and subtle theory about social support and life events. They showed that lack of social support was a major vulnerability factor for depression (Brown and Harris 1978). While social networks involve family members, the non-kin elements of the social networks of depressed individuals are smaller than the same elements in non-depressed individuals (Brugha *et al.* 1982). There is also evidence that it is particularly depressed women who experience their interpersonal relationships as less emotionally supportive than non-depressed persons. From these findings it looks as though people who have depression have few or unsupportive friendships and that this is particularly the case for women as opposed to men (Dean and Ensel 1982; Billings *et al.* 1983).

Depression however is well known to lead to bias in recall and re-porting. Since many of the studies in this area were done on currently depressed women their findings may be consequent on depression rather than being causal. Longitudinal studies aimed at ruling out this possibility followed up depressed women later when their depression had remitted (for example Gotlib and Lee 1989). These studies find some increase in the number of social contacts reported by the recovered individuals but there was still evidence of restricted social networks. This work suggests that reduced social support predisposes to depression and does not recover when depression remits. They also show that social support cannot be the only factor in causing or relieving depression.

The special vulnerability of women to depression in relation to poor social networks is interesting and shows that at least one reason why friendship is important to women is that it is necessary for good mental health. Why should women need and value friendship more than men? One possibility is that the different social locations of men and women partly account for the differing importance of friendship. When male employment was much greater than female employment it would have been possible to suggest that men met similar needs in collegial relations at work not necessarily defined as 'friendships' by them. However this analysis does not stand given the greater equality in modern employment patterns. Possibly understanding the special nature of friendship to women requires a more psychological analysis.

Psychotherapeutic perspectives on women's friendships

One notable exception to the general psychoanalytic silence on the subject of friendship in general and female friendship in particular is the work of Orbach and Eichenbaum (1987). This book devoted to the subject bears the mark of disillusionment with the heady idealism of the women's movement from which it came. On too many occasions the sisterly rhetoric of mutual support and cooperative activity gave way to factionalism and recrimination. Those women who did capitalize on their reproductive and economic freedoms did so by competition in a masculine environment taking on masculine values as a result. Lastly the women's movement had failed to theorize or accommodate childbearing as a life choice. Orbach and Eichenbaum noticed strains in their own friendship and in the friendships of others. The resulting book seeks to apply understandings of female psychology derived essentially from the work of Chodorow (1978) to female friendships.

Orbach and Eichenbaum argue rather gushingly that friendships are particularly important to women because 'a woman without a best friend is a very lonely woman. There is an exquisite intimacy to female friendship, the sharing of experience, of daring of pain, of challenge' (Orbach and Eichenbaum 1987: 18). However despite the 'sense of continuity' a 'deep friendship with a woman' can provide they point out that troubles can occur in women's friendships.

Briefly they theorize that women grow up learning to know what others want and being rapidly sensitive to others' emotional states. This knowledge is derived from the mother–daughter bond which is blissful and problematic. It is problematic because at times the mother must rupture the blissful union to attend to her own needs and thereby be unempathic to the baby, which makes the bond insecure. Within the context of this insecure attachment the mother is able to see her son as different more easily than her daughter. This easy perception of difference allows the mother to encourage her son's independence. In relation to her daughter she experiences a need to merge, seeing her daughter's needs as her own, confusing the two and as a result being more likely to restrict the daughter's needs to be independent. In turn the mother teaches her daughter to be preferentially alive to the needs of others and give up her own needs. Ultimately the whole business of attachment in the daughter becomes characterized by repression and merger and produces a loss of personal identity.

Orbach and Eichenbaum work out the consequences of this psychological situation in all the various situations of adult life. They show how women have difficulty standing up for themselves, may become hugely prone to envy, fear of abandonment and frightened of competitiveness in their friendships. Clinically, for a certain group of patients – particularly the white middle classes from a particular age range – their analysis rings true.

Rebeccah's friend Rachel told her that she was 14 weeks pregnant. Rebeccah was outwardly pleased for Rachel but inwardly she was furious that Rachel had not told her earlier. Rachel had said this was because she wanted to feel sure she would not have an early miscarriage before she told everyone. Rebeccah was livid to be 'everyone' and to be excluded in advance from the possible task of comforting Rachel in that event. She found herself hating the developing baby and wanting to stab it. Rebeccah was the oldest child in a family of three siblings. Her sister was conceived when Rebeccah was 5, the news was kept from her until late in her mother's pregnancy and school was held up as Rebeccah's compensatory reward. Rebeccah's sister combined with school to displace her from her illusion of being her mother's special love, friend, equal and companion. Rachel's pregnancy reawakened these feelings abruptly.

However the chief complaint to be made about this work (and it is churlish at best to criticize the only work in the field) lies in the way that its developmental perspective reduces women's friendship dynamics to those of the mother–daughter relationship. While some sociologists have made similar suggestions, most of the sociological work takes by contrast a synchronic or locally developmental perspective on women's friendships. From within a psychological perspective the absence of a theorization of fatherhood, of alternative family organizations (lesbians are on occasion discussed but dismissed as not showing up the dynamics strongly enough) or of sibling and peer relationships, all of which might be highly important for the dynamics of friendship, is unduly constricting.

Another difficulty with Orbach and Eichenbaum's work centres on its universalizing tendencies. They are alive to the difficulties of this tendency saying for example: 'We are often blind and ignorant vis-à-vis experiences dissimilar to our own, we may deny differences, we may misperceive the circumstances of others or we may collude with stereotypes in our ignorance' (Orbach and Eichenbaum 1987: 108). Other than citing the range of their client group, however, they are not able to give any substance to their awareness of difference. For example there is evidence that the special nature of women's friendships may well be a culturally relative pattern. Berman *et al.* (1988) showed that Indian men's friendships are conducted far more on a 'female' line with for example greater latitude for physical contact. Amongst Hong Kong Chinese students an opposite pattern is found, with women's friendships showing no higher level of self-disclosure than men's friendships (Wheeler *et al.* 1989). However in neither country is there any difference in the largely female dominated pattern of childrearing to account for the different patterns observed.

A more radical analysis of difference in women's friendship would have been exactly a remedy for the tendency to developmental reductionism in Orbach and Eichenbaum's account. Had they been able to include a greater range of friendship patterns they would have been compelled to the view that, while we all have or had a mother, aspects of whose care will be common to us all, the hallmark of our friendships is their range and differences and a single mother dynamic will not serve to account for these differences.

Another psychoanalytic perspective with strong implications for women's friendship is attachment theory. Attachment style is obviously likely to be linked to capacity to form friendships (Birtchnell 1997). If an individual has poor internal working models to represent attachment, intimacy, and social relating they may well have considerable difficulty in forming secure friendships and the difficulties that they have will be consistently related to the exact nature of their maladaptive attachment patterns.

> Janet, a 63-year-old woman, had a lifelong pattern of consistently being unable to form close friendships. As soon as an acquaintance got to a certain level of intimacy she would forget meeting times or lose telephone numbers. As a child Janet had been separated from her mother during an infectious illness. On her return to her mother she had displayed an avoidant attachment pattern.

However the exclusive focus in attachment theory on the style of relationship to a single early figure does not do justice to the diversity of early experience. Nor will a concept of a single attachment template account for the range of attachment styles found in adult life or their development over time (Field 1996; Bartholomew 1997; Gittleman *et al.* 1998). For example women's friendships contrast strongly with the marriage relationship to the extent they may even be described as having a compensatory structure. It is difficult for attachment theory to account for this without an additional theoretical structure. For this reason attachment theory shares with the work of Orbach and Eichenbaum the twin problem of erasing difference and of making universalizing assumptions in this case about the foundational nature of early attachment for all later relating.

Sullivan (1953) outlined a variant of psychoanalytic thinking that was consistently interpersonal in outlook. Buhrmester and Furman (1986) have developed his work to give an account of changes in friendship relationships in childhood. They take as a starting point a range of social needs which Sullivan thought fundamental. These are tenderness, companionship, acceptance, intimacy and sexuality. These needs emerge through childhood, starting with tenderness in infancy and ending with sexuality in early adolescence. The social needs do not replace each other but are layered on top of each other until at last some of each of the five needs is co-present in adulthood. While parents meet the first two needs in early infancy, same-sex friends come successively to meet needs for companionship, acceptance and intimacy as childhood progresses.

Meeting each need requires the development of a distinctive range of interpersonal competencies. If these are not developed it is possible to arrest at each of the stages, and at each stage arrest will lead to a distinctive pattern of loss. So arrest during infancy when tenderness is to the fore leads to insecure attachment, whereas arrest during the juvenile era when acceptance is the developing need will lead to peer group ostracism and possibly compensatory disparagement of others. It is a part of this model that arrest may be due to influences other than parents, including for example, experiences at school.

Buhrmester and Furman have collected some evidence to support parts of this neo-Sullivanian theory. By and large they were able to collect evidence of age appropriate and group appropriate variations in skills associated with each social developmental stage described by Sullivan. Much of their experimental work relies on looking at preferential association with same and opposite-sex friends. This allows them to extend Sullivan's model which makes exact predictions about the ages at which same and opposite-sex friends meet specific needs. Sullivan himself thought his theory fitted boys' friendships best. He predicted a transfer in importance from parents to same-sex friends as the chief providers of intimacy. Buhrmester and Furman found that this occurs in boys and girls but the girls achieve this earlier than the boys (fifth rather than eighth grade) and achieve throughout higher levels of intimacy.

It is a logical consequence of the neo-Sullivanian model that the pattern of adult female friendships will be influenced both by early upbringing but also by friendship experiences in childhood. Thus some girls will bring a burden of poor relating at home to their first social experiences and as a result have difficulty, while other girls may experience at school, or with their peers, upsets that may leave their capacity for adult friendships substantially compromised.

> Frances was moved by her ambitious parents from a large school, where she had been failing academically, to a smaller one. Here she was both brighter than her peers but, more importantly, from a very different class and ethnic group. Faced with ostracism she rapidly developed into a friendless and unlovable swot. Efforts to achieve socially in her next school also failed, partly due to racism. In adult life, although Frances did make friends, she was constantly alive to the possibility of rejection and tended to misread actions as signalling rejection of her.

This neo-Sullivanian view on friendship escapes many of the reductive problems that were associated with the more traditional psychoanalytic perspectives. Crucially it is able to produce a far more complex analysis of friendships' varieties and vicissitudes because it admits of more potential sources of influence in their development. However there are two difficulties with its account. First, as the authors themselves comment, Sullivan's own work is 'poorly organized and often confusing' (Buhrmester and Furman 1986: 41) and add that to modern ears it could seem that the 'concept of "need" to be a bit mysterious and outdated' (1986: 42). Buhrmester and Furman do much to correct these difficulties but the model still lacks clarity. Second it is still like the attachment model committed to a programme of somewhat arbitrary grand stages (albeit with high face validity). As with all such models there is a danger that experimental evidence collected from within the paradigm and based on its assumptions is used in a circular fashion to argue for the existence and validity of the stages or units proposed. Without experimental evidence in which their paradigm is pitted against a rival paradigm, it remains hard to judge the validity of their model.

Arguably cognitive behavioural therapies were developed as a direct response to the complexities and obscurities of psychoanalytic approaches. Young (1986), who extended Beck's work in a more developmental direction, has turned his attention to friendship. Young's core notion is that schemas are responsible for guiding our analysis of any situation. The concept of Schema and the term have been very widely used in a whole range of psychological literature and to cover a wide range of different ideas. For Young however schemas are defined as stable, enduring patterns of thinking that are developed in early childhood. When schemas are maladaptive they may have serious negative effects on behaviour. In friendship relationships Young proposes that self-concept schemas combine with perception-of-others schemas and relationship schemas to govern relating. A negative self-concept schema might be that I am unlovable, a negative perception of others schema could be that they are cold and unemotional, and a negative relationship schema might be that friendships are 'not worth the bother'. All together these would produce an individual with little interest in and hope for friendship. However Young goes on to differentiate the different circumstances in which schemas are laid down. In particular he distinguishes close relationship schemas from social relationship schemas, arguing that the former may be developed in the family setting while the latter are chiefly developed at school or with peers.

Young also introduces the notion of levels of friendship ranging from very intimate (check-in) friendships, in which there may be daily contact or 'checking-in', to acquaintance level and argues that maintaining friendship across the whole range of levels is important. Finally he classifies difficulties in friendships into difficulties initiating friendships, and general problems with friendship – a category that might be better termed difficulties managing friendships.

The distinction between close and social relationship schemas, the delineation of a range of friendship levels and the classification of 'friendship disorders' allow Young to develop a conceptualization of a wide range of friendship disorders and to develop ways of treating them. Young does not consider gendered issues in relation to friendships, however our knowledge of female socialization allows us to predict that women are more likely than men to possess negative schemas about the self than they are about others. Women are also more likely to view aggression and conflict as unacceptable because of underlying schemas about the social acceptability of aggressive behaviour. As a result many women's friendship difficulties centre around doubts about whether they will be liked or around low assertiveness within friendships, leading to a one-sided meeting of needs.

> Jane consulted with depressed mood. Initial enquiry appeared to reveal a large network of friends and a superficially satisfactory set of relationships. However further inspection revealed that Jane felt she was continually putting herself out for her friends but getting little in return. Furthermore she felt that if she did not do as they wanted all her friends would abandon her. The underlying schemas involved were: 'I am unlovable so I must keep up a front', 'other people need to be placated or they will abandon me' and 'relationships are vital, I must keep them up at all cost'. Cognitive therapy centred on gathering evidence to question and revise these schemas.

While the underlying foundations of schema-focused cognitive behavioural therapy seem more secure than those of a neo-Sullivanian approach it still contains at its core universalizing assumptions about the prototypes for human relating. The assumptions Young makes seem eminently reasonable and the conclusions he draws accord with common experiences but they remain unsecured and potentially overgeneral. Maladaptive underlying schemas tend to be listed in cognitive therapy textbooks with no sense that the judgement of maladaptation may be a culturally relative one. Furthermore cognitive behavioural therapy frequently regards the other or the environment with which the individual interacts as an entirely passive object of knowledge. This makes an analysis of relating particularly difficult as there is little room for a view of the contribution of the other except perhaps in a brief discussion of problems in friendship selection.

Cognitive Analytic Therapy (CAT) developed by Ryle (1990, 1998) may offer some escape from these difficulties. It tries to develop an account of interpersonal and intrapersonal behaviour which is based in part on the concept of a reciprocal role. Reciprocal roles consist of two relationship poles united by a relationship paradigm. 'Care giver' in relation to 'care receiver' would be a good example. CAT describes how reciprocal roles are learned en bloc during social experience. A girl in primary school asks if she may join in a skipping game but is told she is not good enough. Later, when playing hopscotch she refuses entry to another girl on similar grounds. Thus the girl is learning, enacting and rehearsing the reciprocal role 'judging and excluding' in relation to 'judged and excluded'. Roles become internalized and form the basis for later relating both with self and others. A key feature of roles is that they exert pressure to reciprocate. Thus if a role is adopted strongly by an individual, others in that individual's orbit find themselves strongly pressed to adopt the relevant reciprocal pole. If, say, an office member begins to sob at her desk at least some of those around her will rapidly adopt a caregiving role.

Except in some severe disorders CAT conceptualizes difficulties in relationships both with self and others as frequently stemming from one or two reciprocal role templates which are malevolent, rigid or undermodulated. These may have been acquired at any point during social life from infancy through to adulthood. Thus the girl in the previous example was well on her way to internalizing 'judged and excluded' in relation to 'judging and excluding'. If this role were too strong or the only pattern available to her she might in adult life suffer from a range of difficulties, for example tending to avoid testing situations for fear of being judged and found wanting.

There has as yet been no specific account of women's friendships in the CAT literature but as the above example shows it is not hard to sketch some initial features from basic principles. To the extent that girls are socialized in ways that encourage intimacy, disclosure and trust they will develop reciprocal role templates that embody these relationship qualities. As we have seen girls and women spend time and energy doing talk and intimacy and this means that the roles will tend to be numerous, flexible, varied, and well modulated. By the same token, to the extent that aggression and assertion are not encouraged in girls, their stock of reciprocal roles for dealing with this will be impoverished and often excessively negative. Difficulties in dealing with aggression will result and may take the form of undue passivity or placation, or outbursts of misplaced or ineffective aggression often followed by an excessive shamed retreat. These two features can combine to account of the cycles of merger and explosive separation described by Orbach and Eichenbaum (1987) and ascribed by them to somewhat different dynamics.

However, unlike Orbach and Eichenbaum, CAT is not committed to the view that women must develop in this way. In different cultural or personal circumstances the pattern of internalized reciprocal roles would be quite different and would not produce the same pattern of friendship styles.

Sasha described having much less difficulty making friends with men than with women. She found she could talk to men about topics of mutual interest such as politics, whereas in groups of women talk turned to the doings of acquaintances and she often lost track. Sasha had been brought up by an uncle who appears to have treated her rather like a small non-sexual adult. Sasha had consulted because she was concerned about her capacity to be an adequate mother and said that she sometimes felt more like a man than a woman. Therapy concentrated on helping Sasha to develop a reciprocal role template for caring and nurturing. When her daughter was born, Sasha's parenting style had elements of traditional fathering and mothering roles, although she never entirely lost her worries about being able to care for her child.

Towards an integrated theory of friendship

Cognitive analytic therapy manages to avoid universalizing assumptions about the particular nature of reciprocal roles and it is both a social and a developmental theory. CAT is emphatic in its insistence on culture and sign mediation as the distinctive features of the human condition. We are born into a culture and CAT gives an account of how we acquire knowledge of norms of interpersonal relating within or in opposition to that culture. But CAT, being an individual psychotherapy without psychoanalysis' long history of application in various kinds of cultural criticism, remains individual in focus and it lacks, as yet, any account of group or cultural processes. CAT happily accepts that we do not simply construct our friendships as we will. We are constrained by cultural and social forms and all that we do or build is in conformity to or in contrast with a complex interacting network of powerful, if ill-defined, conventions. However these norms develop and shift over time. In relation to women's friendship a complete account requires some way of describing, analysing and accounting for these norms and the shifts that occur in them.

Arguably two notions may provide the basis for such an account. The first is the idea that relationships are defined within a field of other relationships in such a way that a large part of what it is to have one relationship can be discerned by contrasting that relationship with others that are similar but culturally distinguished. To this notion must be added the concept of an 'objectified social form' (McCall 1988). Relationships are governed by general norms of behaviour which are not entirely accounted for by their function or nature. On account of this it has been suggested that relationships can be analysed as examples of an 'objectified social form'. This term refers to the idea that a relationship is a kind of conventional social organization that imposes certain rules on the participants independent of and on occasion overruling the individuals involved, their circumstances or their psychological needs. Evidence for the convention-driven elements in these relationships can be found in the kinds of images, rules of conduct and customary modes of behaviour that are appealed to by individuals who are called on to prove the existence of a particular kind of relationship. Objectified social forms are arbitrary conventions of behaviour and nothing overt binds individuals to these forms. However the cultural agreement that maintains them gives them a force that transcends individual wishes. Obvious examples of such forms include weddings and funerals, but less obvious ones include tacit agreements about queuing in banks or occupying seats on buses. In the area of personal relationships each different kind of encounter is undertaken under the regency of some structuring form. Mother–daughter relationships are especially interesting in this regard as the formal structure allows (scripts one might say) a change in dependency levels, and rules of politeness as the daughter first matures and later the mother ages.

Relationships therefore are objectified social forms but they are also set in a network of contrasts which partly, but not entirely defines them. Thus the objectified social form of a relationship will vary over time as innovations (for example produced by prominent figures and reproduced in the media) catch on or as other objectified social forms in the network shift, changing the structure of abutments that its neighbouring objectified social forms experience.

CAT's insights about the cognitive structure of internalized knowledge about relationships might usefully be combined with the concept of objectified social forms and with a structural analysis of the relationships of such forms to each to give a unified account of women's friendships. Again, sadly, space constraints leave only room for exemplary gestures at such an account, but these should serve as examples for the necessary wider analysis. I shall focus on the relationship between kinship and friendship as it applies in the lives of straight and lesbian women. Notice how the change in the structure of one dyadic relationship (the erotic one) reverberates within these categories affecting their boundary.

Broadly speaking it seems possible to define at least three kinds of dyadic relationships between individuals. We have friends, lovers (including stable partners) and kin (that is parent, child, sibling). This division of dyadic relationships is built on the different circumstances that bring them into being. Kin are our genetic (or children's genetic) relations, lovers are those with whom we share sexual intimacy, often with some expectation of exclusivity, and friends are those with whom we choose to become intimate with though generally not in a sexual way.

All these relationships can also be demarcated according to the social psychological functions that they perform. For example relationships with kin and lovers satisfy the need for long term commitment and relationships with friends satisfy needs for peer group enjoyment (Litwack and Szelenyi 1969). These relationships can also be seen as principally fulfilling three different kinds of intrapersonal psychological function: for kin, lovers and friends respectively, nurture and dependency, erotic desire, and identification and reciprocity. Admittedly, these functional distinctions are only relative and in practice all the kinds of relationship fulfil a mix of functions.

When we try to define relationships and particularly when we are arguing about difficult cases, we often use a further device for demarcating different kinds of dyadic relationship. We use the device of contrasting one type of dyadic relationship with another and use their differences to help separate them. Hess (1972), for example, looked at the way that friendships between women relate to marriage and pointed out that friendships might be complementary to marriage – supporting it and help- ing to sustain it; they might be competitive with marriage – undermining and weakening it; or they might act as a substitute for it, especially in the elderly after the death of a spouse. Hess is using the possible abut- ments of friendship and marriage as a way of investigating and defining the nature of friendship. Arguably, this strategy can be taken further, leading to the suggestion that all the abutments of all the different kinds of pairs of dyadic relationships help to define these relationships, and in consequence reciprocally influence their structure.

How do the boundaries define and maintain each other? Consider first the boundary between kinship and friendship. In terms of the 'objectified social forms' demarcated by kinship and friendship the key distinction appears to be between the obligatory nature of duties imposed by kinship and the voluntary nature of duties imposed by friendship. Certainly there is some variability in the strength of the obligations of kinship – one may choose which relatives to whom one is especially committed. By the same token, there may come to be obligation in friendship but participants may well use the analogy of kinship to represent the building up of obligation in a friendship. 'She is like a sister to me, I would do anything for her.' In statements like this people use the borders between different objectified social forms of relationship as ways of grasping at the nature of an unusually strong friendship. This usage however, by defining kin-like friendships as atypical, tends to confirm, even build up a stereotyped view of the objectified social form.

From the perspective of cognitive analytic therapy the many social interactions in which women appeal to friendship relations and kinship relations and use their abutments to define them serve to build upon prototype reciprocal role structures. They do so in a particularly important way. They strengthen the central stereotyped reciprocal role for friendship in general and serve to establish a whole cluster of related reciprocal role structures that describe a wide range of variant forms. From 'friend–friend' (the central role) through, for example, 'friend like older sister guiding and caring–friend like younger sister guided and cared for' and perhaps including variants like 'friend like sister always letting me down–friend like sister ignoring and preoccupied' or 'friend like sister a bit bossy–friend like sister putting up with it'. I have argued elsewhere (Denman 1999) that a key determinant of good psychological functioning is the range subtlety and organization of reciprocal roles.

In modern societies sister–sister kin relationships tend to be more like friendships than do mother–daughter ones. There may be a number of social reasons for this. Sisters are less likely to have economic relations with each other and are less likely to have been in a relationship involving very much asymmetrical practical tending. We mark the closer similarity between sisterly relations and friendship with a variety of verbal forms for close friendship derived from sisterhood. Sister–sister relationships also offer – potentially – a way out of the dyadic relationship model and the importance of this is evident from a consideration of the literary forms that involve three sisters. Three sisters are a girl gang with a special intimacy, rivalry and closeness and the actually or potentially multiple nature of sisterhood has had particular importance for social forms based on female group intimacy, collectively and unsurprisingly known as sororities.

A consideration of sororities and of sister–sister–sister relationships also draws attention to the demarcation between friendship and erotic relationship. It is possible to discern a distinct social strand that uses the multiple nature of the sorority as a guard against slippage into erotic relatedness. Between sisters, because they are kin, we expect and can tolerate reductions of personal privacy and elements of exclusivity. Between friends however, similar reductions of privacy and intimations of exclusivity are not so permissible. They may signal breaches of the friendship ethos of limited interpenetration but they may also signal worrying slippages into an erotic form of relationship. Clearly the female sex of both participants provides some social protection – consider the much stronger limits on the intimacy possible between male and female friends – but perhaps not enough.

Examples include films involving three close women friends, which have had a vogue arguably because the form allows for an exploration of female intimacies that do not threaten with lesbian undertones. Nuns provide another case of anxiety about lesbian overtones in sisterly relations. In various religious orders 'personal friendships' – that is dyadic friendships – were highly discouraged. While there were obvious group dynamic reasons for wanting to tone down the strength of dyadic relationships in small communities living and working together, there were also clear implications of lesbianism in 'personal friendships'.

Friendships, because they are chosen, require maintenance with a reciprocity of gifts, affection and intimacy. In women's friendships there is a particular stress on being with rather than doing with in these friendships, and often where doing with is involved the doing may be some aspect of care of the body, such as shopping for clothes or going to the hairdressers together. Consequently there is potentially room for slippage between friendship and erotic intimacy. There are therefore expectations of privacy that mark friendship off from erotic intimacy. Friends don't declare love, they behave properly, theirs is a contract for talking and listening, remembering and planning. Among straight women there is also the barrier of overt mutual non-attractedness. However with the growth of lesbianism as an accepted social form this barrier may have grown somewhat more tentative. Academics have spent considerable amounts of time reclaiming as lesbian historic female–female relationships previously cast as platonic. In doing so they have pointed to evidence in the form of passionate exchanges of letters, and shared sleeping arrangements. However Faderman (1981) has argued that the passionate friendships found between women in the eighteenth and nineteenth century are not properly read as lesbian. Rather she argues the converse: that the rise of lesbianism has led to a reciprocal fall in passionate friendship between women because of fears of accusations of lesbianism.

Generally the downfall of the passionate friendship has been read in the context of external accusations of lesbianism. However internal voices may also be raised in prohibition. In her essay 'A closet of one's own' about being straight Daphne Merkin (1996) describes this anxiety in passing. She has arranged to go with a female friend who 'had researched an article on women pornographers and thus was a fount of knowledge on such things' to a sex shop to buy a dildo 'in compliance with a request from a man I was trying hard to please'. As they approached the shop her friend 'described the store as lesbianish and joked uneasily that the two of us would be taken for gay by virtue of frequenting it' (1996: 107). In this snippet the two women are wreathed in every kind of protection against mutual desire. Merkin has a boyfriend and is only going to please him, her friend has written an article and her interest is presumably academic. Notwithstanding the two friends stand potentially accused by their own inner voices on the brink of their 'lesbianish' shop.

Returning to a CAT perspective, restrictions in female friendships on account of potential accusations of lesbianism signal a restriction in the reciprocal role relationship repertoire. Anxieties over being thought lesbian when in a close female friendship signals the awakening of reciprocal role criticizing to criticized which is fairly universal. However it suggests that Merkin does not posses a reciprocal template embodying either contented lesbian sexuality or one embodying intimate non-sexual relatedness.

This difficulty can cut both ways. One lesbian writing about friendship muses on the situation created by the break-up of her recent relationship juxtaposed with the reforming of a friendship between herself and a childhood friend who is also now a lesbian.

> I didn't know whether to be envious or not of Nell and her lover. The girlish connection between them seemed wonderful and frightening to me. The relationship I was then painfully disentangling myself from had had that kind of child like element in it . . . My lover was there in a place where Nell had once been, I think many years before, when the connection between two young women was still safe and sexless . . . In that same imaginative place Nell had her girlfriend now. Nell and I were still close, still good deep friends, but we weren't best friends, the kind you have in grade school.
>
> (Brownrigg 1996: 44)

This passage filled with confusions and ambivalences shows how a combination of the insufficient development of the relevant social patterns (objectified social forms) with a wealth of shifting reciprocal roles templates, some only partly formed, produces confusion and subjective distress. Brownrigg's distress results from the shifting of role templates as new ones are created and old ones gain new significances. With luck the resultant pattern will be superior to the old. What happens in a single person's psychology is also mirrored in the development of objective social forms. Because the boundaries between relationships partly define them, when one of the relationship structures is changed all of the boundaries shift somewhat. Lesbians have different patterns of erotic relatedness than do heterosexuals and consequently serve as a good example of change in social forms.

How does the boundary between erotic relationship and friendship seem to lesbians? For straight women their female friends may, as we have seen, compete with, complement or substitute for their marital or erotic relationship. For a lesbian is a female friend always a potential lover? Certainly in some strands of lesbian thought there is no distinction between friends and lovers. Rich (1980) proposed the now famous concept of a lesbian continuum ranging from any kind of women's friendship through to formally 'lesbian' relationships. Later more radical lesbian groups defined as lesbian any woman-identified woman who did not have sex with men. This definition did not require any actual lesbian sex and was attacked by lesbian sex activists like Califia (1994) and who were concerned to re-emphasize that lesbian identity is first and foremost a sexual identity.

The question still engages the lesbian community, however. A survey of sexual preferences among lesbians still found it necessary to ask the question 'What would have to happen between you and another woman for you to call it sex?' The range of answers covered acts such as 'going past heavy petting, naked . . .' as well as 'some form of genital contact' intents or effects as in 'an activity which one or both women try to bring the other to the point of orgasm' and importantly for our purposes, contradistinction from a friendship relation as in 'any physical or eye contact that wouldn't take place with my platonic friends' (Creith 1996: 70).

Issues of definition in the lesbian community have centred therefore around the two questions: Who is a lesbian? What counts as sex? In both cases it is concern to negotiate either by emphasizing or by de-emphasizing the boundary between sexual relationships and friendly ones which is at the fore. The fact that more lesbians retain ex-lovers as friends than heterosexual partners do might be adduced as concrete evidence for the further permeability of this boundary.

> Petra consulted in turmoil. After finishing a long relationship with a man she had just started a sexual relationship with a female friend and work colleague. In her first sessions she was preoccupied with defining herself not as a lesbian (she hated the word) but as someone who had simply happened to have fallen in love with a woman. In later sessions a new anxiety came to the fore as Petra worried that her other female friends might reject her as 'unsafe'. She finds herself reading newspaper articles about gay and lesbian issues; suddenly it seems as if there are an awful lot of these – far more than she can remember having read in the past.

Petra moves suddenly into a new social and emotional area. The objectified social forms shift under her feet, and her reciprocal role repertoire proves inadequate to the task in hand. In the therapy sessions she shows some signs of beginning to expand her range of reciprocal roles to cope with the situation. The role 'someone who just happened to fall in love with a woman to woman who just happened to be fallen in love with' may or may not prove to be a waystation but for the present it is new.

Conclusions

Women's friendships are important for their mental health. They represent a major part of social life and are complex, subtle and varied. This chapter has tried to review some of the large body of work in the field. Noting the lack of deep psychological theorizing in the area it has tried to forge and apply an integrated social and psychological view of relationships to some very limited aspects of women's friendships. At the very least it is to be hoped that future work in the area will try to remedy the deficiencies inherent in both psychological and social conceptions of friendship. To do so will involve being psychological about the social and social about the psychological.

In keeping with this view a central aim of the conceptualization of friendship that has been developed in this chapter has been a welding of the notion of an objectified social form with the concept of a reciprocal role template. Such a union represents an attempt to bring the social and the psychological together. However to do so I have proposed that much of our social behaviour is governed by large structures which govern us and limit freedom. Both objectified social forms and reciprocal role templates are largely given to us by our early experiences and by the social structures of the culture in which we live. Our inner mental structures for perceiving the world of social relationships (reciprocal role templates) largely structure our perceptions and direct our experience. Likewise the objectified social forms we enact mainly lay out the limits of behaviour and exert a palpable force over our actions. It is possible to experience this force by the simple expedient of sitting on a tube train or bus and attempting to shout out loudly the name of each bus or tube stop as it is approached.

However while such a view does set limits to human freedom experience and behaviour it does not result in any form of anti-realism or strong social determinism. While we see the world largely in terms given to us by those who saw it before, those terms arise because of the way the world actually is and they change as the world changes. Thus our view of acceptable dress and appropriate behaviour transform, so also do our notions of the value, nature and objects of love and friendship. Just as our reciprocal role templates represent the result of cumulating interpretations of repeated transactions with people in relationships, so objectified social forms represent the outcome of a perpetual negotiation between all the social actors enacting the form. It is a logical result of this view that objectified social forms and our attitudes mostly evolve with time rather than being radically transformed. Women's friendships can be seen to have evolved in just this way, from intense personal intimacies through a cooler phase inaugurated by the increasing economic independence of women, through to a current phase, which as Orbach and Eichenbaum (1987) note, seems characterized in some circles by a new preoccupation with envy and competition as women have gained social power.

Grand theories, and one that attempts to fuse psychological and social perspectives is in many ways far too grand a theory, suffer from saying everything or nothing. They need experimental grounding and they should justify themselves by signing up to some definite predictions in advance of the data rather than doing a rapid two-step in order to accommodate incoming information. One huge lack in the field of female friendships has been the lack of any attempt to survey their cultural diversity. Honourable exceptions aside, the literature on women's friendships is overwhelmingly a white middle-class literature with whole books on just this topic (Gouldner and Strong 1987). Statistically such friendships account for a small subset of female friendships. It must surely be the case that the white female American college student, however convenient and accessible for study, is no longer an appropriate sampling frame. This gap in the field provides theorists of female friendship with an unlooked for opportunity. It should surely be possible on theoretical grounds to make predictions about the structuring of female friendships in differing cultural settings and then to test these out against a range of different social organizations.

It is beyond the scope of this chapter and the intelligence of its author to outline a full set of predictions for any kind of culture, however two limited and preliminary thoughts can be set out to set the ball rolling. Ryle's (1990) notion of reciprocal role templates is essentially dyadic, based on the notion of self and other. It is central to his theory that this should be so. Does this represent western cultural bias elevating the notion of selfhood and privileging two-person over many-person relationships or is it as Ryle might argue a universal feature of human relating? The nature of marriage – through much of history fundamentally an economic institution – is centrally structured on female friendships. In social organizations (for example some Mormon communities) where both marriage is changed and a further female relationship is added (that between wives) is there a radical restructuring of non-kin female friendships? If there were not this would constitute a major blow for the theory. It is, at the last, no surprise to find that more work will be needed to answer these questions.

References

Adams, R.G. (1985) People would talk: normative barriers to cross-sex friendships for elderly women, *The Gerontologist*, 25: 605–11.

Bartholomew, K. (1997) Adult attachment processes: individual and couple perspectives, *British Journal of Medical Psychology*, 70 (Pt 3): 249–63.

Berman, J.J., Murphy-Berman, V. and Pachauri, A. (1988) Sex differences in friendship patterns in India and in the United States, *Basic and Applied Social Psychology*, 9: 61–71.

Billings, A.G., Cronkite, R. and Moos, R.H. (1983) Social–environmental factors in unipolar depression: comparisons of depressed patients and nondepressed controls, *Journal of Abnormal Psychology*, 93: 119–33.

Birtchnell, J. (1997) Attachment in an interpersonal context, *British Journal of Medical Psychology*, 70 (Pt 3): 265–79.

Blieszner, R. and Adams, R.G. (1992) *Adult Friendship*. Newbury Park, CA: Sage.

Brown, G.W. and Harris, T. (1978) *Social Origins of Depression*. London: Free Press.

Brownrigg, S. (1996) Like cutting off my arm, in M. Daly (ed.) *Surface Tension: Love, Sex and Politics between Lesbians and Straight Women*. New York: Touchstone.

Brugha, T., Conroy, R., Walsh, N. *et al.* (1992) Social networks, attachments and support in minor affective disorders: a replication, *British Journal of Psychiatry*, 141: 249–55.

Buhrmester, D. and Furman, W. (1986) The changing functions of friends in childhood: a neo-Sullivanian perspective, in V.J. Derlega and B.A. Winstead (eds) *Friendship and Social Interaction*. New York: Springer-Verlag.

Buhrke, R. and Fuqua, D. (1987) Sex differences in same- and cross-sex supportive relationships, *Sex Roles*, 17: 339–52.

Califia, P. (1994) *Public Sex: The Culture of Radical Sex*. San Francisco, CA: Cleis Press.

Chodorow, N. (1978) *The Reproduction of Mothering*, Berkeley, CA: University of California Press.

Creith, E. (1996) *Undressing Lesbian Sex: Popular Images, Private Acts and Public Consequences*. London: Cassell.

Davis, K.E. and Todd, M.J.(1985) Assessing friendships: prototypes, paradigm cases and relationship description, in S. Duck and D. Perlman (eds) *Understanding Personal Relationships: An Interdisciplinary Approach*. London: Sage.

Dean, A. and Ensel, W.M. (1982) Modelling and social support, life events, competence and depression in the context of age and sex, *Journal of Community Psychology*, 10: 392–408.

Denman, C. (1999) Introduction to Cognitive Analytic Therapy, in S. Stein and J. Stein (eds) *Psychotherapy in Practice: A Life in the Mind*. London: Butterworth-Heinemann.

Donelson, E. and Gullahorn, J.E. (1977) Friendship, in E. Donelson and J.E. Gullahorn (eds) *Women, a Psychological Perspective*. New York: Wiley.

Faderman, L. (1981) *Surpassing the Love of Men*. London: Junction Books.

Fehr, B. (1996) *Friendship Processes*. Newbury Park, CA: Sage.

Field, T. (1996) Attachment and separation in young children, *Annual Review of Psychology*, 47: 541–61.

Gittleman, M.G., Klein, M.H., Smider, N.A. and Essex, M.J. (1998) Recollections of parental behaviour, adult attachment and mental health: mediating and moderating effects, *Psychological Medicine*, 28(6): 1443–55.

Gotlib, I.H. and Lee, C.M. (1989) The social functioning of depressed patients: a longitudinal assessment, *Journal of Social and Clinical Psychology*, 8: 223–37.

Gouldner, H. and Strong, M.S. (1987) *Speaking of Friendship: Middle-Class Women and Their Friends*. New York: Greenwood Press.

Hays, R.B. (1988) Friendship, in S.W. Duck (ed.) *Handbook of Personal Relationships: Theory, Research, and Interventions*. New York: Wiley.

Hess, B.B. (1972) Friendship, in M.W. Riley, M. Johnson and A. Foner (eds) *Ageing and Society*, vol. 3. New York: Russell.

Lewittes, H. (1989) Just being friendly means a lot – women, friendship, and ageing, in L. Grau and I. Susser (eds) *Women in the Later Years: Health, Social, and Cultural Perspectives*. New York: Harrington Park.

Litwack, E. and Szelenyi (1969) Primary group structures and their functions: kin, neighbours and friends, *American Sociological Review*, 34: 465–81.

McCall, G.J. (1988) The organisational life cycle of relationships, in S.W. Duck (ed.) *Handbook of Personal Relationships*. Theory, Research, and Interventions. New York: Wiley.

Maccoby, E.E. (1990) Gender and relationships: a developmental account, *American Psychologist*, 45: 513–20.

Merkin, D. (1996) A closet of one's own, in M. Daly (ed.) *Surface Tension: Love, Sex and Politics between Lesbians and Straight Women*. New York: Touchstone.

O'Connor, P. (1992) *Friendships Between Women: A Critical Review*. New York: Guilford.

Orbach, S. and Eichenbaum, L. (1987) *Between Women: Facing up to Feelings of Love, Envy and Competition in Women's Friendships*. London: Arrow.

Raffaelli, M. and Duckett, E. (1989) 'We were just talking . . .': conversations in early adolescence, *Journal of Youth and Adolescence*, 18: 567–89.

Rawlins, W.K. (1992) *Friendship Matters*. Hawthorne, NY: Aldine de Gruyter.

Reisman, J.M. (1979) *Anatomy of Friendship*. New York: Irvington.

Reisman, J.M. (1990) Intimacy in same sex friendships, *Sex Roles*, 23: 65–82.

Reiss, H.T. (1988) Gender effects in social participation: intimacy, loneliness, and the conduct of social interaction, in R. Gilmour and S. Duck (eds) *The Emerging Field of Personal Relationships*. Hillsdale, NJ: Lawrence Erlbaum.

Rich, A. (1980) Compulsory heterosexuality and lesbian existence, *Signs: Women in Culture and Society*, 5(4): 630–60.

Rubin, L.B. (1986) On men and friendship, *Psychoanalytic Review*, 73: 165–81.

Ryle, A. (1990) *Cognitive Analytic Therapy: Active Participation in Change*. Chichester: Wiley.

Ryle, A. (1998) *Cognitive Analytic Therapy and Borderline Personality Disorder: The Model and the Method*. Chichester: Wiley.

Sapadin, L.A. (1988) Friendship and gender: perspectives of professional men and women, *Journal of Social and Personal Relationships*, 5: 387–403.

Sullivan, H.S. (1953) *The Interpersonal Theory of Psychiatry*. New York: Norton.

Thorne, B. and Luria, Z. (1986) Sexuality and gender in children's daily worlds, *Social Problems*, 33: 176–90.

Walker, K. (1994) Men, women, and friendship: what they say, what they do, *Gender and Society*, 8: 246–65.

Wheeler, L., Reis, H.T. and Bond, M.H. (1989) Loneliness, social interaction, and sex roles, *Journal of Personality and Social Psychology*, 57: 79–86.

Wright, P.H. (1982) Men's friendships, women's friendships and the alleged inferiority of the latter, *Sex Roles*, 8: 1–20.

Wright, P.H. (1984) Self-referent motivation and the intrinsic quality of friendship, *Journal of Social and Personal Relationships*, 1: 115–30.

Young, J.E. (1986) A cognitive–behavioural approach to friendship disorders, in V.J. Derlega and B.A. Winstead (eds) *Friendship and Social Interaction*. New York: Springer-Verlag.

5 Women and work

Eileen Aird

One of the central objectives of the feminist movement of the 1970s was the transformation of the world of work and of women's place in that world (Rowbotham 1983). This chapter explores the interconnections in women's lives between the public and the private worlds of work. The public and the private are not separate but intimately and intricately related to each other. The daily realities of most women's lives include the bridging of work and home, functionally in the juxtaposition of the necessities of shopping and filing for instance and psychologically in thinking about relationships, needs and feelings both in the home and the workplace.

The feminist struggle to change definitions and experiences of work has included the fight for equal pay and the desire to break down the barriers between the domestic and the public economy through the 'wages for housework' campaign and through an analysis of the economic as well as the emotional costs of mothering and of caring for elderly relatives. Emphasis was given to creating alternative structures for work based on the ideals of collectivity and cooperation rather than on hierarchies of power. The energy for change was rooted in both anger and a sense of injustice and idealism and hopefulness for a different future. In practice collective and cooperative ventures brought their own problematic dynamics where idealization sometimes masked envy and hostility, which was not always successfully recognized and worked through. However collective approaches to work and to decision-making did represent a radical attempt to transform workplace structures, to distribute power throughout an organization and to encompass difficulty alongside positive energy.

Yet from the much less hopeful perspective of the year 2000, with the women's movement dispersed, it can sometimes seem that very little has actually changed. Despite the legislative developments of the last

25 years, which have given women statutory equality at work, the gap in average earnings has not been reduced. Average gross annual earnings for men in full-time employment in April 1999 were about £23,000 a year, while for women in full-time employment they were about £16,000 a year – a difference of 42 per cent (Travis 2000). Many women are still employed in part-time low-paid and insecure jobs. Pension entitlements are less advantageous for women than for men because of breaks in employment and lower levels of lifetime earnings. Maternity pay and leave is less generous than in many European countries.

There are some important gains and some embedding in the mainstream of what once hovered on the radical edge or within the subversive space of alternative thought. Women are represented in middle management positions in many professions now, although their penetration of senior management is rare, even within the woman-dominated caring professions of nursing and teaching. In part this represents a generational issue; some women now in middle management will become the senior managers of tomorrow. It also indicates men's unwillingness to relinquish the strongholds of policy and resources while relying on women's communication skills and capacity for connectedness at middle management level.

Girls at school may still find themselves being directed into nursing, teaching or secretarial work but some of them, at least, are impatient with this advice and enter a range of professions and jobs previously seen as male dominated, from accountancy to refuse collection, engineering to bus driving. The occupational range of jobs available to women is one of the areas of significant change that has taken place since the mid-1970s. About 1.5 million women worked as domestic servants at the end of the nineteenth century; this was the dominant employment category for women. At the end of the twentieth century 800,000 women worked as cleaners and housekeepers. Although women still dominate teaching and nursing the choice of jobs is now as wide for women as for men (Travis 2000). Ideological definitions of the place of work in a woman's life may not have changed as rapidly as the employment profile. The majority of women now spend much of their working life in paid employment beyond the home, often working very long hours in low paid jobs such as night-time office cleaning. Less frequently women achieve highly paid and senior jobs in finance or industry. The price to be paid for entering these traditionally male domains is a whole scale participation in a work ethos that demands 12-hour days followed by two hours in the pub.

While the social and gender construction of work in British society is changing we live still with a split between the public and the private, often translated into the marketplace and the home. Work is defined as belonging to the public arena of employment, while domestic labour is largely invisible and unrecognized. Women, it is assumed, mother, clean houses, shop, cook and look after their partners out of love. Work, however, is defined as a contract where labour is sold for money.

This opposition between home and work is an illusory one, incorporating a number of denials. It suggests that work in the home is not as onerous or repetitive or worthy of financial recompense as work in the marketplace. There is a false supposition that women can freely choose whether to work within or beyond the home, ignoring the evidence that the majority of women have to work beyond the home for economic reasons. Many women have little choice about combining mothering of preschool-age children with part or full-time work. Work in the public arena is opposed to that in the private world, although most women work both beyond and within the home, combining paid and unpaid labour. Although there has been some increase in the number of men acting as primary carers of their young children and there is an easy rhetoric about the sharing of household tasks, surveys consistently show that the number of hours in childcare and domestic labour undertaken by women is still much higher than that undertaken by men. Many women now live on their own, often with their children; without adequate state and workplace childcare they have little choice beyond a double burden of domestic work and paid employment.

We are still living with the faint heritage of the Victorian ideal of the angel in the house (Lown 1990) where women represent the sanctity and comfort of the hearth to which men return from the rude realities of the workplace. This split between hearth and workplace encompasses a denial of class. Many women in nineteenth-century England were forced from an early age to sell their labour in mines, factories, households and brothels.

If the split between home and work is a false one economically and socially, it is also oversimplified as a psychological construct. We transfer our familial experiences from the private world of the home to the public one of employment or voluntary activity. Women still cluster in the caring and helping professions, partly because they are good at looking after the needs of others, having developed skills and capacities in the home and in mothering which can be transferred into the structures of the marketplace. In part, such work may fulfil a psychological need to be a carer of others and not to seek power, authority or be ambitious for change or influence, desires traditionally seen as masculine. This replicates the conventional social and psychoanalytic structure of the heterosexual family, in which mothers represent and embody nurturing, understanding, empathy and connection while fathers hold the boundaries of the family, are more absent, characterize their communication and relationship by thinking rather than feeling and are less likely to meet the emotional dependency needs of their partners or children. Psychoanalytic psycho-therapists writing from a feminist perspective (Ernst and Maguire 1987) have established the extent to which women care for others from the well of their own unmet needs. The vicarious satisfactions of work in the caring professions can sometimes offer an identification with those for whom they care which may seem to meet their own needs. In choosing this vicarious satisfaction women may deny their own individual-ity, agency and subjectivity. Orbach (1997: 48), who has written about these issues over the last 25 years, says: 'A woman's struggle to achieve psychological subjectivity may be stopped in its tracks or constrained by the overwhelming demands of giving to others what she so badly needs herself.'

Of course there is a genuine satisfaction to be gained from giving to others within the boundaries and structures of the workplace, but there may also be involved an emptying of resources and a manic reparation.

Sarah works as a counsellor in a large, run-down college of further education in a northern industrial town with very high levels of poverty and unemployment. The elder daughter of an intelligent and ambitious father, who never fulfilled his own creative potential because he lacked a formal education, Sarah is aware of the privileges of her own university education. She has never been quite able to satisfy her father's conscious desire for her to go from success to success because it is based on an unconscious desire to assuage some of his own frustration, which Sarah shares with her father through her identification with him.

Sarah's mother had an unhappy childhood as the only child of strict parents who expected her to work hard in the house from an early age. She was determined to mother her two daughters well and to give them the love she had not experienced, but found it very difficult to separate from them and allow them to develop independent and intimate relationships of their own. Sarah feels alternately exasperated with and guilty about her mother's need for intimacy and connection with her.

Many of her clients in the college counselling service struggle with poverty, difficult home circumstances and low self-esteem. Many are adult students working with determination to repair previous unsatis-factory educational experiences. Sarah works very hard, exceeding her hours every week and taking on more and more clients. It is as though if she works hard enough and uses her professional skills as fully as possible, she will be able to transform the lives of her clients. She is driven to do this in a way that is exhausting and draining her because she is playing out an internal role as the daughter of a father who overtly presses her to work hard and succeed and a mother who unconsciously sees her daughter as her mother.

There is little space in this scenario for Sarah to consider her own needs, and a manic drive to reparation which transfers Sarah's external and internal family scenario on to her work circumstances. In her conscious striving to provide contexts for change for her clients Sarah is effectively opening up opportunities. She is good at her job and committed to the environment in which she works. Unconsciously she is trying to re-solve cultural, class and psychological conflicts that are integral to her identity.

Work that is seen consciously or unconsciously as reparation may lead to particularly effective contributions. By trying to put right what we have experienced as wrong, internally in our psychological world or externally in a social world structured by differences of class, race and gender, we may strengthen our own good inner objects as well as effect change in the external world. There is a danger of idealization, however, particularly if the drive towards reparation carries a high unconscious component. Colleagues, clients, customers, students or patients may be idealized to such an extent that envy, hostility and competitiveness can-not be consciously admitted. The denial of envy and competitiveness can lead to disappointment and destructiveness as idealization inevitably gives way to a more complex encounter with paradoxical reality.

Winnicott's (1971) conception of good enough mothering is relevant here. As a concept it has been enormously influential in structuring ways of thinking not just about mother–child relationships but about relationships in general. Winnicott (1965, 1971) argued that in order to facilitate the greatest psychological growth of her child, the mother needs to be constantly and delicately attuned to the child's fluctuating need for both connectedness and separateness. Increasingly throughout the first two years of the child's life the mother needs to create a safe psychological context in which the child can explore its environment secure in its sense of the mother's holding. As the child is able to play, initially in the mother's presence but ultimately in her absence, because knowledge of her is now internalized, a secure sense of separate identity begins to emerge. Although Winnicott emphasized that what was needed was good enough mothering, not perfect mothering, his requirements are exacting. He assumed that the mother would be supported in this complex emotional interaction by the child's father. With no gender analysis of socially constructed and psychologically experienced differences between the sexes he underestimated the extent to which women carry with them an internalized and perpetually re-experienced knowledge of the inequality of caring. Mothers, he assumed, would, by virtue of their biological or social role, be able to be carers with no difficulty arising from unmet needs of their own. Feminist scholars and therapists have argued convincingly that few adult women have their own psychological needs met as fully as they are expected to meet the needs of others (Sayers 1986; Seu and Heenan 1998).

Translated into the world of work the idea of good-enough has influentially shaped several work roles, including those of the carer, the manager and the personal assistant. Discussions of management styles and effectiveness now include references to the feminization of management. This describes ways of managing based on empathy, availability and accessibility, the desire to develop the capacities of others and to work through connection and relationship. As a style of management it is recognized as particularly effective in complex organizations where diverse skills and high levels of flexibility and teamwork are required. It is not of course, confined to women managers, nor are all women facilitative in their approach to others. Like good-enough mothering it assumes an unlimited capacity to provide a healthy and secure environment for the growth of others. It is undoubtedly productive of good working relationships and encouraging of creativity and development.

Difficulties can arise when confrontation, clarity or difficult decisions about restructuring, redundancy or substantial changes in work objectives are needed. A manager previously seen as open and consultative who has to make changes that deeply affect the dynamics and emotional life of the workplace may then be seen as tough and uncaring. The defensive splitting of good and bad, which allows the denial of a more painful but mature acceptance of ambivalence, can seriously distort perceptions in the workplace as elsewhere.

> Barbara had an interesting and well paid job as the head of a small research unit in a government office. The daughter of schoolteacher parents she had been brought up in a house run rather like a well ordered classroom. Reason, routine and common sense prevailed, displays of emotion of any kind were not encouraged and displays of overt affection, either verbal or tactile, were rare. Barbara was a bright enquiring child and her parents expected her to do well at school while not seeming particularly pleased by her success. Her glowing school reports were quietly received and read with little comment and her parents did not always manage to attend school functions. Barbara understood from early on that she was meant to succeed but not to take too much pleasure in her achievements.
>
> On leaving university she had a series of jobs in administration and then management. As a manager of the research unit she was

well liked by her staff whom she encouraged to take on and develop interesting projects. While she genuinely wanted them to do well, supported their professional development and was supportive of any personal dilemmas which impinged on the workplace, she also felt a lack of satisfaction in her work. She thought that it was inappropriate for her as a manager to take on any of the research projects and sometimes felt a sense of loss as she handed over interesting topics to her colleagues.

Her own manager, Sue, had a very different approach to management, relying on last minute demands rather than carefully supported delegation. Instead of involving Barbara in the development of initiatives she would often send terse memos with unrealistic timescales. At the same time she needed a lot of personal support in her own very senior role and would expect Barbara to listen to her problems. A difficult situation arose in the research unit because of changes in both policy and funding which meant that two people would need to be made redundant. Barbara received a memo from Sue instructing her to make two of her research officers redundant as quickly as possible. Barbara reacted with sudden and uncharacteristic fury and stormed into Sue's office accusing her of lack of cooperation and of shifting the responsibility for difficult decisions onto others without involving them in initial discussion and planning. Sue responded by describing her own dilemmas about the restructuring and repeating her order that Barbara should carry out her instructions. Barbara's anger rapidly turned into distress as she felt that her identity as a responsible and caring manager was being attacked.

As long as Barbara was able to encourage the development of others and so repair her own lack of parental encouragement, she was able to contain her disappointment at the lack of direct creativity in her own work. She saw herself as a good enough manager, effective, fair-minded, competent and stimulating. Although she was irritated by Sue's peremptoriness and neediness she was able to manage her own unit without too much disruption. When she was asked to make staff redundant with no proper process of consultation and planning she was rightly angry. The anger gave way to distress as she feared the loss of her reputation as a good-enough manager. At the same time she recognized, how little she herself was supported by her own manager. Indeed she had to function as a good-enough mother to Sue on several occasions. Both the anger and the distress awoke the conflicts of her childhood, where her energy and creativity had been subordinated to the rather repressive culture of her family. Like many mothers she was trying hard to be a good-enough manager without sufficient support or attention to her own needs. She was also carrying one aspect of an organizational split in which Sue was the bad manager and Barbara the good one – a split that was reflected in both workplace projections and their individual personalities.

Individuals at any level in an organization do not work in a vacuum, isolated from others. The organizational culture and structure of the workplace influence individual transactions and everyone both contributes to, rebels against and is shaped by the cultural dynamics (Segal 1985). Failure at work may be signalled on an external level: not meeting targets, misunderstanding systems or carrying out procedures inaccurately for instance. Failures of this kind may reinforce earlier experiences of not succeeding at school or in training or previous work environments. Much will depend on how this is handled by managers and colleagues as to whether it can become a learning point leading to future development or simply a rather dismal experience, reducing self-esteem and job status. A more complex kind of failure sometimes stems from an ambivalence about what success means and what implications it may have for personal life. Is there a conscious and unconscious choice involved between being a manager and being a woman? If career development involves competitiveness with both men and with other women will this be too uncomfortable? These conflicts are particularly likely if women have been brought up in families where they have been encouraged to be self-effacing in the care of others.

As women are still the main carers of young children a common and repeated dilemma arises in relation to the needs of the workplace and those of children. In the absence of workplace crèches women who work long hours and perhaps also travel some distance to work may have to arrange alternative childcare with a childminder or nanny. Mothers with older children at school may have to stay at home when children are ill. Usually seen as personal and individual dilemmas these issues are embedded in the structure of work and family; they arise from a split between the woman as 'worker' and the woman as 'mother'. As a worker the woman has a public role, as a mother she has an invisible role which is taken for granted economically and socially. There is a real tension between these roles of 'worker' and 'mother' which raises fundamental questions about the value of public and private work. Mothering belongs to the private world of the home but is vital to the maintenance of the public world of work.

Important issues for any organization are: Who wields the power? What are the decision-making processes? Who is involved in making decisions and who owns them? Who does the caring and who holds the boundaries? Is the ethos competitive or collaborative? Power and decision-making are often identified consciously and unconsciously as masculine, while caring, servicing and collaborating are characterized as feminine. Women taking on responsibility in the workplace may find that they have a voice, confidence or authority that surprises them. Sometimes this is in conflict with a caring, serving role and they may become too anxious to carry out the managerial or supervisory role. It is not uncommon for very able women to reject power and influence, preferring to remain as assistants or workers. This may be a realistic or creative choice but it can also indicate an abdication of the responsibility for changing structures, cultures and to some extent oneself. Women making these choices often find themselves in supportive roles within the workplace: listening to their overstretched manager, male or female, looking after the boss, making quietly facilitative contributions in groups where the assertive leadership comes from elsewhere. Alternatively they may be left with a freedom to rebel or criticize, nursing the belief that 'of course I could do it better but I choose not to', or they may eschew as far as possible the conflicts, politics and structural demands of the workplace.

The rejection of power may be based on a fear of one's own destructiveness and on an anxiety that the aggression which is sublimated in the caring or creative role will emerge in a way that is damaging to the self and others.

Karen, who worked as an administrative assistant in a large business organization, was sent on a residential management training course by her line manager. The culture of her organization was aggressive and competitive; people were expected to work long hours, sick leave was regarded as an indication of weakness and the emphasis was on productivity and achievement. A competitive culture was developed through a system of bonuses and rewards. Karen was pleased that she had been selected for the management training and was keen to do well.

Early on in her course participants, who came from several different organizations and were mostly unknown to each other, were asked to play a game based on the barter and exchange of tokens, where the exchange rate constantly changed so there was no fixed value to the currency. The objectives changed as different tokens acquired more or less value. Success in the game depended on the ability to win individual barters. Karen found herself playing the game with great enthusiasm and energy, her quick mind kept up with the implications of the changing values and she was effective in exchanging tokens to her own advantage.

Eventually the trainer halted the bartering process and all participants organized themselves into three groups: top, middle and bottom, according to the current value of their tokens. The top group, of which Karen was a member, was then asked to draw up rules for exchange of membership between the groups.

Karen led her own group into making draconian rules which kept her and everyone else in rigid structures, with an even more complicated bartering system that intensified the hierarchical culture. Her usually caring and responsive self was swallowed up by the demands of the game, which revealed her pleasure in her capacity to influence and even dominate others. She was immediately horrified and upset by the response from members of the other groups, who refused to accept the rules and the hierarchy which she had been so instrumental in reinforcing.

Under the pressures of the training course the split between her need for power and her clarity in achieving ends and her sense of herself as a carer and server became apparent. This behaviour also reflected the management culture within which she worked which valued competitiveness rather than collaboration. The game was an important learning experience for her, allowing her to think of ways in which she could combine decisiveness and caring and bring together within herself stereotypically masculine and feminine strengths. She was still left with a struggle in trying to work in an integrated way in an organization that valued competitiveness above all other things.

Women who have competed and achieved senior manager or chief executive roles have to find a way of combining what is characterized as a feminine mode of communication and connectedness with what is characterized as a masculine mode of authority and overall responsibility. Individuals inevitably tend to emphasize one style rather than the other, although both are needed for effective senior management. Women in positions of power are likely to receive both feminine and masculine, maternal and paternal projections. They may be unconsciously expected to be at one and the same time a source of support, understanding and mothering and also to be the holder of boundaries, the financial expert and the person who makes and implements tough decisions. Although a woman in a senior position is often admired as the role model who has broken through the glass ceiling, unconsciously she can also be the target of envy for both women and men.

Envy (Klein 1975) is a destructive force attacking what is perceived as good in others. It functions within a dyadic relationship, unlike jealousy which belongs to a three-person dynamic and is based on one person feeling excluded from an intimacy which two others have. Envy is thus the opposite of gratitude, yet related closely to it. Conscious gratitude may mask unconscious envy. Equally envy may be a defence against gratitude. The projections of colleagues, where they contain complicated and shifting combinations of envy, gratitude, the desire to be taken care of and the desire to be given boundaries, meet the conscious and unconscious desires, conflicts and anxieties of the senior manager. Because a woman's psychology is based more on connectedness than separateness, she is more likely than her male counterpart to experience a conflict between the desire for closeness to her colleagues and the knowledge of her inevitable isolation within the role. Weeramanthri (1997: 224) describes this well:

> Women in leadership roles are at a particular disadvantage as there are relatively few role models to draw on. For many women, they will be the first in their families to take up such roles in the outside world. Some may identify with traditional male models of leadership, basing their leadership style on a masculine identification. Other women leaders may simply try to reverse male patterns of leadership by an overemphasis on caring and egalitarianism, by blurring role boundaries and by paying less attention to the task (or to necessary role differentiation in the service of the task).

In environments where work is developing well and there are high levels of creativity and collaborative development, the balance between maternal and parental projections and identifications is easier to manage. In an organization in difficulty, where finances are overstretched or policy and structure are undergoing a period of fundamental change, then the maternal and paternal projections onto managers may be complex and difficult to handle. Particular difficulties can arise in women-only organizations or organizations with a majority of women workers. Without the indication of otherness created by gender difference, feelings, conflicts and anxieties which might have been projected onto men have to be worked out between women. Competitiveness has to be acknowledged as well as support. The balance between connectedness and separateness can be difficult, and quite primitive material from early infantile experience may at times dominate the workplace culture. Other factors of difference such as race, class and sexual orientation may then become more active within the dynamics of the organization.

The safe context of women-only organizations is vital for work of various kinds. The Women's Therapy Centre (1999) in London, for instance, had about 5000 calls in 1999 from women seeking therapy, 80 per cent of whom gave as their reason for contacting the centre that it is women-only. Careful attention needs to be given to the dynamics of women-only organizations or organizations with a feminine culture to preserve this context for the work.

The gender split between supposedly maternal functions of support, caring and nurturing and paternal functions of clarity, logical thinking and the maintenance of law and order cannot be sustained in a women-only organization. Instead these functions have to be acknowledged and shared between the women working in the organization. The process of identifying and apportioning both tasks and approaches, if it goes well, can lead to the breakdown of stereotypes. If the organization cannot bear to see this process through, then a split will develop between women seen to be carrying the maternal function and women seen to be carrying the paternal function.

In this context it is important to consider the role of secretaries and administrative staff. From the late nineteenth century onwards a work role usually adopted by women rather than men (although there is some change in this more recently) has been that of secretary or personal assistant. Much is demanded of the secretary/personal assistant and while she does not wield direct institutional power she often has considerable influence. Expected to be the holder of secrets, confidences and plans for the future she sees and hears things and is required to be discreet about them. Both men and women bosses may, consciously and unconsciously, see their secretaries in a conventional wife's role: the helpmeet, the organizer, the carer, the person who recognizes what is required before it is requested. Stories are commonplace of secretaries expected to buy birthday presents, send flowers, organize family outings, book hair and dental appointments and generally smooth the personal as well as the professional pathway of their manager. Women secretaries may comply with these demands, enjoying the insight it gives them into someone else's life and the apparent intimacy it contributes to the relationship. They may feel this to be a necessary, even indispensable, way to reinforce the influence of their position. Alternatively they may feel angry at being asked to undertake personal tasks beyond their job description and find it difficult to challenge the request because of the power differential.

Enabling others to do their jobs with creativity brings its own job rewards but it may also make the enabler feel deprived or envious. If a secretary who is trying to be a perfect helper gains her own satisfaction through the identification of herself as competent in the support of another, she allows herself and is often allowed by others little space for anger or a sense of her own boundaries. All organizations rely on the effectiveness and flexibility of their administrative structures without always recognizing the energy and reliability which goes into their maintenance.

As more women have moved into positions of power in middle and senior management the traditional relationship between a male manager and a female secretary has widened to include that between a female manager and a female secretary or more rarely, a female manager and a male secretary. Complicated by the push–pull of gender dynamics, which can result in an uneasy closeness between women including both warmth and connectedness and the desire to separate, the relationship between a woman manager and her woman secretary is often multifaceted. At its best it allows the possibility of a more democratic and sharing approach, and a positive identification between women that can work to the advantage of both, but it may also have undertones of merging or of envy.

Janey, Catherine's secretary, was 28 while Catherine was 50. Janey was bright but had left school unsure what she wanted to do; she was creative and painted and played the clarinet well but had not felt confident enough to pursue a professional training in either art or music. She came from a large working-class family where the norm was for people to leave school at 16 and find a job. Catherine came from a similar background and had been the first person in her family to go to university. She had had a variety of jobs at different times, where she tended to work much too hard; as the head of public relations in a large city firm she was clear about her own ability but not always confident that it would be recognized by others. She needed Janey's support on a personal as well as a professional level. Janey admired Catherine's capacity to think fast and respond clearly both verbally and in writing but felt very anxious about Catherine's emotional state. She identified with her and when Catherine was tired, angry or upset, Janey often thought that it was her fault. She tried to deal with this by working harder and harder herself but also felt angry about the extent to which Catherine appeared to lean on her. Negotiating a working relationship was difficult for both women, although they were committed to trying to do this in a way that was both mutually supportive and recognized the difference in their organizational roles.

If splits develop in organizations between women carrying maternal and paternal projections this may be played out through hierarchy as well as personality. Administrative staff might be consciously and unconsciously seen as the people who smooth things out, anticipate others' needs and are unobtrusively ready to fulfil a range of functions, including being supportive personally as well as professionally. If this happens they will fulfil an often unacknowledged role for the institution as good-enough mother.

Conclusion

Throughout a lifetime of work, in and out of the home, women experience a range of roles, responsibilities, rewards and dissatisfactions. These shift throughout their lifetimes and are affected by structural issues of class, race, sexuality and by whether women are mothers or not. How happy and successful women are at work, in both the public and the private domains, is dependent on both external and internal factors. The economics and the dynamics of the workplace are, in general, still more favourable to men than to women and structural power is still, in the main, in men's hands. This is changing.

The experiences women have within the structures and dynamics of the family, particularly as children and adolescents, are internalized and then used to construct the worlds of home and work. The experience of the family, of parental and sibling relationships, is transferred on to the world of work. Desires, tensions, disappointments and strengths arising from the roles of mother, daughter, sister or partner are alive within the workplace. In turn being employed affects a woman's self-image, introducing contradictions and ambivalences which may or may not be easily resolved, and which may reflect back into personal life. These complex and shifting interrelationships, between work and home and external and internal perceptions, particularly characterize women's experience of work from both a sociological and a psychological perspective.

Perhaps the greatest contribution that women make to the changing face of employment is their complex and frequent negotiation between the demands of the home and the demands of work. Passing between these previously separate worlds and effecting change in both in the process, women can demonstrate the necessity of bringing together the public and the private.

References

Ernst, S. and Maguire, M. (eds) (1987) *Living with the Sphinx: Papers from the Women's Therapy Centre*. London: The Women's Press.

Klein, M. (1975) Envy and gratitude, in *Envy and Gratitude and Other Works, 1946–1963*. London: The Hogarth Press and the Institute of Psychoanalysis.

Lown, J. (1990) *Women and Industrialisation: Gender at Work in Nineteenth Century England*. London: Polity Press.

Orbach, S. (1997) Women's development in the family, in M. Lawrence and M. Maguire (eds) *Psychotherapy with Women: Feminist Perspectives*. London: Macmillan.

Rowbotham, S. (1983) *Dreams and Dilemmas*. London: Virago.

Sayers, J. (1986) *Sexual Contradictions: Psychology, Psychoanalysis and Feminism*. London: Tavistock Publications.

Segal, J. (1985) *Phantasy in Everyday Life: A Psychoanalytical Approach to Understanding Ourselves*. Harmondsworth: Penguin.

Seu, I.B. and Heenan, C.M. (1998) *Feminism and Psychotherapy*. London: Sage.

Travis, A. (2000) How gap between rich and poor has grown, *Guardian*, 11 May.

Weeramanthri, T. (1997) Managing anxiety and the practitioner's role, in M. Lawrence and M. Maguire (eds) *Psychotherapy with Women: Feminist Perspectives.* London: Macmillan.

Winnicott, D.W. (1965) *The Maturational Processes and the Facilitating Environment: Studies in the Theory of Emotional Development.* London: The Hogarth Press and the Institute of Psycho-Analysis.

Winnicott, D.W. (1971) *Playing and Reality.* Harmondsworth: Tavistock Publications.

Women's Therapy Centre (1999) *Annual Statistics.* London: Women's Therapy Centre.

6 Women and intimacy

Marie Maguire

Some women clients talk obsessively about their failure to find the ideal partner. Yet if, after listening for a long time I ask a prosaic question such as 'What kind of partner do you want? What do you imagine yourself doing with them?' they reply surprisingly often, 'Good question. I don't really know'. They have not thought much about what it might be like to have a partner around on an everyday basis. They wish simply to be swept off their feet by a Mr or Ms Right. These clients are expressing a deeper need – for a feeling of perfect harmonious fusion with a maternal figure whose life revolves only around them. Heterosexual women often say 'There are no men around – or at least no suitable men'. What they mean is 'There are no men in my internal world, or if there are I am quite uninterested in them. I am so overwhelmed by what went wrong with my mother that, despite my conscious obsession with men, I really want a feeling of complete unity with her.'

Similarly a lesbian client told me 'My friends say, "Why can't you find a nice woman partner?" But I simply never meet anyone'. She actually meant, 'Only women who are like my mother really attract me. I don't notice the available ones, only those who are tantalizingly unsure of their sexual orientation'. Obsessed with trying to rescue her mother from an unsatisfying marriage, she constantly found herself in triangular situations. With her female lovers she played the role of her father who had waited around for her glamorous mother to notice him. Unconsciously though, these withholding partners were less threatening to my client than those who offered her constant attention. In psychotherapy she revealed an overwhelming fear that if she really allowed herself to depend on me or any other woman she would lose her sense of identity as she felt she had with her mother. Another client I discuss later in the chapter initially avoided all discussion of intimacy through talking about her confusion about her sexual orientation. She needed to work through her wish to remain forever enmeshed in an eroticized attachment to a mother-figure. While in fantasy she imagined herself cocooned in a loving maternal embrace she did not have to face her terror of an abusive male sexuality. This fear stood in the way of her heterosexual wishes.

Such problems in forming or sustaining intimate relationships may reflect experiences of emotional rejection, separation or abuse in early childhood. The infant needs to feel secure in an emotionally containing 'maternal' relationship where she can gradually come to tolerate, think about and understand her own powerful feelings and fantasies. As the little girl becomes increasingly aware of Oedipal difference – between the sexes and the generations – she struggles to separate herself psychologically from her mother. At this point she needs help with her own anxieties about her own envy and destructiveness towards those she loves. As I show later, there is a particular danger at this stage that the girl who is not helped to form her own autonomous identity may defend against envy and rivalry towards her mother by idealizing her father and masculinity. Other women – regardless of sexual orientation – state their preference for their mothers, projecting a caricatured version of their own 'masculine' aggression onto their fathers and men. One lesbian client had to re-own these aspects of herself before she could form a new partnership with a woman where each could recognize the other as different, equally capable of moving freely between a range of cross-gender identifications.

The difficulties many women have in experiencing themselves as individual beings with their own needs and desires are compounded if the girl cannot identify with so-called 'masculine' qualities. She may then seek out an extreme form of masculinity in others – for instance an emotional independence akin to ruthlessness – in her male or female lovers. If there is no actual father in the family, what is crucial is the mother's internal relationship to her own father and the male aspects of her psyche.

What do I mean when I speak of masculinity and femininity, mothering and fathering? The roots of gender expectations lie in our ideas about the psychological division in parenting. What is seen as masculine and feminine varies between cultures and historical epochs, but it is still true that masculinity tends to be associated with activity in our society and femininity with passivity, as Freud argued. Power relations between the sexes are in flux, but women's major sphere of influence is still over the mind of the human infant. Men may be losing their pre-eminent position but they continue to control most major cultural institutions – political, economic, legal and medical. In our society the mother is expected to look after the baby's physical needs and help her to contain and think about feelings. Fathering is associated with boundary-setting and offering the child a pathway out of the symbiotic preoccupations of infancy into the wider world. The daughter – as I show later – needs to identify with the agency and potency associated culturally with men if she is to be able to acknowledge her own needs and desires. I assume that the capacity for mothering and fathering exists in all of us. Indeed fathers are sometimes more conventionally maternal, whereas mothers may be more confident at fathering.

Currently we need theories that contribute to a more active view of female identity, one where women can sustain intimate attachments while remaining agents of their own destinies. Traditional psychoanalytic and feminist critiques often focus mainly on the girl's relationship with one or other parent giving an unbalanced view of the female psyche. In this chapter I outline some quite polarized psychoanalytic perspectives, showing that no one theory offers a complete understanding of sexual identity. I am especially interested in those theorists who integrate the role of maternal and paternal power in the mind of the girl. I argue that we need to link object relations insights about mother–daughter identification with a feminist Freudian Oedipal perspective if we are to understand women's conflicts about intimacy and independence. Drawing on the work of Luce Irigaray, Janine Chasseguet-Smirgel and Jessica Benjamin, who each seek to integrate mother and father-centred theories, I explore the way culture structures sexual inequality into the psyche at the crucial point where the daughter struggles to form an autonomous identity.

Penis or womb-envy? opposing theories of female identity

In the twentieth century two periods of psychoanalytic controversy about female identity coincided with rapid shifts in women's social position. Between 1919 and 1935 Freud's theory of female penis envy provoked a vigorous debate amongst psychoanalysts about the nature and origins of all identity. In the 1960s psychoanalytic clinicians, influenced by an embryonic new feminist movement, returned again to those questions. What is sexual identity? they wondered. Are we born with a certain kind of male or female identity, with tendencies towards heterosexuality or homosexuality, or with a desire to produce children? Opposing factions from the first debate coalesced into theoretical tendencies which continue to dominate psychoanalytic thinking about sexual identity. I structure my survey around the 1919–35 debate, beginning with the polarized views of Freud and his major opponent, Karen Horney, on gender power relations.

Freud's theory revolves around the child's relationship to the father and the girl's struggle to come to terms with patriarchal authority and privilege, a process in which the mother becomes almost a bystander. Karen Horney accused Freud of 'male bias', of creating a theory that devalued women. Horney's view was that each sex has something uniquely valuable which arouses fierce envy in the opposite sex (Horney 1924, 1984). This argument won influential support from colleagues who later transformed the role of the mother in psychoanalytic theory. For British object relations theorists and North American ego psychologists, women – far from being deficient – have enormous emotional power based on their reproductive capacities and the utter dependence of the newborn infant. From this perspective women's influence over the psychic lives of infants is far more significant than men's political and economic power. At issue here are different notions of power and control and arguments about which parent is viewed by the child as most potent and enviable. Mother-centred theorists such as Klein and Winnicott emphasize that ambivalence towards maternal power underpins female envy of male privilege as well as men's repudiation of femininity. Most crucially for my discussion, early psychoanalytic interest in the erotic life of women has faded and been replaced by a preoccupation with their maternal function. In much contemporary clinical discussion the mother may well dominate her children in indirectly sexualized ways, but is not the subject of her own desire. Ironically, given women's increased sexual independence, there has been a long period where we have heard little about their actual sexual relationships with men or other women.

Can female sexuality change?

Feminists have remained divided as to whose views on sexual identity were the more radical – Freud's or Horney's. They disagreed fundamentally about whether women were born heterosexual, with a desire for motherhood, or whether femininity was created through culture. For Freud the girl only begins to desire men sexually and to want their babies once she realizes she can never be male. In contrast Horney argued that women are born with tendencies towards heterosexual femininity. By emphasizing innate womanliness in this way Horney intended to defend women against the Freudian charge that we are all men manqué. Present-day feminists, however, have pointed out that she threw the baby out with the bathwater, abandoning one of Freud's most subversive insights, his theory that sexual identity is formed through personal history and culture, rather than biology (Mitchell 1974).

We all know consciously that the world around us is altering, but psychoanalysts have always had very different views about whether cultural change impinges on the depths of the psyche immediately, after a time-lag, or not at all. My personal view is that we are formed primarily through culture but that anatomical differences between the sexes do impact upon the psyche, affecting our unconscious fantasies and anxieties. Because male and female bodies are constructed differently and we have different sexual and reproductive capacities, our experience of sex, reproduction and the physiological lifecycle will inevitably be different. However I do not think that we are born with tendencies towards heterosexual femininity or masculinity. Neither do I believe that there is a core of 'real' personality that transcends culture. I am saying then that sexuality is shaped within culture but mediated through the body. Desire cannot exist outside prevailing social structures, but neither can psyche and soma ever be seen as distinct from each other. Language-patterns, belief-systems, cultural symbols and values will fundamentally determine how we interpret physiological sensation in any given society.

Freud, Lacan and female identity

In spite of his provocative tone Freud was preoccupied with questions that are still relevant for women. For instance he noted that girls of 3 seemed more intelligent and lively than boys of that age. He asked how those confident little girls came to lose their intellectual curiosity and assertiveness (Freud 1933). Freud did not know whether it was through nature or nurture, but he was sure that it was at the point where the little girl becomes interested in the father and men that she becomes more passive. His explanation was that the girl – unlike the boy – has the painful task of giving up her primary love-object and renouncing her active (masculine) love for her mother for a more submissive conventionally 'feminine' attachment to her father and men. As she becomes more passive the girl often loses much of her own sexual desire. From these painful renunciations 'difficulties and possible inhibitions result which do not apply to men' (Freud 1931). The girl simultaneously has to come to terms with belonging to the less valued sex – a fate she may never fully accept. She may well turn her 'masculine' aggressive urges inwards, becoming self-sacrificial, prone to tolerating unhappy situations. Feeling a sense of internal lack, women look for a sense of value through being desired by others – especially men.

Not surprisingly, Freud thought that many girls never do become fully heterosexual, even if they think they are. They might identify with their fathers, wanting to be seen as 'one of the boys' whether they desire men or women. Or they may retain their primary attachment to the mother, becoming lesbian or establishing only a very unstable veneer of hetero-sexuality. 'Some part of what we call "the enigma of women" may perhaps stem from this experience of bisexuality in women's lives', Freud observed (1931: 385). Such women, according to Freud, might marry and quickly lose interest in their husbands, transferring their love entirely to a baby.

Lacan: a return to the father

Some feminists have turned to Lacan's theories, arguing that we need to look again at Freud's father-centred theory to understand how gender inequalities continue to reproduce themselves in our minds however family life is structured (Mitchell 1984). Attempting to reinstate the father at the heart of psychoanalytic theory Lacan was deeply critical of the contemporary preoccupation with the mother–infant relationship.

He disagreed particularly with object-relations theorists and ego psycho-gists who chart an ideal line of development from infantile satisfaction at the breast through to adult heterosexual fulfilment. Describing some relationships or states of mind as 'mature' or 'healthy' romanticized conventional ways of structuring sexual and family life, Lacan argued. Instead he stressed that adult sexual relations are inevitably unsatisfying because the loved one is always a substitute for the primal maternal lost object. Desire comes into existence through experiences of absence or lack (of the breast or the mother initially), not as the result of satisfaction. There is then something intrinsically painful and insatiable about desire itself. Any later experience of satisfaction always contains that first loss within it. As Freud said, 'We must reckon with the possibility that some-thing in the nature of the sexual instinct itself is unfavourable to the realisation of complete desire' (Freud quoted in Mitchell 1984: 255).

While rejecting the idea of the 'natural' or pre-given, Lacan seems to echo Freud's uncertainty about whether women really are in some way inferior. Certain feminists argue that neither Lacan nor Freud were sup-porting patriarchy. They were simply describing what they saw around them: a world where women were second-class, their social position unenviable (Mitchell 1984). To arrive at this conclusion, however, Freud and Lacan must be read in a very selective way. Both are fundamentally phallocentric, focusing primarily on male subjectivity.

Nevertheless Freud's emphasis on the tenuous nature of all sexual orientation is useful in understanding those women who, while appearing utterly obsessed with men, are unconsciously preoccupied with creating a more perfect version of the mother–infant dyad. The link he draws between women's tendency to tolerate unhappiness and the cultural stereotype of heterosexual womanhood is still of crucial significance for contemporary psychotherapy. Similarly Lacan's critique of psychoanalytic idealization of conventional ways of structuring sexual and family life is enormously helpful in a climate where women appear to have many choices but are still under enormous pressure to conform to prevailing norms of femininity. The relevance of these father-centred theories will be obvious to the client I describe next.

I can't choose a partner because I don't know whether I want a man or a woman

Some clients resist intimacy through dilemmas about which sex they desire. One woman told me 'I spent my 20s saying I couldn't settle down with a man because I might be lesbian. Now in my 40s I'm saying I can't get involved because I might want a man.'

What lies behind this kind of chronic indecision about sexual orientation? Annika came into psychotherapy unable to decide whether she was lesbian or heterosexual. She came from a very conservative small-town Scandinavian family, where the women had always married young and devoted themselves to their husbands and children. Her bohemian parents had deviated from this pattern during her teens. Annika had witnessed violent rows and torrid reconciliations but now the family view was that her parents had weathered these storms, while retaining their sexual passion for each other. Following in her mother's footsteps Annika had married her first boyfriend at 19 but found his constant sexual demands and angry moods unbearable. After a year she left him, came to London and began a highly successful career. When she entered psychotherapy at 26 she had had no other sexual experiences with men, and wondered whether she was a lesbian. Hers was a long and complex psychotherapy, structured like a Chinese box, with one secret hiding another.

One day she told me this dream:

> I come to your house for a session with three of my friends, Susan, Linda and Jenny. You are very polite but they are not – Susan goes and has a bath, Linda is rude and cheeky and Jenny falls asleep. I'm split between you and them – it is a disastrous session. Then a man starts banging on your front door. You let him in. He's foreign, out of control, shouting, unshaven, coat flying everywhere. I immediately dislike him. You try to calm him down – he is your husband. By the time you've shut him in a room my time is up. My friends all write out cheques whilst implying they won't come again. I feel I must make up for their rudeness, whilst I feel not part of it, and know that I will come again.

Annika immediately said that the friends must represent parts of her. 'They behave as I would like to. But I've always felt I must be compliant, grown up, good at talking.'

I said, 'What you really want is to be a messy child with me as you could not with your mother, to wander around my house, get inside my mind and body.'

She said, 'I suppose so.' She did not, she admitted, want to keep on talking politely. Her dream reflected a fantasy that I might tolerate her bathing and messing about and devote myself to meeting her primitive bodily needs. She was, she said, angry at the idea that she should spend her sessions with me talking about men as she had initially felt she should. The man banging on the front door represented a sexual man who she feared might take me over and have a noisy abusive sexual relationship that would exclude her. Indeed she had felt that her father and brothers prevented her from getting the feeling of intense closeness, of bodily unity she needed from her mother in childhood.

When she first came into therapy she saw herself as the only member of the family who could not create a lasting sexually harmonious partnership. After a visit home Annika realized that she found her parents' insistence on sexual openness oppressive and intimidating. This was very difficult for her to think about and she needed my support in contemplating the idea of her parents' relationship as less than ideal. Eventually she decided that aspects of her parents' behaviour might well have contributed to her fear of male coercion. Her dread was that heterosexual relationships could only be maintained if the woman submitted to constant sexual demands.

After a holiday break Annika told me, 'I had a dream about coming back here – I was living in an attic flat, and there were two women there, a mother and daughter. They seemed part of each other, as if their bodies were not separate. They both had the same Christian name, and only the mother had a surname. I realized who she was – that famous actress who has written about how disastrous her marriage was, even though they had often been described as an idyllically happy couple.' The daughter also reminded her of a childhood friend who was now seen as the vulnerable problematic child by her parents, but who was 'worth more than the rest of the family put together'. Annika knew that I wrote books about sexuality and identity. She wondered whether she was yet again getting entangled with a mother-figure who pretended to be wise in the ways of the heart, but was actually hiding a deep unhappiness. Could I help her to find her own path to sexual intimacy or would I draw her into an eroticized state of collusion?

While some members of her family covered up their emotional inadequacies, Annika hid her strengths and capacity for change like the daughter in the dream. Early on in therapy she behaved as if she found anything I said about her transference relationship with me particularly uninteresting. This proved to be a smoke-screen. For instance, early in her psychotherapy she talked a great deal about a woman friend with whom she had secretly fallen in love. Her sessions were dominated by questions such as, what does she feel? Will I lose her friendship if I declare my desire for her?

I listened for a while and then said, 'Perhaps your feelings for Lucy have grown in intensity because of feelings that you can't express towards me. You wonder whether there is an eroticized element to your relationship with your mother. Perhaps you might have some sexual feelings towards me but be afraid of expressing them in case you lose the therapeutic relationship with me.'

'Maybe', Annika said. When I made a similar interpretation in the next session, she said 'I don't know'.

Her responses continued to be low-key and non-committal. I found it increasingly difficult to persist in this vein, even though I suspected I was right, so undermined was I by her unresponsiveness. Eventually Annika announced that she wanted to marry again and have children, while also maintaining her successful career. When she did begin a sexual relationship with a man, she returned to the subject of Lucy, telling me of her friend's obvious jealousy and pain. 'I did have a crush on Lucy' she said, 'But of course the feelings became more intense because I couldn't tell you how passionately I felt about you.'

I was astonished and could not help showing it. 'So you knew that Lucy reciprocated your feelings,' I said.

Annika admitted that she had. She went on to tell me that she had also secretly agreed that I, like her mother, aroused a kind of eroticized love in her. Annika now said, 'Of course I knew you were right. I just couldn't tell you so.'

With her new boyfriend Annika saw herself as being like her father – simultaneously withdrawn and aggressive. She dreamed of a box of toys under the therapeutic couch, including a rabbit she had lost in childhood that she had endowed with her 'feminine' characteristics. In the dream I pronounced the session over but she felt she could not leave the room until she had re-owned her lost 'feminine' side – sweet and gentle. Her boyfriend had nightmares of her as a 'chaotic dangerously violent sexual being'. Annika said 'I am very cruel to any man I get involved with. I make them cry.' She now realized that she had witnessed her parents being very cruel to each other.

'So your cruelty is an identification with both of them. But interestingly you do not bring that part of yourself here,' I said. We had been talking about how demure and timid she so often appeared in the sessions.

Annika agreed and went on to say, 'People at work know I can be tough and frightening. And here I often feel it is you who are cruel.

I wonder sometimes if you are really interested in me. That was how it was in childhood. My father seemed detached and my mother was preoccupied with her own problems.'

In therapy she needed to relocate her lost 'feminine' vulnerability if she was to temper the 'masculine' harshness that was driving her lover to tears. Ultimately, however, she decided that they were not compatible, since he, like her mother, made constant demands for emotional support. She could not help behaving like her rejecting father when she was with him. Nevertheless the relationship had confirmed her heterosexuality and given her a new confidence in her desirability and sexual responsiveness.

As more family secrets emerged, Annika discovered that many of her female relatives had been depressed. She said, 'It's not surprising. The men are emotionally protected and then there's the idea that they're stronger. They don't have to sort out family problems. I'm expected to listen to everything but not get upset. Then I'm seen as the sensitive one.'

Later Annika began to explore how her identification with her father had helped her professionally. She always had difficulty feeling herself to be like her glamorous mother since she felt asexual and boyish. Now for the first time Annika admitted that she knew she had her own kind of beauty. In the family it was said that Annika's father loved little girls, but found adult women difficult. He adored her until puberty, when the relationship became distant. Annika described her painful early teens, where she inflicted injuries on herself, hoping vainly that her parents would notice her anxiety lest her father injure her mother or leave the family. Given the tenuous nature of the marriage and her mother's personal fragility sexual rivalry had never seemed safe. Annika worried about how she would manage a career when her mother had never been able to work outside the home. She decided quite consciously that she would have to model herself on her father, who was a successful businessman. But the problem with that, she realized even then, was that her father constantly made derogatory remarks about women, saying, for instance, that they were all hysterical. Could she take her father as a model when he held her sex in such contempt? In the next section I relate some feminist psychoanalytic theories about mothering to Annika's difficulties. I return later to the difficulty many girls have in identifying with their fathers in a culture where women are routinely denigrated.

Women's lack: a feminist perspective on mothers and daughters

What does Woman want? Freud demanded in 1933. At this point Freud located the origins of women's narcissistic wounds in an ambivalent early relationship with a mother who could not adore her daughter as she did her son since the girl could not provide her with masculinity by proxy. He argued that this failure to arouse idealized desire in the mother later becomes organized into penis envy, a narcissistic wound which leads women to become highly dependent on the love and esteem of others. Women love in order to be loved, to compensate for their own feelings of inferiority, according to Freud, in contrast to men who love in order to satisfy their instinctual needs (Freud 1914).

A half century later Eichenbaum and Orbach (1982) strongly refuted this theory, arguing instead that a girl's sense of inadequacy originated in the mother and daughter's shared identification as second-class citizens. They offer a clinical scenario that resonates absolutely with Annika's experience of hiding her messy emotional needs beneath a façade of daughterly compliance. Eichenbaum and Orbach's little girl strives from infancy to nurture her emotionally deprived mother (with whom she identifies). With the hope of gaining love vicariously she becomes a compulsive carer. As Annika describes, however, these skills of feminine caring are devalued in a society that prizes 'male' characteristics, such as emotional detachment and rationality, more than 'feminine' attributes such as empathy and intuition (Eichenbaum and Orbach 1982).

Contemporary feminists remain utterly divided about the nature of female identity and the means whereby women can effect change. Eichenbaum and Orbach's theory originated in a period of optimism after the cultural flux of the 1960s, when it was believed that female and male identity might change over several generations if family life were reorganized. They stress the necessity for fathers to share childcare equally, so breaking the cycle of emotional deprivation between mother and daughter. This theoretical approach assumes a fluid interchange between the psyche and the external world, a certainty that as culture changed, so would internal reality. Identification is complex and contradictory, however. A daughter may simultaneously resist and absorb the awareness that she is female, knowing she is a woman yet feeling that she is in some way masculine psychologically – and mothers may identify strongly with a son rather than a daughter.

It is also obvious from Annika's account of her teenage identification with her father that the child does not simply remain passive while outside forces stamp themselves on its personality. Identification – through which one person assimilates attributes of another and is transformed partially or entirely after the model the other provides – is a process in which the child engages actively, although unconsciously. She takes inside herself – introjects – bits and pieces of experience infused with fantasy. The child's view of the world around her is also structured through what she projects onto it from inside herself. Identifications are formed through a subtle and intricate process of layering and fusion of memory, fantasy and desire. Fragments of language and image are constantly worked over, influenced always by fantasy.

It seems clear to me that expectations and wishes that are transmitted from generation to generation cohere around bodily experience. How are we to understand the way emotional and sexual experience is mediated through the body without arguing for inborn tendencies towards certain kinds of femininity? Indeed some orthodox object mother-centred theories have been used to pathologize those women who choose not to live in conventional ways. It is widely recognized that girls often have profound difficulty in separating psychically from their mothers, who have the same body and gender. This was illustrated graphically in Annika's dream of sharing her mother's body. The girl's psychic separation is a lifelong process, played out through her body, and expressed through crises at each physiological phase of the lifecycle. While the boy can use gender difference to cut off consciously from his early emotional experience, girls often remain constantly preoccupied with difficult feelings about their mothers.

This process is reinforced in adolescence. Janet Sayers (1998) discusses the way teenage boys can consciously detach themselves from conflictual childhood feelings, fantasizing instead about marvellous things they may accomplish. Girls, in contrast, remain more in touch with highly ambivalent loving and hating feelings about close figures. After the age of 11 girls become more prone to depression – as Annika did – whereas boys are if anything more depressed before that age. Teenage girls tend to idealize boys, while boys idealize themselves. This means that girls typically see no other means of escape than fantasies of being rescued by heroic figures, usually male. Sayers links increased depression amongst female adolescents to the massive changes in their bodies, combined with the fear and contempt that exists towards women's physicality. Girls, like Annika who mutilated herself, use their bodies to re-enact their conflictual feelings towards their mothers and their selves. Sayers argues that a close confiding relationship with an emotionally supportive mother is an antidote to this teenage desolation.

Many feminists argue that the only way to break into the cycle of suffocating merger between mother and daughter is for the father to intervene in childcare from the beginning. In contrast Luce Irigaray, a French feminist psychoanalyst, believes that women themselves must alter their position in society by creating new ways of speaking about and for their sex. This may mean existing separately from men for a time.

Irigaray (1984) claims that Freudian and Lacanian psychoanalysis recognizes only masculine desire and sees all desire as masculine. Psychoanalysis reproduces one of the 'sexual theories of children', Irigaray argues: the phantasy that there is only one (male) sex, and that women are castrated, defective versions of men. Irigaray argues that the first problem for women is that the relationship to the mother and the mother's body is not symbolized often or adequately enough in our culture. At the moment women exist in a state of 'dereliction', outside society and the symbolic order, as if abandoned by God. Deprived of their own symbols, gestures, imaginary, denied access to their own auto-erotism, the mother–daughter relationship is the 'dark continent of the dark continent, the most obscure area of our social order'. Without that 'interval of exchange, or of words, or gestures, passions between women manifest themselves in a rather cruel way' (Irigaray 1984: 103, quoted in Whitford 1989). Both mothers and daughters must create a new language in which their identities as women can be articulated. At the moment the daughter has no woman with whom to identify.

Irigaray points out that Freud and Lacan constructed their theories around the boy's experience of his body while denouncing as biologist anyone who attempted to do the same for the girl. She explores the female body made meaningful in language, articulating the ways in which it is used as a site both for patriarchal power relations and for symbolic representational resistance.

Obviously Irigaray is right in arguing that our culture represents all agency and power in phallic terms and there is no equivalent symbol to suggest female desire or potency. Does the hidden nature of women's sexual and reproductive organs reinforce this cultural inequality? Psychoanalysts have often suggested that men may find it easier to mobilize intense feelings, including aggression and desire, because they can symbolize these powerful emotions through the more visible penis, which they can imbue in fantasy with magical powers for destruction or reparation (Freud 1924; Klein 1975). It may be easier to control anxiety through a symbolic and physical focus of sensation. Women often experience intense sexual excitement as dangerous, frightening and destructive, perhaps because they cannot so easily link it to any external organ that would localize it in space and allow them to visualize control of its duration. This lack of anatomical anchoring could have a correlative effect at the symbolic level (Noel Montgrain, quoted in Benjamin 1988). The difficulty for women is in recognizing our desire as truly inner. Spatial images can be used to convey images of female desire, as opposed to phallic activity. We need metaphors for describing inner space, which emphasize holding and self-exploration as the active side of receptivity. Women need to recognize the sensual capacities of their whole bodies, the totality of space between and within our bodies as the site of pleasure.

As I have shown, theory is still polarized between mother and father-centred perspectives. Each theoretical tendency has strengths, while neglecting crucial aspects of female psychic life. Lacanian feminism provides a powerful challenge to conventional ideas about identity, power and language, and a counter-balance to the idealism and romanticism of object relations theory. Study of the role of the (symbolic) father is also vital for understanding how patriarchal structures reproduce themselves even when parents make a conscious effort to avoid reinforcing them. Like Freud's theory, however, it is constructed from the perspective of the male, and women tend to be ignored or denigrated. As in Freud's theory it is the mother who is associated with boundless narcissism and regression to archaic early experiences. The possibility of early paternal receptivity or the father 'holding' the baby emotionally is ignored in these theories. Neither is it considered that the mother – or the child itself – may have urges towards moving out into the world, although many mothers are heavily committed to employment outside the home as well as to childcare.

In contrast object relations and post-Lacanian feminists struggle to articulate women's previously hidden experience as mothers, daughters and autonomous sexual subjects. It is obviously true that the girl has particular difficulty in separating herself psychically from the much-envied early mother, who is initially experienced as omnipotent. This is exacerbated by the problems many girls have in identifying with the father and qualities seen as 'masculine'.

What kind of lesbian? what kind of intimacy?

How far can psychotherapy help us to change such psychic patterns given that gender power inequalities have permeated sexual and emotional life for so long? These questions are all the more acute for contemporary women who often feel intense conflict between what they want for themselves and conventional images of femininity. This was particularly the case with one lesbian client who felt she had to chart an entirely new path for herself since she did not fit in with any group she knew. She had a complex racial history, lesbian sexuality was invisible in her culture, and she increasingly felt herself to be unusually single-minded about her career as compared to her female colleagues and friends. When, after an apparently fruitful beginning, her psychotherapy reached an impasse, we had to unravel an intricate knot of cultural and psychic complications.

This client, who I will call June, sought psychotherapy at 26 because she could not settle down professionally or emotionally. A series of unhappy love affairs had undermined her capacity to use her considerable talents. Her lovers were usually married and bore a striking resemblance to her tantalizingly inconsistent mother. At first she saw me as being very much in the same mould – the desirable, unattainable older woman who followed my own rigid professional rules, to the detriment of her emotional needs. Initially I was struck by June's scorn for men. She had no social contact with heterosexual men and would even avoid conversation with her male colleagues if at all possible. When she did begin to discuss the taboo area of heterosexuality we uncovered a previously buried but very positive relationship with her father. In the transference she began to see me as being suddenly like him – interested in her life, appreciative of her wit, intelligence and good looks.

It became clear that one reason for her avoidance of men was that she did not want to think about their obvious attraction to her or to consider the possibility that she might reciprocate in any way. As she came to trust and to internalize me as a more consistent maternal figure, we explored all aspects of her sexuality, including her eroticized transference to me, her feelings about men, and her fantasies about her parents' relationship. Through this process June became even more certain of her attraction towards women, but her interest in unavailable older women declined. In fact, after a period of deep depression she was slowly developing a more equal relationship with a woman of her own age. Another major change was that she now enjoyed supportive friendships with male colleagues. In fact her professional life was now utterly transformed and she was rapidly moving up the hierarchy in her organization. So when June told me that her increased work schedule made three weekly sessions impossible, and she would like to cut down with a view to leaving at the end of the year, I was not surprised. However the months passed and June said little more about leaving, even though I would sometimes acknowledge our previous discussion.

Now June was less preoccupied with rescuing her mother she was able to think more freely about what kind of woman she was and who she wanted to be close to. She talked again about her dislocated childhood, which had been punctuated by long family visits around the world and relatives who became close and then disappeared. For instance in her first year of life she had been looked after intensively by an aunt who had then moved to another continent. During the early years of therapy she had recurring dreams of searching for an address or a person through alien foreign cities.

Soon after she mentioned leaving psychotherapy June told me 'I had an utterly different dream last night. Unlike my other dreams I wasn't searching for something or someone. I was in a room, neither modern nor traditional and it was the right room. I was by myself.' I linked the room to my consulting room, which has a mixture of modern and traditional features, but she was non-committal about this, stressing that she was by herself. She seemed to be trying out the idea of living alone and leaving therapy.

She went on in the session to express her disappointment with the group of lesbians who had once been her closest friends. 'They're all talking about nappies or playing golf.' She had always known she did not want children, partly because she wanted a woman all to herself. And parenting, always a difficult venture, was, she said even harder for lesbians who often lacked the support and social approbation that heterosexual families took for granted. Nowadays she had to continually resist her friends' and colleagues' attempts to attach her to their families as an honorary aunt. She could now recognize the strength of her own ambition, knew she was fascinated by her work and did not want lovers or family members to distract her from her career. June had once relied on gay men as a source of support, but in this session she described her increasing disenchantment with the lifestyle of a homosexual couple she had known since college days. 'I said to them, "I don't want to talk about pornography, not while I'm eating my dinner." They said, "Oh June, you're so buttoned up." I don't know why they want to use pornography. Why, when they've got each other?'

I said 'You are alone in the dream, but you don't want to be isolated. You wonder who you can find things in common with. You wonder, does a shared sexual orientation or history give you a sense of belonging with these people even if you don't share their values?'

June reflected a bit more on this and then told me about her boss who wasn't looking after her interests. They had a meeting to talk over departmental problems but since then nothing had changed. Someone junior had appropriated her desk and her boss had not supported her when she ousted the newcomer.

I suggested that she might have similar feelings about me – that I was not helping her to resolve some fundamental problem about intimacy and belonging. June insisted that if this was so she was quite unaware of it. At the time I accepted that, but I felt rather uneasy about this session and later events offered a basis for my unease. I felt that she was telling me through the dream that I had helped her to feel freer. She was no longer desperately seeking mother-figures and wanted to choose whether and who to engage with. I also sensed that she was annoyed or disappointed with me though. Had I, like her boss, failed to hear what was wrong? Certainly I had not understood how profoundly ambivalent she was about leaving psychotherapy.

A few weeks later June told me that she'd bought a very expensive new car. I was surprised she hadn't told me before. It seemed to represent some new 'masculine' self-sufficiency. 'I love driving my new car. It's like being in an aeroplane. Everyone gets out of the way.' Karen, her new lover, had laughed, saying how butch the car was. June had made things up with her male boss who had teased her about buying the car to attract women. 'You don't understand. It's a substitute', she told him. I wondered what the car was a substitute for. June said, 'For a woman.' I thought this rather odd, since she apparently felt so optimistic about her new sexual relationship. In retrospect I think she might have been lining up the car as a substitute for me. It was a cocoon-like space, where she was sealed off, high above other people who got out of her way so that she did not have all the difficulties of negotiating with them. I also thought at the time that perhaps June was afraid of arousing my (maternal) envy. The car, as she suggested, was definitely a luxury item and marked her out as a successful woman who had a purchasing power more often associated with men.

In this session June commented that her boss alone had the 'feminine intuition' to notice her growing attachment to Karen, who he thought very attractive. 'But Karen is not a girlie. My friends are going to be shocked when they meet her. She's not my usual type, not femme and into opera. And she wears trouser suits.'

I said, 'Your previous lovers expected you to be more masculine than you felt comfortable with, to take the lead when you didn't necessarily want to. Now you feel more genuinely powerful and assertive, but you don't think Karen will expect you to wear the trousers.'

June said, 'I used to associate assertiveness with men, but now I think I can be a strong woman. You talked about having something in common with people. I've been thinking. Karen knows she's a lesbian – unlike my past lovers. And she's also passionate about work. And she quite likes living alone.'

Around this time June's state of mind deteriorated dramatically. She rapidly became so depressed that for a while she could not leave the house. She found it all but impossible to maintain her professional commitments or to come to psychotherapy. There followed a long period where all the changes June had made in therapy seemed to evaporate.

What had led to June's regression? Here I can only make a few comments relevant to the themes of this chapter. Previously June had taken up a rather masculine role in relation to a series of maternal figures (including myself) and this had enabled her to hide her own conflicts about what she might really have to offer another woman sexually and emotionally. Her new partner had a more equal balance of 'masculine' and 'feminine' identifications. This new relationship, combined with her decision to cut down and eventually leave therapy, had triggered a re-emergence of the desolation and emptiness she had felt in her infancy. It was difficult to know what her babyhood had been like, though her mother was obviously well-meaning but distracted, and her devoted aunt had left suddenly.

Part of her wanted to stay in psychotherapy for a long time, perhaps forever. Because I had not recognized the intensity of her need, June felt pushed out, an abandoned and enraged baby. There was also a part of her that could not allow recognition of the work she still needed to do psychically, however. Most significantly June did not feel able at this point to face the rigours of intimacy and separation. At work, in therapy and in every significant relationship June felt that the ground-rules were already set, and that they enraged her, as she had felt infuriated by her mother's unwillingness to structure life at home around her needs. She was asking whether it was possible for her to assert her needs and be close to me or anyone else. Was her identity strong enough to have a struggle with me and maintain the relationship? Or could she only assert her independence by leaving suddenly?

Earlier on in psychotherapy June had drawn on the strengths of her identification with a father who had been very successful professionally in his early life. She had also identified with his vulnerabilities, however, including his tendency to depression and self-sabotage. During her teens her father had become bitter and isolated because of an inability to assert his personal and professional needs at home or at work. Perhaps she felt guilty about succeeding more fully than he had in a traditionally male sphere? June also agreed with me that her mother might have been ambivalent about her daughter's greater opportunities for professional fulfilment, simultaneously encouraging and enviously undermining. She might also have felt that I would be envious if she really allowed herself the kind of life she wanted. Certainly it cannot be a coincidence that June collapsed into depression at the point where both personal and professional fulfilment seemed within her grasp.

In the following section I discuss some psychoanalytic and feminist theories about the vicissitudes of the girl's struggle for psychic autonomy and identification with the (real or symbolic) father in a culture where women and femininity are still regarded with profound ambivalence. At this Oedipal phase, envy, guilt and rivalry play a key role.

Why do women tolerate sexual unhappiness?

Gender power inequalities are woven into our fundamental passions and desires at the point where we struggle to understand the difference between the sexes and the generations. The narcissistic wish to avoid confronting our ultimate helplessness in the face of psychic pain, loss and death exists unconsciously in all of us. The most important aspects of existence elude our control. Recognizing that both sexes are anatomically different yet equal would mean facing up to the fact that our mothers and all later love-objects are separate individuals beyond our control. As a defence against this girls are still brought up to maintain an illusion of ecstatic fusion with others – the traditional stereotype of femininity – while boys are encouraged to cut off from their own 'feminine' dependency needs and project them onto women.

During the 1970s American feminist Dorothy Dinnerstein (1978) described how both sexes tacitly collude in a gender-based division of power and labour, once a social necessity, but now a threat to the race, since biotechnology has become dangerously out of control. At the basis of this collusion is an unwillingness to face the original loss of the illusion of blissful unity with the mother, which would also mean confronting the inevitability of human frailty, psychic pain and death. Because of their particular difficulties in separating from the all-powerful early mother, daughters welcome the apparently more limited authority of the father. Later they attempt to recapture their original feeling of fusion with the maternal body by retreating into motherhood and family life, so avoiding responsibility for the challenges of history-making. Men develop a capacity for mastering the universe and a compulsive preoccupation with what can be predicted, possessed, piled up and counted in order to deny the strength of their early physical and emotional link with the mother.

While girls often have particular difficulty in separating psychically, the boy, in contrast, can assert his physiological difference and privileged place within culture, thus triumphing in fantasy over a mother experienced as omnipotent. Daughters who cannot overcome problematic experiences in infancy can remain unconsciously stuck in a state of ambivalent subservience towards their mothers, unable to build a viable lesbian or heterosexual identity. The girl dreads that in fighting for autonomy or expressing Oedipal rivalry she will destroy her mother – the mainstay of her identity. She may feel terrified of arousing her mother's envious retaliation if she is more sexually contented, or manages to combine motherhood and work in a way her mother could not. Here the parents' unconscious wishes and expectations are crucial. If the mother or father is indeed envious, the daughter's anxieties about rivalry will be greatly magnified (Maguire 1995, 1997).

Some daughters – including those who appear obsessed by disappointing relationships with men – remain tied in a quasi-erotic way to their mothers. Others try to cut off from early pain and deprivation by resorting to the culturally favoured solution of denigrating their mothers and their own sex. 'Basically penis envy is the symbolic expression of another desire. Women do not wish to become men but to detach themselves psychically from the mother and become complete autonomous women,' argues Chasseguet-Smirgel ([1964] 1985: 118).

To the girl fathers represent difference. Male influence in the external world may appear more limited than the mother's all-encompassing emotional power, but the girl who idealizes men may be fighting against a particularly virulent form of envious guilt towards both parents, which can lead to profound sexual and creative inhibitions. She will then project her own destructiveness and her ensuing dread of parental retaliation onto her own female sexuality. Consequently she might be unable to enjoy sex because of an unconscious fear that her own vagina is dangerous or that any kind of penetration will damage the inside of her body (Chasseguet-Smirgel [1964] 1985: 97).

Envious guilt can leave the woman feeling profound contempt for her own female sexuality. Yet she may simultaneously be unable to fully utilize her own 'masculine' qualities if she feels paralysed by guilt about having stolen what rightly belongs to her much-envied father. If she does allow herself success in the outside world she may sabotage her personal happiness through extreme passivity, even subservience within intimate relationships. As I noted earlier, June could not allow herself the pleasures of loving dependency while maintaining her highly responsible professional life.

Jessica Benjamin, the North American psychoanalyst, explores this dynamic in her account of 'ideal love', where the woman yearns for an unattainable 'heroic sadist' who alone can arouse her desire. Daughters who could not form an identificatory love relationship with a paternal figure are particularly prone to idealizing 'masculine' qualities. They may seek out men or women who are extremely ruthless or emotionally independent so that they can experience those qualities vicariously while consciously disowning them. Or, like June they re-create the unresolved triangular scenarios of childhood. Distant, controlled relationships offer the woman an opportunity to surrender her will so that she can feel both excited and contained, an experience she lacked in childhood. She feels that such a detached lover won't overwhelm her or be destroyed by her intense emotion as once she feared her mother would be. Nevertheless beneath the sensationalization of power and powerlessness lies a distorted wish for recognition and intimacy with an equal other (Benjamin 1988).

How can a daughter separate psychically without entering into another relationship where she relinquishes her will and desire? First we need to recognize that the girl gains strength from her early identification with the mother. Then we can explore how the daughter might form an identificatory relationship with the father without idealizing his sex.

Theories that assume that only the father's authority can protect us from irrationality and submission reinforce the devaluation of women and motherhood. Real mothers devote most of their energy to fostering independence, inculcating the social and moral values that make up the superego. It is usually they who set limits to the child's desire for erotic closeness and wish for omnipotent control.

It is necessary then to combine the object relations emphasis on how women's second-class status is structured into the personality through early maternal identifications, with a feminist analysis of the Oedipal phase, where the girl's perception of sexual difference becomes distorted. At these two points of interaction between culture and the psyche, fundamental questions arise about the girl's capacity to symbolize and act on her own desires.

The girl needs to be recognized as being like both parents psychologically. She also needs to have access to images of women as active sexual beings and agents of their own destinies. It is women themselves who must continue the fundamental task of creating new ways of symbolizing female experience.

Conclusion

I have argued that we need to combine different elements of orthodox and feminist psychoanalytic thinking to create a more active image of female identity, where the woman feels able to sustain her own pattern of intimate attachments while knowing that she remains the centre of her own life, the agent of her own destiny. Most valuable are those theories that seek to understand the interaction of 'maternal' and 'paternal' power in the girl's psyche. We need to draw together new ways of symbolizing and articulating the mother–daughter relationship and integrate this with feminist theorizing about Oedipal triangular issues. This will enable us to understand more about how the girl can come to 'own' her powerful emotions, to experience them in her mind and body in a way that later allows her to assert her desires in all spheres. We can then integrate this with a deeper analysis of how, at the point where the girl struggles to form her own female identity, the cultural devaluation of womanhood is structured into her psychic and sexual life.

In therapy, as in childhood, the woman needs to play in fantasy with a range of cross-sex identifications, accepting difference by making it familiar. We need to recognize both the 'holding' mother and the exciting father as elements that make up desire. As I showed through my clinical examples, female identity can be enriched if we re-own some of the qualities we so often prefer to project onto men. Ideally the girl should have paternal figures (who might be female), to help her gain a sense of herself as psychically separate, and find a way out into the external world. It is crucial that parents protect daughters from their own envy and rivalry, instilling in girls a sense that they can succeed both in conventionally 'masculine' and 'feminine' activities. This parental belief in the daughter's capacity for personal fulfilment is a vital antidote to the cultural devaluation of femininity. We must bear in mind though that female identity will not alter through psychological change alone. The girl will have to struggle to synthesize any sense of independent selfhood with the reality of living in a society where there are so few images of womanhood as active and autonomous. Only then will girls and boys come to see women as full subjects with their own needs and desires.

References

Benjamin, J. (1988) *The Bonds of Love: Psychoanalysis, Feminism and the Problem of Domination.* New York: Random House.

Chasseguet-Smirgel, J. ([1964] 1985) Feminine guilt and the Oedipus complex, in J. Chasseguet-Smirgel (ed.) *Female Sexuality.* London: Maresfield.

Dinnerstein, D. (1978) *The Rocking of the Cradle and the Ruling of the World.* London: Souvenir Press.

Eichenbaum, L. and Orbach, S. (1982) *Understanding Women: A Feminist Psychoanalytic Approach.* New York: Basic Books.

Freud, S. (1914) *On Narcissism: An Introduction,* Pelican Freud Library 11. Harmondsworth: Penguin.

Freud, S. ([1924] 1979) *The Dissolution of the Oedipus Complex,* Pelican Freud Library 7. Harmondsworth: Penguin.

Freud, S. (1931) *Female Sexuality,* Pelican Freud Library 7. Harmondsworth: Penguin.

Freud, S. (1933) Femininity, *New Introductory Lectures in Psychoanalysis.* Pelican Freud Library 2. Harmondsworth: Penguin.

Grosz, E. (1990) *Jacques Lacan: A Feminist Introduction.* London: Routledge.

Horney, K. (1924) On the genesis of the castration complex in women, *International Journal of Psycho-Analysis,* 5: 50–65.

Horney, K. ([1926] 1984) The flight from womanhood, in J. Baker Miller (ed.) *Psychoanalysis and Women.* Harmondsworth: Penguin.

Irigaray, L. (1984) *Ethique de la difference sexuelle.* Paris: Minuit.

Klein, M. ([1928] 1975) Early stages of the Oedipus complex, in *Love, Guilt and Reparation and Other Works 1921–45.* London: The Hogarth Press.

Maguire, M. (1995) *Men, Women, Passion and Power: Gender Issues in Psychotherapy.* London: Routledge.

Maguire, M. (1997) Envy between women, in M. Lawrence and M. Maguire (eds) *Psychotherapy with Women: Feminist Perspectives.* London: Macmillan.

Mitchell, J. (1974) *Psychoanalysis and Feminism*. London: Allen Lane.

Mitchell, J. (1984) *The Longest Revolution*. London: Virago Press.

Sayers, J. (1998) *Boy Crazy*. London: Routledge.

Whitford, M. (1989) Rereading Irigaray, in T. Brennan (ed.) *Between Feminism and Psychoanalysis*. London: Routledge.

7 Nine-tenths of the pleasure: sexual expression and the female body[1]

Geraldine Shipton

> *Jupiter:* This love of male and female is a strange business
> Fifty-fifty investment in the madness,
> Yet she ends up with nine-tenths of the pleasure.
>
> (Hughes 1999: 9)

In the introduction to his *Tales from Ovid*, Ted Hughes situates those strange, seminal stories about 'bodies . . . magically changed by the power of the gods, into other bodies' (1999: xi), in that unique moment in the history of the Roman Empire reckoned to be the time of the birth of Christ. It was a mythopoeic time when ecstatic cults flourished and the Empire was:

> at sea in hysteria and despair, at one extreme wallowing in the bottomless appetites and searching higher and higher for a spiritual transcendence – which eventually did take form, on the crucifix. The tension between these extremes, and occasionally their collision, can be felt in these tales. They establish a rough register of what it feels like to live in the psychological gulf that opens up at the end of an era. Among everything else that we see in them, we certainly recognise this.
>
> (Hughes 1999: xiv)

Ovid's ancient poem *Metamorphoses*, from whence the stories originate, explains the origins of the everyday world in which we live and how it had come about through the cruel and passionate relations between humanity and the capricious gods. We seem, at the beginning of the twenty-first century, to be at a similar historical juncture when what went before will no longer suffice in terms of moral codes, explanatory power and transcendental potential (though this may also be a myth).

Nevertheless, our understanding about sexuality has been undercut by a shift in consensus about what constitutes 'normal' sexual desire and behaviour and our own cultural artefacts seem to push us into rethinking the body as something to be performed or worked on in a variety of new as well as older, more established, ways. This involves not only fasting, dietary control, exercising, and cosmetic surgery but the whole gamut of transient popular cultural forms which are expressed via the body such as piercing and tattooing. The performance artist Orlan's operations to transform her appearance by means of the creation of facial bumps through surgical reshaping of her features, filmed and displayed at her 'Conférences', or less stomach-churning virtual alteration of her image into a replica of a pre-Colombian god, represent a more systematic and thought-provoking illustration (see Adams 1996: 140–59; Ayers 1999: 171–84 for an introduction to the work of Orlan).

The basic category of the body, with its own unique face which signifies identity and which we are used to considering as the bedrock for the formation of a self, is being put under question as a given. Gender-reassignment operations seem to offer the possibility of being a man and a woman in one lifetime. In Ovid's tales from Roman mythology, Tiresias, who was changed from a man into a woman and then changed back by the angry gods when he claimed women had more sexual pleasure than men, as referred to in the title of this chapter, suffered the consequence of being made blind by his rash comment, though he was given insight and soothsaying or 'nightscope' (Hughes 1999: 11) as a compensation.

This chapter discusses women's sexual pleasure and how it is expressed in the era that is opening up to us against a background of shifting attitudes to the body, sexuality and gender. Always hovering on the edges are the unanswered questions 'what is a woman?' and 'what is the significance of anatomy?' which are far bigger issues.

First, I would like to start from the context of a sociology of embodiment which, like psychoanalysis, is concerned with the lived experience of the body as well as the constructed nature of our attitudes to it. Like Tiresias, it seems to me that we are somewhat blinded if we rely purely on our psychoanalytic insights, garnered as they are from our everyday experiences of patients in therapy and our own capacities to reflect upon them as they affect us in both psychological and visceral ways, if we do not also look at what might be going on in the world outside our consulting rooms and the wealth of thinking about the body that has gone on in the last few decades.

The body and embodiment

Feminists put the body at the centre of their project to change the world and women's place in it when they set up myriad workshops, women's health centres, study groups, and consciousness-raising groups. They did this without especially theorizing what they were doing from the perspective of abstract ideas about bodies, yet looked at how the personal was political and their female bodies were both uniquely personal and very political subjects. Bordo (1993) has decried the subsequent writing out of feminism's contribution to the history of the body in society by contemporary social theorists and academic feminists who have stressed the work of Foucault in particular. Such writers, she suggests, seem to have forgotten earlier generations of activist women for whom thinking about the body and its relation to oppression was always geared to bringing about change. She quotes Mary Wollstonecroft's writing from 1792: 'Women are everywhere in this deplorable state . . . Taught from their infance that beauty is woman's sceptre, the mind shapes itself to the body, and, roaming around its gilt cage, only seeks to adorn its prison' (in Bordo 1993: 186). Nonetheless, Foucault's work has made a big impact on feminists and non-feminists who have wanted to study the shape of power by studying the shaping of bodies by society.

Foucault's analysis of power relations took him away from a conceptualization of power as held by people or groups, like a possession, towards the idea that power was operated by a network of non-centralized forces that are constituted by the economic and ideological forms of a historical period (we can imagine, for example, the rise of the factory-age and the need to produce a workforce that is adapted to the machine) (Ramazanoglu 1993). Such networks are not designed from above but are ushered in by a dynamic process that has different origins and sources and that operates by elements of the construction of time, space, desire and embodiment. A mechanism that orchestrates this impersonal process is self-surveillance and self-correction to fit the individual to prevailing norms through a discipline of the self and the body. There is thus no precultural or transhistorical feminine body or sexuality but discourses and practices that produce the body as a site and expression of power-relations which correspond to the particular time and place. The medical study of sex in the nineteenth century by the developing profession of medicine produced 'sexuality', which created a new kind of knowledge as a result of a new kind of power which in turn influenced what could be further produced. Thus sexuality was not employed initially as a purposeful way of controlling the rising working class but 'to define that which was unique and superior about the bourgeoisie, to serve the positive role of differentiating them favourably from the debauched, blue-blooded nobility and the naturally degenerate lower classes' (Bailey 1993: 113). As we know, it was the delicate 'gentlewoman' who suffered from weakness and fainting fits, not the scullery maid or the mill girl. However, where there is power there is also resistance and Foucauldians have emphasized the subversive potential of individuals to resist essential categories and fixed identities. For example, cross-dressing could be seen in the light of such an approach as a challenge to norms concerned with disciplining men and women into fixed gender stereotypes.

Brian Turner has developed a sociology of embodiment, rather than of the body, based to some extent on a critique of Foucault's work and its emphasis on the discourses that structure thinking about the body but taking special note of the historical relationship between religion and the body (Turner [1984] 1996). He illuminates the lived experience of bodily practices, performed in social space as opposed to a reification of the body as a thing-in-itself and has developed the notion of a 'somatic society' in which 'major political and personal problems are both problematized in the body and expressed through it' (Turner 1996: 1). The body, in our current epoch of late capitalism and its promises of pleasure through consumption, 'emerges as a field of hedonistic practices and desire in a culture which recognises that the body is a project' (Turner 1996: 4). The postmodern self is closely linked with the development of consumerism and satisfactions that are not simply associated with traditional sexual functions but are connected to desire saturated with fantasies of unlimited consumption of material goods, food, and signs. The self as a major concept has given way to the pre-eminence of the desiring body and technology has contributed a promise of eternal plasticity and therefore endless possibility. However, Turner holds on to a view of the body which maintains that, although it is a socially constructed metaphor – the 'natural body' is always already a cultural and historical phenomenon – there are also ontologically given aspects to bodies (he gives left/right-handedness as an example). In other words, the body is both natural and cultural. Using the concept of bodily practices enables him to approach embodiment phenomenologically and yet take account of how it is socially and historically constructed. He has set the stage for an exploration of the communal and collective nature of embodiment while clinicians have tended to find particular and special instances of individual trajectories of personalization and embodiment in work with patients.

This chapter does not attempt to integrate or harmonize psychoanalytic and sociological perspectives but it puts them against each other to give a wider view of the sexual body in contemporary life. Clinicians tend to hear little about sexual relations when they are happy and satisfying, unless they are being mentioned in such a way as to represent an acting-in on the part of the patient, who may be trying to pull the therapist into a discourse which transgresses the patient's partner's sexual privacy. The emphasis is more usually on unsatisfactory or shameful experiences, fantasies, infantile sexuality and perverse sexual states of mind (Meltzer 1973). Clinicians do not have direct knowledge of the sexual expression of their patients unless it is mediated retrospectively by discourse or acted out in some other way.

Sexuality and psychoanalysis

Unruly passions, as described by Ovid, come quite late in the development of the individual's sexual maturation and sexual identity in psychoanalytic accounts of subjectivity and sexuality which start from a polymorphous sexuality, as Laplanche and Pontalis (1973: 149) commented:

> If one sets out with the commonly held view that defines sexuality as an instinct, in the sense of pre-determined behaviour typifying the species and having a relatively fixed *object* (partner of the opposite sex) and *aim* (union of the genital organs in coitus), it soon becomes apparent that this approach can only provide a very inadequate account of the facts that emerge as much from direct observation as from analysis.
>
> (original emphasis)

They go on to discuss the limits Freud came up against in trying to understand the nature of sexual energy itself – he hoped biochemistry would shed some light on the mystery – but he was clearly persuaded that sexual life existed virtually from the beginning. However, by dint of deferred action, it meant that subsequent meanings were constructed about experiences that were not originally construed in the same way. Infantile sexuality, taken as the foundation for all sexuality, is puzzling:

> it cannot be accounted for either by an approach that reduces it to a physiological function or by interpretation 'from above' that claims that what Freud calls infantile sexuality is the love relationship in its varied embodiments. In fact it is always in the form of *desire* that Freud identifies infantile sexuality in psycho-analysis: as opposed to love, desire is directly dependent on a specific somatic foundation; in contrast to need, it subordinates satisfaction to conditions in the phantasy world which strictly determine object-choice and the orientation of activity.
>
> (Laplanche and Pontalis 1973: 421, original emphasis)

Thus, sexuality and fantasy are forever wrapped around each other in much the same way as are the psyche and the soma.

The sexual instincts

Few psychoanalytic writers discuss sexuality in terms of precise sexual function (see Alizade 1999: 61–111). There is more interest in infantile sexuality and sexual disorders than in the mechanics of successful and so-called mature genital sexual expression, which has become the domain of the sexologists. Alizade (1999) mentions that Freud refers to orgasms only about a dozen times in the whole of his oeuvre. Freud, though, was at pains to correct the popular misunderstanding that only what was genital was sexual since some people made use of anything but the genitals for sexual gratification. Others, such as children, gained sexual pleasure from other body zones from birth onwards and only in maturity in heterosexuals did the genital zone come into play in the service of reproduction, and then the two did not always coincide. However, Freud's analysis of the fusion of the sexual instincts is of great importance in trying to understand how an object or its substitute is being used sexually. Freud's understanding of the instincts went through considerable changes in his lifetime and, as all students of Freud soon come to realize, he tended not to throw out previous bits of theory but to leave them unused but undiscarded. In his 'Outline Of Psychoanalysis' Freud (1940: 379–80) puts his final theoretical position clearly:

> The forces which we assume to exist behind the tensions caused by the needs of the id are called *instincts*. They represent the somatic demands upon the mind. Though they are the ultimate cause of all activity, they are of a conservative nature; the state, whatever it may be, which an organism has reached gives rise to a tendency to re-establish that state as soon as it has been abandoned . . . We have found that instincts can change their aim (by displacement) and also that they can replace one another – the energy of one instinct passing over to another . . . After long hesitancies and vacillations we have decided to assume the existence of only two basic instincts, *Eros* and *the destructive instinct*. (The contrast between the instincts of self-preservation and the preservation of the species, as well as the contrast between ego-love and object-love, falls within *Eros*). The aim of the first of these two basic instincts is to establish ever greater unities and to preserve them thus – in short, to bind together; the aim of the second is, on the contrary, to undo connections and so to destroy things . . . In biological functions the two basic instincts

operate against each other. Thus . . . the sexual act is an act of aggression with the purpose of the most intimate union . . . Modification in the proportions of the fusion between the instincts have the most tangible results. A surplus sexual aggressiveness will turn a lover into a sex-murderer, while a sharp diminution in the aggressive factor will make him bashful or impotent.

(original emphasis)

Freud's description of the flow of instinctual energies, a mixture of life and death instincts, fused together in an unstable way, stimulated by and enlivening different erotogenic zones and directed at different aims, objects or part-objects paints a compelling picture of what it is to be a live complex sexual being.

Female sexuality

If sexuality in general is a subtle admixture and is hard to fully comprehend, female sexuality is even more enigmatic since it has suffered from a tendency to be considered on the basis of its similarities or differences to male sexuality. Asking 'what do women want?', as Freud did in 1926, put men in charge of the question and women on the margins and, as R. Horacio Etchegoyen notes, 'the persistent attempt to accommodate the female of the species in the procrustean bed of the male orgasm is a way of constraining, dominating and controlling her' (Foreword in Alizade 1999: xiv).

Many analysts in the 1920s and early 1930s, such as Horney, Jones, Deutsch, Klein, Riviere and others, developed Freud's theory of sexuality to explain the material they came upon in psychoanalytic practice both with adult women and female children (for access to a collection of important papers from that period see Grigg *et al.* 1999). Freud himself confessed that he found the first attachment to the mother in infancy to be particularly shadowy 'as if it had succumbed to an especially inexorable repression' (1931: 226). He wondered if the girl's relationship to the father might be construed in some cases as a refuge against an earlier problematic attachment to the mother and, especially towards the end of his career, grew unconfident about his grasp of the psychology of women: 'It is admittedly incomplete and fragmentary, and sometimes it does not sound altogether flattering'. To know more, he suggested: 'you must interrogate your own experience, or turn to the poets, or else wait until science can give you more profound and more coherent information' (Freud [1933] 1967: 173–4).

Numerous writers since Freud have, indeed, interrogated their own experience and offered different understandings of the development of female sexuality. Indeed, the term female sexuality is confusing since gender identity is also closely linked to sexual practice, as Person (1999) has discussed and as continental feminists have elaborated in their explorations of femininity and feminine sexuality, particularly stressing the cultural connotation by using the word feminine.[2] In the rest of this chapter I will not attempt to engage with the fullness of the complex debate but will instead focus on those strands that make sense to me in relation to a woman's sexual use of her own body. This, in effect, amounts to a discussion of some of the work of psychoanalysts who have disagreed with Freud's claim that the girl's genital anatomy is completely unknown to her until it is discovered at the age of 3 to 5 years and found to be wanting in relation to the boy's penis and she presumes herself to have been castrated by the mother. It is the area of what is lived but perhaps not yet named that interests me in thinking about sexual expression in women. I want to think about the conscious and unconscious knowledge the girl has of her own body and her mother's body and how the lived experience of being a girl in a social world where the feminine body is shaped not only by anatomy but by the power structures which predominate might influence her desires and their expression.

Unconscious phantasy

Klein differed from Freud in that she supposed the female child to have some innate knowledge of her genitals; just as in elaborating the concept of unconscious phantasy on behalf of the Kleinian group, Susan Isaacs (1948) had posited the infant's innate knowledge of the mouth and an accompanying expectation of a nipple which will be found to fill it with milk, so Klein (1932) thought the girl had an intuitive knowledge of the vagina and of the penis. Such unconscious intuitions were called imagos. Klein went further though and proposed that all infants were preoccupied with the contents of their mother's body, which they partly intuitively knew could contain babies, but which also appeared to the infantile mind to contain the father's penis. These phantasies being primitive and based on part-object conceptions are frightening and may lend themselves to a fear that mother is damaged and potentially damaging, while at the same time she is the source and object of love. For girls in particular this situation, if unmitigated by love and reparation, may leave behind a legacy of hostile feelings towards a mother with whom she identifies and towards parental coupling, which may be felt as dangerous as well as excluding. As Hinshelwood (1991: 89) succinctly writes:

> It lays the seeds for the adult woman's anxieties about her bodily attractiveness, or lack of it, and the ravages of the ageing process . . .

The girl suffers from the fear that there is something wrong with her body (signified by the small external genital) [which] will be manifest in the fears, during pregnancy, of giving birth to deformed babies, all of which matches the deformities to the babies and the penis which the little girl has attacked in phantasy, inside mother.

This way of understanding the girl's unconscious anxieties and fears complicates her response to each psychosexual libidinal organization (oral/anal/phallic) and makes her passage through the Oedipus complex and onto particular choices of love objects and sexual aims fraught – there will always be concerns for her own insides being worked through in her sexual relations, as well as concerns and love for her external objects. Of course, the same can be said for boys but two significant factors obtain for girls: they identify with the mother, their first object, and are identified with her by the rest of the world. Even if an identification with mother is rejected in favour of an identification with father, it has normally still been the first identification.[3] This would suggest that identity and sexuality are both connected with archaic phantasies about the mother and her body, for both men and women.

The sexual development of the girl is especially affected by the unconscious fears she has about the inside of her own and her mother's body. When the girl is weaned she is left with an unresolved resentment towards her mother, the quality of which will be important in how she adapts to the father as a substitute – in unconscious terms taking father's penis in lieu of mother's breast, but finding in it a greater potential for gratification. Klein believed that in this equation of the penis with the breast, that the vagina took on the receptive role of the mouth in a 'displacement from above downwards' (Klein 1932: fn 196–7). This beginning of activation of the vagina as an erogenous zone is not complete until puberty, of course. The girl's interest in the father's penis is assisted by oral, urethral, anal and genital impulses, and is made covetable also because, according to Klein, mother has been perceived as possessing father's penis inside her body. The girl may take up a revengeful attitude to the penis on this account or be submissive to men sexually because of it: two opposite responses. The power attributed to this penis may also undermine her confidence in it as a good alternative to the breast and it may become a 'bad' dangerous penis. Klein believed the child introjected a good and bad breast and in a similar way a good and bad penis. A fear of the bad penis inside can encourage her to keep trying to introject a good one to counteract the bad one and if, when she is older, heterosexual intercourse allays her anxieties by giving her the opportunity for libidinal satisfaction and reassurance she is likely to benefit doubly – such a scenario is likely to make her want a partner who treats her well.

If the situation is less propitious it may strengthen a desire for real punishment to appease her fears about the bad penis in her mind and could result in her choosing sadistic partners to destroy the even worse bad penis inside. Klein (1932: 202) puts it this way: 'Thus the deepest root of feminine masochism would seem to be the woman's fear of the dangerous objects she has internalised; and her masochism would ultimately be none other than her sadistic instincts turned inwards against those internalised objects'.

Klein agreed with Freud that the girl desires a child and that this takes over from a desire for a penis but her clinical work made her come to the conclusion that wanting father's penis is the forerunner of this development, and that sometimes the girl's next equation may be between child and faeces, not child and penis. When the faeces are the link, Klein thought the girl's later attitude to her child is likely to be more narcissistic and much more identified with her own body and with her excrement, and forms the basis for hatred to the child.

There is not space here to describe the full extent of Klein's sexual theory but I would like to mention what Klein has to say about menstruation, the girl's relationship to her appearance and the relationship to her child when she becomes a mother. Menstruation when it arouses anxiety, as it does to some extent in all adolescent girls, is equated in the unconscious with other bodily substances, including excrement. Bleeding makes the girl fear that she has damaged the inside of her body or that mother or father has spoiled her in retaliation for whatever phantasies may have been going on – stealing father away, filling mother with excrement, masturbating and so on. The flow of blood makes it seem as if her genitals are indeed injured, her internal objects may be damaged, or that phantasy babies inside have been killed off. When anxiety can be managed and femininity has been accepted, menstruation can be met with satisfaction – proof that the girl is fertile and womanly and can expect gratification and, in principle, babies.

Klein also noticed how small girls have a particular sensitivity about beautifying their own bodies and their dolls' or imaginary babies' bodies. She linked this to a fear that in the anal phase they have put dangerous faeces into mother – thus they sublimate along a pathway of beauty and cleanliness, wishing for a lovely home and grooming themselves to create a beautiful body so that they can feel they are good and lovely on the inside of the body. Contemporary exhortations to women to be thin and forever nubile, and the availability of advanced technologies combine to produce new opportunities for surgical interventions to come to the aid of both sublimation and self-mutilation.

Finally, Klein discussed the opportunity afforded the girl when she has a baby and can breast feed and return to the point of onset of all her ambivalent feelings towards her mother and when she can feel her phantasies have not come true and that she is full of good things to give her baby. Caring for the baby rewards her pleasure twofold: by being able to fulfil her earliest desires and by being able to identify with the baby and its satisfaction. The girl has many routes by which she can reinforce the good mother imago. Klein was able to identify not only what the girl lacked, as Freud had done, but what she possessed, and could elaborate her ideas about sexual development on a distinctly feminine basis. Klein's ideas combine cultural expectations about heterosexual femininity as well as biological and unconscious processes which come together in a rich mix but which leave women who do not want babies or hetero-sexual relations in a position that could be construed as 'abnormal' or 'unfulfilled', both of which are now seen as questionable. Nonetheless, in terms of explaining why heterosexual relations and having babies remain powerfully attractive to most women, Klein's account is persuas-ive, to my mind, and a balance to the Freudian emphasis on woman as failed man.

Chasseguet-Smirgel sums up Freud's theorizations on feminine sexuality from the standpoint of archaic phantasies about the mother:

> Female sexuality is therefore a series of lacks: the lack of a vagina, lack of a penis, lack of a specific sexuality, lack of an adequate erotic object, and finally the lacks which are implied by her being devoid of any intrinsic feminine qualities which he could cathect directly and by her being forced to give up the clitoris . . .
>
> *Now the woman as she is depicted in Freudian theory is exactly the opposite of the primal maternal imago as it is revealed in the clinical material of both sexes . . .*
>
> *The theory of sexual phallic monism (and all its derivatives) seems to me to eradicate the narcissistic wound which is common to all humanity, and springs from the child's helplessness which makes him completely dependant on his mother* [sic].
>
> (Chasseguet-Smirgel 1993: 115, original emphasis)

Helplessness

Brennan (1993) argues that psychical processes based on a false notion of monism are acted out over time and geographical space, and proposes that this is rooted in our capitalist economic system. She presents several foundational phantasies about how we think about our being in the world, which deny our dependence on the environment and on each other. One is that we phantasize ourselves as active and the environ-ment as passive and under our control. We also phantasize that we are energetically contained – we foreclose knowledge of connections between ourselves and other beings and entities. Western technology can fulfil some of the omnipotent desires expressed in these phantasies and so tends to encourage an acting out on a global scale that reinforces the power of the phantasy. The prime example is how we use up the earth's resources greedily as if they are replenishable.

On an individual scale, the freedom that modern technology promises us in relation to health, well-being and longevity is also available to be harnessed to unconscious phantasies, the nature of which might be quite opaque to us. The benefits of cosmetic surgery, for example, may be matched by their accommodation to perverse desires for mutilation or for emptying out of a part of the body which might be associated with a maternal function and its link to dependency. Here, I am thinking of the apparently (apart from health risks associated with both surgery and silicone) benign nature of breast enlargement operations which seem relatively understandable, and, at first glance, seem to suggest a positive feminine identification with the 'good' breast. Although women may still breastfeed after the operation, it means that they do so with a breast that could be construed as deceptive; it contains silicone and milk. Whether or not this matters and what is expressed is linked to what it means in the mind of the mother – perhaps silicone is just silicone, though it will always also be 'not milk'. Anatomy most clearly is not destiny but it is both the product of culture and our vehicle for participating in culture, and, if Wollstonecroft is correct, it shapes the mind, though we may be as unconfident about how this happens at the start of the twenty-first century as Freud was 70 years ago.

Sensuality

Other psychoanalytic writers have emphasized different aspects of the special experience of the girl child in her relationship to her mother and what this means in terms of her particular sensual use of the body. Women who have written about this area seem to have taken up the lyricism of the challenge from Freud to 'turn to the poets' and have often been influenced by the work of Jacques Lacan, even if, like Luce Irigaray, they have ultimately rejected it.[4] In her work in this area, Alizade (1999) represents a point of view that draws upon Lacan but opts for a Tiresian assertion of the superiority of feminine sexuality. Although her work is an unusual blending of contemporary French psychoanalytic theories as much as more familiar Freudian theory, and both her reference points and her own views probably lose something in translation, it evokes the woman's enjoyment from a perspective that is less visible in the masculine outlook that Etchegoyen warned had been predominant. Alizade (1999: 10) outlines the following frame of mind in which to approach women's sensuality:

> To listen to erotic demands from the psychoanalytic point of view implies shedding prejudices and ideologies and accepting a wide variety of needs and inhibitions that range far beyond convention. Vicissitudes in object-relations, the dimension of human love, conflicts of loyalty – all these divert the course of the erogenous impulses and allow for successful sublimations and forms of erotic relationship that challenge the physiology of sexuality, bringing substitute satisfactions, and ego-orgasms (Winnicott [1958] 1990) that offer profound well-being in the context of indirect instinctual satisfactions.

Alizade quotes Didier Anzieu's work extensively, in particular the development of a set of ideas about 'psychic envelopes' (Anzieu 1990) and the skin-ego as they have been elaborated by him and his colleagues in France. Anzieu points out the special tactile nature of the skin which is both endogenous and exogenous at the same time – both active and passive – keeping inside in and outside out, and which is also the container for the nascent ego and, according to Alizade, a 'primal starting-point for thinking of the trophic flow of sensuality' (1999: 17). She follows Anzieu in positing the skin-ego as the point in the biological body of coincidence of sensation, affect and instinct, enveloped in a covering of skin which protects the emergent organizing capacity of the ego. The skin-ego is an intermediary between mother and baby in both fusion and individuation as mother's body and mind deliver up a separate individual. Mother and mother's skin connect to and hold the infant and the holding capacity becomes a support to the formation of the ego as well as a highly sensitive integument. This tactile basis of the ego puts an affective sensuality at the core of well-being and Alizade positions feminine sensuality as most closely linked to it, particularly through the mother–infant link: 'I am interested in bringing out the ... intimate association between sensoriality and erogeneity. The two elements form a sort of Moebius strip such as the external body forms with the internal body' (1999: 23). It is this Moebius strip quality that Orlan shows us when her skin is cut and pulled about and that engenders such emotion in the spectator and which disturbs our thinking about the female body when it is modified in surgery, whether for justifiable reasons or not.

Alizade argues that the fact of female anatomy is that the girl's own genitals are not easily visible to her and she cannot readily see that she has not been mutilated, despite her unconscious attacks on her mother's body, or masturbation and fears of retaliation. However, this is not merely a lack, as proposed by Freud or Lacan, but a benefit, since it encourages the diffusion of eroticism over the entire surface of the body – this may be why Tiresias was right in thinking that women have nine-tenths of the pleasure. Furthermore, it is the woman whose body undergoes the most mysterious of changes throughout life: menstruation, pregnancy, childbirth, breastfeeding, menopause – as well as genital orgasms. Women have, therefore, even more opportunities for the free play of sensual and sexual expression available to them. The image conjured up by Freud in his famous description of the baby feeding blissfully at the breast, its cheeks suffused with a warm glow, is a universal emblem of pleasure, but some mothers gain as much sensual pleasure from the feeding as the baby. Indeed, some women say they have orgasms from breastfeeding.

Whereas Freud would have categorized the clitoris as an inferior organ, interest in which 'should' be transferred eventually to the vagina, otherwise too much delay over it by the developing girl or the attentive lover would be construed as pathological, Alizade considers the nature of transference of erogeneity itself. She moves the debate away from whether or not clitoral orgasm is inferior to vaginal orgasm and depicts the whole genital area of the aroused woman as partaking of sexual pleasure during orgasm. Many psychoanalytic commentators have discussed this transferability. Ferenczi (1989) used the term 'amphimixis' to describe the fusion of energies developed as one erogenous zone lends its sexual energy to another in a surge towards discharge (e.g. the bladder to the anus) so that the localization of sexual pleasure becomes difficult to identify. Thus, feminine anatomy itself, amphimixis and the endless capacity of the mind to transfer desire from one object to another, from one aim to another, from one source to another combine to provide women with 'an easy path to voluptuousness' (Alizade 1999: 61). Specifically feminine sexuality, according to Alizade, is one of diffuse eroticism – a kind of delaying over oneself – with an accompanying narcissistic reflux to the ego.

The picture painted by Alizade is tempting – it makes femininity synonymous with being in a potentially constant state of sexual arousal. This is not to undermine the basic message, which seems to evoke a sexuality that is not simply based on a negative template of masculine sexuality, as outlined by Freud, and which is constantly shaped by the evolution of the female body through the many changes it undergoes. However, it plays down the more destructive instincts that are part of the fusion of life and death instincts which infuse sexual experiences. Alizade does discuss feminine masochism but in such ecstatic terms that it is difficult to differentiate it from orgasm in general. Alizade's evocation of the sensual woman also comes perilously close to the male fantasy of 'the omni-available woman' (Person 1992: 333–43). Such a fantasy bolsters up a fragile male ego for the man who would feel threatened by a real sexually active woman with her own needs and differences and so he takes refuge in a fantasy of the woman who is aroused and waiting for him. This fantasy erases the differences between individual women and between her needs and his needs; it is also an increasingly popular icon spread across advertising billboards worldwide. Representations of femininity and sexuality make an impact on us all but their exact effect cannot be predicted and research in this area is inconclusive.

Furthermore, many women profess to have sexual difficulties of one kind or another so there are problems in believing that the road to voluptuousness is so easily travelled for them. In fact, one study (Dunn *et al.* 1998) was carried out by postal questionnaire to 4000 adults in four general practices in England to discover the prevalence of sexual problems. The results showed that 41 per cent of women respondents reported having a current sexual problem. However, men did not fare enormously better – 34 per cent of them reported having a sexual problem. The most common problems in women were vaginal dryness and infrequent orgasm. Men reported erectile dysfunction and premature ejaculation as the most common problems. This would suggest that a large number of men and women are not sexually happy (Dunn *et al.* 1998).

In my own experience as a clinician, there are three main problems described by women in relation to sex, all of which cross the heterosexual/homosexual divide, though women have not usually presented them as the motive for seeking psychotherapy. These are: lack of pleasure in sexual encounters, disgust with the woman's own body, and the use of sexual encounters and activities as a way of expressing self-loathing. I do not have permission to include sexual case material from psychotherapy patients but assume other clinicians, like me, are accustomed to hearing women routinely say they hate their bodies and therefore imagine that this state of mind is widespread.

It may be, as Alizade hints, that what we define as 'sexual' does not include the many varieties of sexual pleasure she has outlined, or that women choose sexual partners who fail to facilitate their sexual becoming. Indeed, a survey of the early 1990s, media interest in which has been prompted by President Clinton's initial denial in 1999 of having sexual relations with 'that woman' (Monica Lewinsky) and his subsequent argument that fellatio did not constitute sexual relations, produced the surprising finding that most of the survey population questioned (American college students) also did not count oral–genital contact as sex (Sanders and Reinisch 1999).[5] What is considered as sexual or indeed a sexual problem is not always clear for women, whose mature sexuality has been seen as running parallel to male sexuality, with a similar emphasis on achievement of penetration and genital orgasm. This has also affected how women's destructive use of their sexuality has been seen, or, more precisely not seen, until relatively recently.

Female destructiveness and sexual practice

Increasingly, a woman's use of her body for perverse reasons has come under scrutiny, particularly by Welldon and the groundbreaking work she has done at the Portman Clinic in London. Perversion has been defined in several different ways, mainly in light of clinical work with men and has shifted over time from a normative definition that focused on compulsive adult sexual behaviour where genital heterosexuality was not the aim (thus rendering homosexuality, for instance, as always perverse) to a more inclusive and humanizing view of perversion as 'the erotic form of hatred' (Stoller 1975) which is 'the result of an essential interplay between hostility and sexual desire' (Stoller 1975: xi). Perversion understood in this way may have all sorts of outcomes in terms of sexual practices and does not define same-sex love as perverse unless there is an erotic form of hatred involved, but which can encompass heterosexuality as potentially perverse where there is hostility enacted compulsively through sexual intercourse. Some psychoanalysts think it is now time to drop the word perversion altogether and to assign some of the sexual problems to the conceptual framework of the neuroses or some other framework which avoids the word being used 'to inflict a negative moral judgment on sexual disorders' (Person 1999: 165).

However, Welldon, writing earlier than Person, in 1988, concurs with Stoller's emphasis on hostility and retains the term, using it in the same way. She compares male and female forms of perversion as she has encountered them in her clinical work:

> I have observed that the main difference between a male and female perverse action lies in the aim. Whereas in men the act is aimed at an outside part-object, in women it is usually against themselves, either against their bodies or against objects which they see as their own creation: their babies. In both cases, bodies and babies are treated as part-objects.
>
> (1988: 8)

Welldon argues that the whole of the female body can be considered as a sexual organ, thus the woman may attack any aspect of it as in anorexia, bulimia or self-mutilation and furthermore may use any aspect of function as part of a sadistic revenge attack on an unconscious phantasy of the all-powerful, robbing mother. This unconscious attack may be enacted through means that conform to normative expectations about how 'unremarkable' adult women behave, such as in heterosexual inter-course, pregnancy, and childbearing, and can involve behaviours related to mothering and prostitution. For example, women may sexually abuse their children directly, indirectly through partners and other men, or expose their own bodies to abuse in prostitution as a way of attacking or denigrating their reproductive organs. Similarly, getting pregnant may sometimes represent a triumphant attack on the mother, and termina-tion may, on occasion, be a way of getting rid of mother's babies or of attacking dependency itself.

Generally speaking, the notion that mothers could be involved in the abuse of their own children has only recently gained ground in the public mind though mythology, as Ovid's tales depict, is full of murderous and incestuous parents as well as heroes and heroines. As a consequence of modern prejudice the reproduction of perverse mothering has often gone on unchecked. Again, Welldon (1988: 151) puts it concisely:

> The clinical histories of my patients relevant to this theme include seduction and emotional deprivation, being seen and treated as part-objects, being prevented from individuating themselves from parental figures, and being prematurely sexualised by their parents.

This leads to depression, which is masked by compulsive sexual activities which Welldon thinks are motivated by revenge. The accounts she gives of her patients' lives and the tragic failures of parenting to which they have been subjected, and which they often repeat, demonstrate that the 'other' most intimate of unions – mother and child – can also be supplied with 'a surplus sexual aggressiveness' (Freud 1940: 379–80). However Welldon's argument that the whole of the female body can be used in a perverse way is confusing when it comes to eating disorders – anorexia and bulimia do seem to have very important sexual dimensions that need to be explored (particularly in relation to sadomasochism) and both can be compulsive, but they strike me as being in a different category. While they are attacks on a vital function that is linked to the imago of the breast and hence to the mother, they seem related to a much earlier sense of mother than the mother–madonna–whore figure.

Violence and the female body

So far we have looked at the contemporary situation and the shifting nature of what we have come to understand as expressions of female desire. Some areas have been left out because they seem related but too unwieldy to incorporate into this chapter. Alizade, for example, identifies a relationship between sexuality and the sublime that is beyond the scope of this discussion and which has extensive roots going back to, at least, the thirteenth century in terms of 'fasting girls' (see Malson 1998) and the sanctified transcendence of the corporeal body (though historic- ally, masochistic self-denial would be the route to the sublime and not Alizade's deliriously sensual heterosexual coupling). However, there is another kind of violence that constrains feminine sexual expression apart from self-inflicted pain; many women are afraid of male violence towards them and some have been victims of it, particularly within intimate and sexual relationships. Inhibition of the expression of sexual desire or availability may be at a conscious level, indeed adolescent girls have to learn to defend themselves as well as express themselves sexually, but it may also be at a less conscious level. For example, Young (1990) analysed the way that a girl will throw a ball in comparison to how a boy throws a ball. There is no obvious anatomical reason for a different style of throwing, no schooling in it, no apparent advantages. Young concludes from her applied philosophy study that 'throwing like a girl' is linked with an idea the girl has in her mind about the space she inhabits – she cannot move freely and expansively through it like a boy because she must constantly guard her personal space to keep herself safe from violence or intrusion. The girl lives through her body but it is also perceived as an object to others in a sexist society. Keeping a private space allows the girl to exist as a subject and not just as a mere object. Hence, she will throw in an underarm way to avoid lifting her arm up and stretching into the air beside her in an open but more vulnerable posture. The boy, on the other hand, will throw a ball through space with a slicing motion, unhampered by fears of violation. How women use their bodies and move through social space, let alone how they express their sexual feelings and desires will always be affected by constraints made upon their freedom by the conventions and ideologies of the culture in which they live, and to which they may discipline themselves to conform.

Conclusion

This chapter has mapped out some aspects of sexual expression in women against a backdrop illuminated by some contemporary sociological ideas about the body. Foucault's power analysis approach helps us to recognize that 'sexuality' is a relatively recently constructed concept, produced by the discourses of the nineteenth century (Ramazanoglu 1993). Psycho- analysis emerged in relation to the medicalization of hysteria, in particular, and has gone on to produce its own powerful discourses and practices and which are themselves products of a power–knowledge regime. However,

Foucault's approach gives little weight to the lived experience of the body in space. Turner's foundational work on embodiment in 'somatic society' offers a more phenomenological understanding of the body which is seen as both natural and cultural. This helps to situate psychoanalytic understanding of female sexual expression, which has shifted since Freud's famous query 'what do women want?'

A phenomenological approach fits well with the Kleinian account of experiences and phantasies in relation to sexual expression, providing the norms of feminine behaviour evoked by Klein can be recognized and situated as such, and not as the essential transhistorical destiny of girls and women. A specific sensuality of women has been outlined as exposited by Alizade but contrasted with a more perverse use of sex, the female body and mothering by Welldon.

In conclusion, it seems that how a woman expresses herself sexually is endlessly imaginative and complex. Indeed, this limited discussion of sexual expression takes us up to the edge of the category of sexuality since sexuality:

> without being the object of any intended act of consciousness, can underlie and guide specified forms of my experience. Taken in this way, as an ambiguous atmosphere, sexuality is co-extensive with life . . . There is interfusion between sexuality and existence, which means that existence permeates sexuality and *vice versa*, so that it is impossible to determine, in a given decision or action, the propor-tion of sexual to other motivations, impossible to label a decision or act 'sexual' or 'non-sexual'.
>
> (Merleau-Ponty 1962: 169)

The way we understand the body and sexuality is changing all the time and despite a resurgence of biological reductionism which seeks the answer to so many mysteries in the genes, the idea of the 'natural' body is dying away, and a view of the socially constructed body is becoming more dominant. However, the idea of the lived body can straddle both of these extremes. Nonetheless, sexuality remains enigmatic and femin-ine sexuality even more so. This is rightly so, despite the ability of psychoanalysis to shed light on the plasticity of the sexual and on the role of unconscious phantasy in creating an object or aim of desire out of the most ordinary or the most bizarre of opportunities. Sexuality still challenges psychoanalysis as it did a hundred years ago.

Notes

1 This chapter title refers to the statement made by Tiresias who lived as both a man and a woman in Ovid's story and who found the former status to be the

happier one in relation to sexual pleasure. I am not implying that woman's sexual pleasure is only available in relation to a man, indeed Tiresias' capacity to be a man and then a woman and to switch back again to be a man destabilizes the very notion of 'man' and 'woman'.

2 See 'feminine economy' by Judith Still in Wright (1992: 90–92) for the beginnings of a discussion of the usage of the term 'feminine'.

3 The discussion of the impact of the early relationship for boy and girl and its impact on the relationship between the genders has been extensively written about by American feminists, in particular by Nancy Chodorow (1978).

4 See Irigaray's work as exposited in the reader edited by Margaret Whitford (1991) or explained by Elizabeth Grosz (1989).

5 The survey was carried out in 1991 and involved a random sample of 599 students of the undergraduate population of a mid-west state university. Fifty-nine per cent of respondents indicated that oral–genital contact did not constitute 'having had sex' and 19 per cent did not think penile–anal intercourse constituted 'having had sex' (Sanders and Reinisch 1999).

References

Adams, P. (1996) *The Emptiness of the Image*. London: Routledge.

Alizade, A.M. (1999) *Feminine Sensuality*, trans. by C. Trollope. London: Karnac.

Anzieu, D. (1990) *A Skin for Thought*. London: Karnac Books.

Ayers, R. (1999) Serene and happy and distant: an interview with Orlan, *Body and Society*, 5(2–3): 171–84.

Bailey, M.E. (1993) Foucauldian feminism: contesting bodies, sexuality and identity, in C. Ramazanoglu (ed.) *Up Against Foucault: Explorations of Some Tensions Between Foucault and Feminism*. London: Routledge.

Bordo, S. (1993) Feminism, Foucault and the politics of the body, in C. Ramazanoglu (ed.) *Up Against Foucault: Explorations of Some Tensions Between Foucault and Feminism*. London: Routledge.

Brennan, T. (1993) *History After Lacan*. London: Routledge.

Chasseguet-Smirgel, J. (1993) Freud and female sexuality: the consideration of some blind spots in the exploration of the 'Dark Continent', in D. Breen (ed.) *The Gender Conundrum*. London: Routledge.

Chodorow, N. (1978) *The Reproduction of Mothering: Psychoanalysis and the Sociology of Gender*. Berkeley, CA: University of California Press.

Dunn, K.M., Croft, P.R. and Hackett, G.I. (1998) Sexual problems: a study of the prevalence and need for health care in the general population, *Family Practitioner*, 15(6): 519–24.

Ferenczi, S. ([1924] 1989) *Thalassa, a Theory of Genitality*. London: Karnac Books.

Freud, S. (1931) Female sexuality, in J. Strachey (ed.) *The Standard Edition of the Complete Psychological Works of Sigmund Freud* (24 vols), Vol. 21. London: The Hogarth Press.

Freud, S. (1940) An outline of psychoanalysis, in *Historical and Expository Works on Psychoanalysis*, Penguin Freud Library, Vol. 15. Harmondsworth: Penguin.

Freud, S. ([1933] 1967) *New Introductory Lectures on Psycho-Analysis*, translated by W.J.H. Sprott. London: The Hogarth Press.

Grigg, R., Hecq, D. and Smith, C. (eds) (1999) *Female Sexuality*. London: Rebus Press.

Grosz, E. (1989) *Sexual Subversions: Three French Feminists*. Sydney: Allen and Unwin.

Hinshelwood, R.D. (1991) *A Dictionary of Kleinian Thought*. London: Free Associations Books.

Hughes, T. (1999) *Tales from Ovid*. London: Faber and Faber.

Isaacs, S. (1948) On the nature and function of phantasy, *International Journal of Psychoanalysis*, 29: 73–97.

Klein, M. ([1932] 1989) The effects of early anxiety situations on the sexual development of the girl, in *The Psychoanalysis of Children*. London: Virago.

Laplanche, J. and Pontalis, J.B. (1973) *The Language of Psychoanalysis*, translated by D. Nicholson-Smith. London: The Hogarth Press.

Malson, H. (1998) *The Thin Woman: Feminism, Post-Structuralism and the Social Psychology of Anorexia Nervosa*. London: Routledge.

Meltzer, D. (1973) *Sexual States of Mind*. Strathtay: The Roland Harris Trust, Clunie Press.

Merleau-Ponty, M. (1962) *Phenomenology of Perception*, translated by C. Smith. London: Routledge.

Person, E.S. (1999) *The Sexual Century*. New Haven, CT: Yale University Press.

Ramazanoglu, C. (ed.) (1993) *Up Against Foucault: Explorations of Some Tensions Between Foucault and Feminism*. London: Routledge.

Sanders, S.S. and Reinisch, J.M. (1999) Would you say you had sex if . . . , *Journal of American Medical Association*, 281(3): 275–7.

Stoller, R. (1975) *Perversion: The Erotic Form of Hatred*. New York: Pantheon Books.

Turner, B. ([1984] 1996) *The Body and Society*. London: Sage.

Welldon, E.V. (1988) *Mother, Madonna, Whore: The Idealization and Denigration of Motherhood*. New York: The Guilford Press.

Whitford, M. (ed.) (1991) *The Irigaray Reader*. Oxford: Blackwell Press.

Winnicott, D.W. ([1958] 1990) The capacity to be alone, in M. Khan (ed.) *The Maturational Processes and the Facilitating Environment*. London: Karnac.

Wright, E. (ed.) (1992) *Feminism and Psychoanalysis: A Critical Dictionary*. Oxford: Blackwell Press.

Young, I. (1990) *Throwing like a Girl*. Bloomington, IN: Indiana University Press.

8 Creating space: women without children

Susannah Izzard

> The childless women who successfully transform a culturally
> prescribed absence in their identities into a creative space are
> unlinking the necessity of motherhood from a fulfilling female
> identity.
>
> (Ireland 1993: 130)

In this chapter I shall explore the nature and prevalence of pronatalism
as a fundamental human phenomenon, and introduce a way of thinking
about adult female gender identity which is independent from the cultural
assumption that motherhood is intrinsic to female adult identity. The
literature divides women without children into three groups – those
who cannot for physical reasons bear children of their own (Ireland's
1993 'traditional women'); those who delay the decision about whether
to have children until it is too late (Ireland's 'transitional women' and
Veevers' 1973 'postponers'); and those who make a conscious choice
not to have children (Ireland's 'transformative women' and Houseknecht's
1979 'postponers'). I shall be exploring the particular tasks that face
each group of women in creating an identity for themselves. Finally I
shall argue that, as each of these women addresses the task of fulfilling
her symbolic capacity to reproduce, they collectively challenge society
by offering this new identity, occupying a 'transitional space' between
the genders, and invite all people to explore their own identity in a
new way.

Pronatalism

Veevers (1980) discusses the widespread nature of pronatalism. The
meaning of the term 'pronatalism' has developed over time, but it is

now considered to describe the pervasiveness and power of the norm that all couples should have children, and involves emphasizing the advantages or positive consequences of having children. Veevers maintains that virtually all societies are pronatalistic, in that parenthood is normative in all societies, and that acceptance of the norm of having children appears to transcend divisions of age, sex, race, religion, ethnicity and class. There have been studies exploring the impact of pronatalism in South India (Kohler Reissman 2000), Zambia (Biddlecom and Fapohunda 1998), Israel (Hartman 1984) and Brazil (Sampaio and Daly 1976) that highlight the global nature of this phenomenon. Pronatalism, Veevers suggests, pronounces that being a parent is a civic and religious obligation; is being moral and responsible; gives meaning to marriage; is proof of femininity or masculinity; is a sign of normal mental health; and contributes to a person's social maturity and stability of personality.

Conversely, those who desire childlessness are seen by pronatalism as flouting religious authority; avoiding their civic duty; are immoral and irresponsible; destroying the meaning of marriage; rejecting their gender role; lacking femininity (or masculinity if male); displaying signs of abnormal mental health and are seen to be associated with social immaturity and emotional maladjustment. Given that Veevers' study was published in 1980, it could be argued that this view is now dated; more recent research however does not support this argument. Callan's (1983) Australian study compared the experience of those who made early explicit decisions not to have children with others who reach voluntary childlessness through a series of postponements. The 'early deciders' reported more negative reactions to their childlessness than 'postponers', highlighting the experience of being labelled as selfish and as child-haters. Lampman and Dowling-Guyer in their 1995 study conducted in the USA into attitudes towards those without children, conclude that their results confirm that voluntary childlessness is discrediting. 'Being a member of a couple planning to remain childless appears to make one vulnerable to a host of negative attitudes, including being viewed as lazy, insensitive, lonely and unhappy' (1995: 221). Morrissette and Spain (1991), in a review of the literature, conclude the existence of prejudice against women who choose to remain childless. Likewise, Campbell (1985) in a Scottish study of couples who have chosen not to be parents, supports the prevalence of a stereotype of a woman without children as unfeminine, hard, cold and brittle. In writing of the sample's experience, Campbell describes the difficulties the voluntarily childless encounter in the attitudes of others: 'faced with an image of themselves as selfish, immature, unnatural, weird, odd, they may attempt to mask their identity, to evade awkward questions, to manage situations which for some women at least are a trial, if not an ordeal' (1985: 109).

Ireland (1993) in her study of 330 women representing all three groups of women without children, found support for the existence of prejudice and negative stereotyping towards women who do not have children. Woollett (1991) studied women's experiences of infertility, and discovered evidence of pronatalism in society, although she does not term it such. Woollett remarks that the terms for childlessness like 'infertile', 'barren', and 'sterile' are derogatory, implying a failure not merely in reproductive terms but as women. The lives of childless women are also seen as 'empty', and Woollett suggests that the way in which childless people become legitimate targets for questions about their fertility as well as for disapproval of their relative affluence, supports the existence of negative attitudes. She quotes Busfield:

> Childless couples are liable to a variety of strictures implicitly condemning their behaviour. One argument uses the idea that children reduce a couple's freedom to suggest that married couples without children cannot cope with such restrictions and are somehow less mature and less adequate than those who can . . . Similarly, spending on consumer durables and evening entertainment, though generally regarded as pleasurable, desirable and a symbol of status, becomes reprehensible if substituted for childbearing.
>
> (Busfield 1974: 17, quoted in Woollett 1991: 60)

Veevers analyses pronatalism and distinguishes three components: cognitive (the belief that having children has positive consequences, and not having them has negative consequences; the belief that parents are *different* from non-parents); evaluative (judgements about those perceived differences, with favourable attitudes towards parents and critical or negative attitudes towards non-parents); and behavioural (the translations of those beliefs and attitudes into actions, such as the pressure put on couples to have children, or taxation policies that favour parents with children).

Pronatalism is like a prejudice in that it operates at many levels from the personal to the cultural. At a cultural level it is seen in media portrayals of the idealized family, advertisements that seem to sell parenthood as well as the baby product it features, and in the pervasiveness of the view that parenthood is inevitable. Campbell (1985) argues that wanting to please oneself by not having children may be defined as 'selfish' and morally reprehensible within a cultural framework that projects an image of parenthood as duty and also demands parental sacrifice. Yet in western society, that same cultural framework enjoins and applauds the acquisition of pleasures (of all kinds) and stresses a person's right to pursue their own destiny.

The sin the childless commit is to abuse this right by choosing a destiny that bypasses what appears to be a higher value: parenthood. The norm of parental sacrifice is so deeply embedded in our consciousness that even the childless appear uncertain as to whether their actions justify the 'selfish' label.

(Campbell 1985: 114)

It has been suggested that pronatalism may also be related to a form of social control (Nelson 1978), or to nationalism (Heeren 1982; Moroney 1992), or to the need to preserve a cultural or religious identity.

Pronatalism involves judgements about the mental state of the women who cannot and the women who do not want to have children; Woollett (1991) in her study of 60 women unable to have children, states that 'childless women are believed to reject or fail to reach the ultimate and proper goal for all women and hence must be mad, inadequate, or somehow at odds with themselves and society' (1991: 60). She cites the studies of Callan and Hennessey (1989) and Cook *et al.* (1989) which show that the 'inadequacy' of these women is sometimes used to 'explain' infertility – they are overanxious, reject their femininity or are not well adjusted. Statements have been made that define infertility as one of nature's failsafe mechanisms in those who are not psychologically healthy enough to nurture (Bardwick 1974). Helene Deutsch, who wrote extensively about the psychoanalytic understanding of motherhood, also discusses the psychic meaning of infertility in women (1947). I am not arguing here that the physical inability to bear a child is *never* influenced by psychological factors; it is the generalization and labelling that reveals the existence of prejudice that is harmful. As long as childbearing for women is seen as essential for physical and emotional maturation, there will always be negative attitudes towards those to whom this is denied.

Women who do not want children attract greater attention and analysis – Peterson (1980) in a study of US college students and parenthood intentions found a higher frequency of psychopathology among the sample of young intended non-parent subjects. He concludes that the intention to be a non-parent appeared to be associated with general maladjustment. Morrissette and Spain (1991) recount that traditional psychoanalytic theory presents motherhood as a developmental stage whereby maturity is attained. In reviewing the literature they conclude that studies have suggested that rejection of maternity is a symptom of deep psychic conflict (Carmel 1990). However they also cite studies that have countered this view (Teicholz 1977; Veevers 1979; Baum 1983), and supported the choice to remain childless as non-pathological. I examine the origins of the pathologizing views a little later, but there

can be no doubt that the impact of being on the receiving end of prejudicial attitudes is considerable.

Studies show that society has a more tolerant, even sympathetic attitude
to women who cannot bear children. Campbell (1985) however suggests
that the response of pity often shown in relation to women unable to
have children originates in convention rather than rational consideration
and as such reflects a prejudicial view. She suggests that the infertile are
deemed victims and therefore are not responsible for their situation – if
people thought it was rational choice it would be different. Lampman
and Dowling-Guyer (1995) however, contend that, in the absence of
any information, people do indeed assume others' situations to result
from choice not circumstance, and suggest that women unable to have
children are judged as harshly as those who choose not to, when the
details of the situation are unknown to observers.

In a study of older women who had not borne children, Alexander
et al. (1992) explored the nature of these women's regrets. All three
groups of women without children were represented in the sample, and
a feature common to all seemed to be that the women were made to feel
incomplete when faced with dominant cultural definitions of gender,
self and life course. 'They questioned whether they have had [*sic*] a
whole life and by extension, whether they were whole people' (1992:
622). These women felt marginal, and 'different' – experiences that
inevitably lead to questioning one's own identity.

These experiences seem to indicate that what lies at the heart
of pronatalism is a conception of 'woman' that is defined by a
culturalization of the biological capacity to bear children. There is an
implicit assumption that motherhood is intrinsic to female adult identity
and an implication of lack for any woman who is not a mother.
This notion is rooted in classical psychoanalytic concepts of feminine
identity.

There are two approaches to the place of motherhood in the analytic
theory of development of gender identity in a woman. One is Freud's
view (1917, 1924, 1931, 1933) where the girl child's wish for a baby is
seen as a resolution of penis envy. The process is brought about by the
castration complex, when the girl discovers that she has no penis and
believes this to be a result of it being taken away as a punishment.

> The renunciation of the penis is not tolerated by the girl without
> some attempt at compensation. She slips . . . from the penis to a
> baby. Her Oedipus Complex culminates in a desire, which is long
> retained, to receive a baby from her father as a gift – to bear him a
> child.
>
> (Freud 1924: 321)

Freud goes as far as to say that without this desire, the female is not fully mature: 'The feminine situation is only established, however, if the wish for a penis is replaced by one for a baby, if, that is, a baby takes the place of a penis in accordance with an ancient symbolic equivalence' (1933: 128).

For Freud the baby and the penis have 'symbolic equivalence'; in terms of the primary process of the unconscious, the baby *is* the penis. The wish for a baby is not a defence against penis envy but a translating of it into a form which offers the possibility of fulfilment. Ireland (1993) points out that the woman's wish for a child is seen here not as a uniquely female drive but a displaced wish for a missing male penis. According to this understanding the wish not to bear children is seen as an identification with the masculine, a wish not to give up the penis, or a wish to be male, and implies more general difficulties with gender identity. However there was in Freud some ambiguity that prefigured the second strand in analytic opinion – that of 'anatomical destiny' (Deutsch 1930: 200). The wish for a baby is seen here as a basic expression of femininity. Research (Ireland 1993) tends to support the view that feminine interest in babies and motherhood is biologically based, preceding the Oedipal stage. Horney (1926) rejects Freud's account of the wish for motherhood in terms of penis substitution and puts forward the idea of it as a fundamental female capacity. This view is supported by Kestenberg (1956) and Parens *et al.* (1976). In addition, Tyson and Tyson (1990) view the wish for a baby as a manifestation of gender role identification, occurring early on, when the girl child identifies with her mother's care-taking and nurturing interactions with her.

The centrality of biology is seen most clearly in the work of Helene Deutsch (1925), who put forward childbirth as a developmental stage in the life of a woman: 'A woman who succeeds in establishing this maternal function of the vagina by giving up the claim of the clitoris to represent the penis, has reached the goal of feminine development, has become a woman' (1925: 171). All sexual acts for Deutsch result in pregnancy, actual or fantasy, such that the sexual act equals reproduction, which is a single process divided into two by time – coitus and parturition.

Therefore we are left with two approaches – a child as a symbol for the missing and desired penis, or 'anatomy as destiny'. Both, I suggest, are unhelpful and provide little hope for the childless woman. The child as the 'missing penis' carries with it all the feminist critiques of Freud's patricentral views, and devalues woman as possessing intrinsic qualities of her own. It suggests that the only way a woman can come to terms with her childless state is to seek to obtain that which was symbolized in the child – the penis, so that a masculine identification is the only avenue open to her. However the 'anatomy as destiny' approach, while it accords value to the unique reproductive function within women, is restrictive, and places heterosexuality out of the range of analytic enquiry and roots it in nature, and results in the kind of concrete thinking that lies behind pronatalism.

I suggest that a way forward can be made by extracting aspects of each approach, to retain the power and uniqueness of the reproductive possibilities of the female body, but to follow Freud in reinterpreting this capacity as symbol or metaphor, which opens up multiple possibilities of expression and fulfilment. There is a move in postmodernist thought to detach the body from sexuality, moving from fixed and stable identities to fluid and mobile understandings. Writers such as Schwartz (1995) see this as a way of honouring what he describes as 'Freud's inclusion of a pervasive *instability* in his theory of human motivation' (1995: 121, original emphasis), which potentially encourages respect for difference. Schwartz argues that sexuality and gender must be deconstructed to move away from the confines of the gendered body and permit elasticity in our erotic capacities. I suggest this argument could be extended to our understanding of a woman's biological capacity to reproduce, such that the metaphorical meaning of the capacity can stand apart from the body. This can then lead us to assert the value and potency of the existence of biology without having to be concrete about its expression.

Ireland (1993), in her discussion of separating female identity from motherhood, draws on Lacan's (1978) view that it is the unique symbolic capacity of humans (epitomized in language), not the physical body, that shapes identity development. The acquisition of language in developing infants functions in Lacanian terminology as a 'third term' – that which enables and acknowledges separateness. This is akin to the Lacanian function of the father in the young family, who provides a 'third term' to facilitate separation of the mother/child unit, and enable the infant to acquire an identity of their own. Clearly the 'father' can be interpreted symbolically here. As a result of the fact that historically the mother has been the primary parent who must be left, femaleness is thereby associated with 'loss and the unspeakable' (Ireland 1993: 105), because as we acquire language and are facilitated by the (masculine) third term, we leave behind our infancy which remains only in the unconscious and therefore cannot be spoken of. Ireland (1993: 106, original emphasis) concludes that

> male and femaleness are *positions* in relation to language in identity and not inherently *biological facts* . . . To hold a female position is to be identified with all within ourselves that is unconscious and/or cannot be consciously spoken; a male position is to be identified with a conscious identity and all that can be spoken.

Ireland develops this idea to suggest that women without children are reflecting to society that which is unconscious in our definitions of 'woman'. The woman without children is an 'absence' in society – they tend to be invisible, and carry with them an association of 'lack' or incompleteness in the eyes of our culture. Ireland suggests that the existence of a woman without a child urges us to look at what is absent from our concept of woman. Each category of woman without children has the task therefore of creating for herself an identity that results from her capacity to take a 'masculine' position in relation to the question of motherhood – to consciously address her symbolic capacity to reproduce and interpret its meaning for herself. Ireland (1993) describes the task as 'unhooking' the reproductive capacity from female identity. I would suggest that it is not unhooking that needs to take place but a reinterpretation away from the concrete to the symbolic meaning of that reproductive capacity. The psychoanalytic view, that a symbol can only come into being when the object it represents is absent, is pertinent here. Childlessness makes it possible for a woman to symbolize the absent child or childbearing potential. In many cultures, absence is experienced as just that – but the contributions of analytic writers such as Winnicott (1971) calls us to see absence as *space* – space in which something creative can occur, whether it is the capacity to symbolize or the encounter with undiscovered aspects of the self.

Let us now look closer at the task which faces each individual category of women without children.

The woman who is unable to have children

Ireland (1993) suggests that this group of women has a stronger identification with the stereotypical gender role identity and therefore are more vulnerable to negative social judgements regarding their childless state. This is supported by Callan and Hennessey's (1989) study, in which they found that infertile subjects described themselves in terms of traditional feminine attributes more than the sample of mothers and married women who were childless by choice. Society also sympathizes with women who cannot have children, even pities them and this can exacerbate their feelings of being 'defective'. Mourning is the key dynamic with this group of women, as they come to terms with the fact that what they had planned, hoped and assumed would happen will not now take place. The fact that the 'bereavement' happens over a prolonged period of time, with a cycle of hope and despair, serves to exacerbate the process and can contribute to a feeling of life being on hold while hope still remains. This process can be further heightened by prolonged involvement with infertility treatments. Even if a child is adopted, the loss of the experience of pregnancy, giving birth, and raising a child of one's own may be keenly felt.

Ireland (1993) points out that when raising children has been presumed to be the major activity of marriage, the realization that it is not going to happen shakes the gender identity of both partners. Ireland suggests that there will be a need for role flexibility within the heterosexual relationship. If these women have a stronger identification with a traditional gender role then the shift to less traditional gender role expectations will be demanding. This group of women feel most keenly the 'something missing' in their lives, and often experience efforts to fill the space as a tacit admission that there is no longer any hope. However, drawing on Ireland's (1993) concept of taking a masculine position with regard to motherhood, the task of these women needs to be a dwelling in the space, with all its attendant pain, in order to discover what the space potentially contains for them in terms of a symbolic understanding of their reproductive capacity. Ireland describes this space as 'full of generative possibilities' (1993: 139), and it encapsulates a woman's creativity, which the symbolism of reproduction indicates is essential to female identity. Raphael-Leff (1997) draws attention to the 'generative identity' within each gender, and it is to this aspect of the self that attention must be given.

Part of the mourning process for a woman who cannot have children is the shift in her subjective position in relation to her childless state – from absence to space. Freud (1917) describes how a person's emotional energy and attachments must be withdrawn from the lost object in every association and memory before it can be reinvested. Accordingly the woman who is unable to have children needs to mourn and relinquish the myriad fantasies of motherhood before the emotional energy can be reinvested. Freud (1917) also suggested that in mourning, the lost object can only truly be given up when significant features of the object were incorporated into the grieving person's identity. Ireland (1993) stresses the importance of creative work in this regard – activity that can express innate creativity, and her study revealed the manifold ways in which women had explored and expressed their creativity. She makes the point that some women will retain a maternal identification in their creative work (caring, nurturing), others will place the energy withdrawn from the concept of motherhood elsewhere.

In Ireland's study the women who were unable to have children reported that their role in the family of origin had changed to accommodate their childless state. One woman took on a role in the family characterized by giving a quality of attention to her nephews and nieces and taking responsibility for a family newsletter. All women testified to the importance of having a supportive network of friends and family and

Ireland stresses the necessity of having friends whose lifestyles are similar to the woman's own.

A woman in Ireland's study highlighted the invisibility of the pain of the lesbian woman who is unable to have children. Lesbian women experience less social pressure to have children but also do not find the kind of sympathy regarding childlessness that heterosexual women in relationships attract. In addition they may have had to overcome considerable resistance in health care settings to be included in donor schemes, let alone fertility programmes, so their grief and disappointment will be complicated. There is also the impact of internalized homophobic attitudes which may make the woman feel she 'deserved' this outcome as she was not fit to be a mother in the first place.

Postponers

Those who delay the decision about having children until it is too late are understood by Ireland (1993) to be ambivalent about the question. In her study this group of women appeared to have the most difficulty in maintaining a positive or coherent sense of female identity. There was a feeling of 'drifting' – a feeling of not doing what they felt they 'should' yet not able to fully relinquish or embrace motherhood. It seemed easier for these women to anticipate motherhood as an eventual element in their lives than to take it on in the present, address the meaning of the absence of motherhood so far, or to find 'alternative fullness' (Ireland 1993: 44). It appeared that consciously addressing the meaning of their reproductive capacity did not actually take place until such time when motherhood was no longer an option. In the study, the women delayed addressing the question as they were engaged in exploring themselves in other ways (for example work, study, politics, feminism), or were trying to resolve a conflict over being in a partnership that satisfied their immediate needs yet did not feel right for the raising of children. For many of these women there was the dawning realization that non-maternal work satisfied their creative capacities.

Ambivalence regarding motherhood has traditionally been seen as resulting from conflicts regarding one's own mothering, but Ireland argues that this originates from a restrictive view of gender identity and pathologizes the pathway of being without children. Ireland states that there are now new and different places for women to occupy in life and this will inevitably mean that other places (including motherhood) are left unoccupied by some women.

However like the woman who is unable to bear children, the 'postponer' needs to *address* the space in her identity, to wonder what it might mean that motherhood is absent, and discover what, if any, void is created by the absence. Ireland argues: 'So long as the transitional woman remains in a state of unconsciousness regarding her child*less* or childfree circumstances, a process of defining and claiming her own life will be inhibited' (1993: 67). This raises the question of where women can address this task. Psychoanalytic psychotherapy has traditionally been a place where motherhood is assumed to be a 'given' for women and its absence is regarded as an indication of conflict. How then can therapy provide a *neutral* space in which a woman can discover her own meaning of having a body redolent of symbolic offspring? The question of forming an adult female gender identity separate from a concrete understanding of the biological capacity to bear children thus becomes an important one for the analytic world, not just for those women for whom it is personally pressing. It is important to acknowledge that for some women, an ambivalence regarding motherhood *may* arise from unresolved infantile conflicts or a rejection of feminine aspects of themselves. A neutral therapy will then allow the space for these things to be faced and worked with, with the result that the woman may now feel free to *make a choice* about whether to have children – or not. Pregnancy is not necessarily an indication of 'successful therapy' (an opinion I myself have witnessed in a supervision setting). It is equally possible that the desire for children may originate in unresolved conflicts – but our cultural conditioning and classical understandings of adult female identity often preclude this being approached neutrally in the clinical setting.

A common misconception is that creative and nurturing energies are absent in women who are not mothers, but this is not necessarily the case – it is more that these energies are not expressed through bearing and raising children. Women who do not want children, but have internalized guilt or prejudicial feelings about this, will often deny altogether their 'maternal instinct' for fear that others will pounce and denounce them as secretly or unconsciously desiring children.

Ireland (1993) makes the point that the frequently asked question 'have you children?' can become a prompt for self-exploration, and confrontation of the woman's self-concept. The point that is important here is that unless consciously addressed, a woman's reproductive capacity can lie dormant and uncelebrated.

Childfree by choice

Ireland posits that there is societal resistance to recognizing the female identity of this woman, seen by many as having a masculinity complex and attracting the stereotypes described earlier in this chapter. This category, more than the others, challenges us to reconsider the traditional understanding of gender roles and characteristics.

> When the transformative woman chooses to remain childfree, she is saying to the world that she is on a personal quest in which motherhood plays no part. She is making a conscious decision to explore other avenues of expression for whatever maternal feelings she has.
>
> (Ireland 1993: 71)

Ireland's study revealed that the fact that a child was not anticipated produced a different approach to these women's intimate relationships. Many of the sample of 'transformative women' expressed a concern about the loss of intimacy that parenting would exact, and some said that the valuable quality of connection to their mate had been a factor in the decision not to have children. Relationships for these women were markedly egalitarian, with both parties expressing non-traditional gender roles. Other research supports this, finding that voluntarily childless women were less traditional in sex role orientation (Bram 1984), and childless-by-choice couples tend to have less traditional attitudes toward women and to interact more with each other than the parents in the sample (Feldman 1981).

The couples in Veevers' (1980) study spoke of many influences in their decision not to have children. Veevers was curious as to how these people were able to question the 'parenthood mystique' and what had happened to have destroyed or discredited the mystique. Searching for causes can collude with a pathologizing view – we tend to ask for explanations when something is seen to be deviant. Veevers' study strives to take a neutral approach, however, and her sample did reveal those who had a distaste for pregnancy, who had disturbing early experiences, who were in the thrall of dichotomous thinking – *either* children *or* work; *either* children *or* a good relationship; *either* children *or* being debt-free. One aspect of dichotomous thinking which society's view of women seems to encourage is the erotic–maternal split. Women are seen as *either* motherly, fecund, pregnant *or* possessing erotic appeal. The split between these two expressions of femininity seems irreconcilable and in existence from earliest times – the whore/madonna split is well known, and may have its root in the incest taboo. Veevers' study revealed some women were loath to lose their erotic appeal, which they saw as inevitable if they were to have children.

Others in her sample revealed a wish to dis-identify with women who were mothers, holding prejudicial views regarding the competence of women who became mothers. Indeed the effects of parenthood were couched by some in very negative terms, that bright, competent women are ruined by motherhood. There seemed a perception that motherhood reduces the bright (masculine?) woman to the rest of the female race, which some women in the sample assumed to be uneducated and not very bright to begin with (and hence not people with whom one identifies). These comments support the existence of a group of women who do not wish to have children because they fear they will become 'woman' – a creature to be despised and looked down on. How far this is to do with maternal identifications with mothers experienced as incompetent, or internalized misogyny, or difficulties with one's own feminine identity it is hard to say. What it seems to indicate however is once again a need for a *neutral* therapeutic space in which these things can be explored.

Veevers' study also found that in many cases, women chose not to have children because there were other things that were more attractive or fulfilling – this lifestyle was characterized by the quest for experience – spontaneity, travel, learning, work or experiencing not-working, and the opportunities that affluence provides. Veevers points out that for a number of childless people the initial decision to postpone childrearing was unconnected to the alternative lifestyle which being childfree makes possible. However, once this lifestyle was experienced, it became more dominant in the decision to remain childless.

Veevers contrasts the dynamic and roles within partnerships with and without children, pointing out that in most families, the partnership dyad is one of many pair-bonds. In contrast the dyad between partners *without* children is the only pair-bond and therefore carries different dynamics. Couples in the sample in the Veevers study were characterized by a greater intensity of interaction, some tendency to self-sufficiency within the partnership, egalitarian relationships, and 'considerable freedom from sex-typed behavior repertoires' (1980: 105). What many of the respondents in the study attested to was that the wish for their partnership to *continue* in this way was instrumental in the decision not to have children.

It is possible to make judgements about the internal worlds of Veevers' respondents – to analyse and deem their attitudes and choices to be defensive, regressed and symptomatic of pathology or conflict, and this has been done (see above). However the need to do this springs from the classical understanding of adult feminine identity such that ways of experiencing or expressing that do not include childbearing are forever seen as 'substitutes' or deviant. Psychoanalytic psychotherapy has prided itself on its neutral analytic stance, yet there are many areas where internalized societal prejudice (homophobia, misogyny, racism) interfere with the capacity of the therapist to provide a truly neutral space in which analytic, evenly held curiosity is the dominant tone of the session. I suggest that pronatalism could be included in such a list of prejudices that distort evenly held curiosity in the therapeutic encounter. Ireland (1993) suggests that exploration can help a woman to move from the position of 'I just can't' or 'I just must' in relation to childbearing, to a conscious, considered choice.

Women who choose not to have children are often seen by others as 'masculine'. Ireland suggests that it is these women's capacity to hold on to a non-maternal desire which is seen as 'masculine' energy. What the existence of these women highlights is the question 'why is this energy seen as masculine? Could it not be a reclaiming of a hitherto unrecognized aspect of feminine energy?' In any case, there are many men who want children, so the wish for a child cannot solely be the preserve of the female.

Rethinking adult feminine identity

The presence of childfree and childless women who lead fulfilling lives points up the lack in our current thinking on the meaning of woman. There is a prevalent view of woman that sees her identity as inextricably linked to motherhood. Even amongst women who are at ease with their childfree state and have few regrets speak in isolated moments of 'feeling a fraud', fearing criticism, not really belonging. The lack of positive images of women without children in the media emphasizes the invisibility of the childless or childfree woman and makes it harder for women to feel that they can identify with the 'woman' that is widely portrayed. Women without children are not alone in this, of course, but they do carry a particular load here.

Ireland's study drew attention to the impact of one's own mother in drawing women away from or to motherhood, and the need for there to be identifications with other significant females – not necessarily mothers – in the girl's early life. Pines (1993: 132) writes of the power of the identification with the pre-Oedipal mother: 'First pregnancy affords a woman a further stage of identification rooted in a biological basis. She enters upon the final stage of being like her own mother, a psychologically mature woman, impregnated by her sexual partner'.

However the girl may be helped to have more creative identifications if there is a variety of women in her life. Ireland suggests that other significant females can act as a 'third term' in the girl's life, creating a space between the daughter and her mother in which other female identities might be imagined. Many of the women who were able to create for themselves a new feminine identity in Ireland's study had had women like this in their lives.

Ireland's study also highlighted the importance of paternal identifications to facilitate a more creative feminine identity. Many of the childless-by-choice sample had fathers who were able to recognize and encourage the daughter's emerging independence and agency, who gave her freedom in her identity not to be restricted to traditional roles. For these women 'gender developed as a salient category for identity, but a category neither fixed in meaning nor limited to particular roles she might assume in later life' (Ireland 1993: 122).

Ireland suggests that the metaphor of a childless woman confronting what is absent or unconscious in her life through not being a mother can also be a challenge to society to do the same in its image of what it means to be woman. As the woman must encounter absence, interpret it, and use it as a metaphor in order to act creatively, so society must wonder about the concrete definitions of woman that leave much of woman's experience as an absence. Female childlessness, argues Ireland, is *not* a question of gender identity or concerns about a woman's sense of femaleness. It is a broader question: 'How does a woman fulfil her own personal identity (to be a subject with desire) when the prescribed gender role for all women remains tied to their biological capacity for reproduction?' (1993: 128). Childless women present a challenge – Ireland sees them as a 'third element' destabilizing our binary arrangement of gender definition and traditional gender roles. They are a metaphor for the dialectic of absence and presence in human identity, because it is in the absence of fulfilling the prescribed gender role that fullness and presence may be experienced. They hold a 'third position in our gender role schema; they are not being the lack, the position that women have traditionally held, nor are they denying the lack and claiming wholeness, the traditional position held by men in patriarchal societies' (Ireland 1993: 146).

I suggest that women who have used their childless or childfree state to explore and express previously unconscious aspects of themselves occupy a transitional space between the genders, being free to be a woman with a unique identity, fluid and mobile yet female. Occupying the transitional space, the childfree woman calls each gender to explore their own 'lack' – the unconscious aspects of the self that are masked by an attachment to traditional gender roles. Ireland (1993) discusses the impact on male gender identity of the existence of women who are not mothers, brought about by their rendering invalid the universality of the restricted female identity. The idea that the childless woman reaches her new identity through a process of conscious engagement with what has been unconscious leads Ireland to call for a model of identity that sees gender and gender roles as fluid and discontinuous and as a dialectic between the conscious and unconscious rather than singular and fixed concepts. Ireland makes the interesting point that society's rules for gender, sexuality and other social roles are in part 'an attempt to minimise the disruptive influence of the unconscious on our identities' (1993:

148). Traditional gender roles are attempts to sustain the illusion of wholeness and sufficiency, but in so doing denies the absent (unconscious) aspects of both genders.

Conclusion

In this chapter I have explored the widespread nature of pronatalism in our society, and the implications of this for how women who do not have children are viewed. There is little doubt that childless women can experience prejudice, and can feel excluded from the accepted cultural norm of what it means to be an adult woman.

This cultural norm is defined by the biological capacity of the woman to bear children. It seems timely to challenge this: women without children are traditionally seen as experiencing a 'lack' and are therefore often invisible, rarely evident in media portrayals of women unless it is as the hard headed career woman on her way to the top of her profession. It is time to expand our understanding of 'woman' through a symbolization of that which has been seen in a concrete way to be at the heart of her identity – the biological capacity to carry eggs, and grow those fertilized to birth. An absence of a concrete expression of this potential through childbearing creates an opportunity to explore what it means as metaphor. Irrespective of the route by which a woman is without a child, the 'space' within must be experienced and reflected on, and used to bring forth new possibilities of expression and creativity. This activity is not the exclusive prerogative of the woman who does not have a child, but perhaps these women undertake the task and stand as an encouragement to others – mothers, fathers and men who are not fathers, to explore the unconscious and unexpressed potential within them. Just as the woman who does not have a child challenges society to rethink their notion of female gender identity, so might they individually challenge all people to explore where they are restricted by narrow definitions of their own gender.

References

Alexander, B.B., Rubinstein, R.L., Goodman, M. and Luborsky, M. (1992) A path not taken: a cultural analysis of regrets and childlessness in the lives of older women, *Gerontologist*, 32(5): 618–26.

Bardwick, J. (1974) Evolution and parenting, *Journal of Social Issues*, 30: 39–62.

Baum, F. (1983) The future of voluntary childlessness in Australia, *Australian Journal of Sex, Marriage and Family*, 4: 23–32.

Biddlecom, A.E. and Fapohunda, B.M. (1998) Covert contraceptive use: prevalence, motivations, and consequences, *Studies in Family Planning*, 29(4): 360–72.

Bram, S. (1984) Voluntarily childless women: traditional or nontraditional? *Sex Roles*, 10(3–4): 195–206.

Busfield, J. (1974) Ideologies and reproduction, in M.P.M. Richards (ed.) *Integration of the Child into a Social World*. Cambridge: Cambridge University Press.

Callan, V.J. (1983) Factors affecting early and late deciders of voluntary childlessness, *Journal of Social Psychology*, 119(2): 261–8.

Callan, V.J. and Hennessey, J.F. (1989) Psychological adjustment to infertility: a unique comparison of two groups of infertile women, mothers and women childless by choice, *Journal of Reproductive and Infant Psychology*, 7(2): 105–12.

Campbell, E. (1985) *The Childless Marriage: An Exploratory Study of Couples who Do Not Want Children*. London: Tavistock.

Carmel, M. (1990) *Ces Femmes Qui n'en Veulent Pas*. Montreal: Saint Martin.

Cook, R., Parsons, J., Mason, B. and Golombok, S. (1989) Emotional, marital and sexual functioning in patients embarking upon IVF and AID treatment for infertility, *Journal of Reproductive and Infant Psychology*, 7: 87–94.

Deutsch, H. (1925) The psychology of woman in relation to the functions of reproduction, reprinted in R. Fliess (ed.) (1950) *The Psychoanalytic Reader: An Anthology of Essential Papers with Critical Introductions*. Madison, WI: International Universities Press.

Deutsch, H. (1930) The significance of masochism in the mental life of women, reprinted in R. Fliess (ed.) *The Psychoanalytic Reader: An Anthology of Essential Papers with Critical Introductions*. Madison, WI: International Universities Press.

Deutsch, H. (1947) *The Psychology of Women: A Psychoanalytic Interpretation*, Vol. 2: Motherhood. London: Research Books.

Feldman, H. (1981) A comparison of intentional parents and intentionally childless couples, *Journal of Marriage and the Family*, 43: 593–600.

Freud, S. (1917) On the transformations of instinct as exemplified in anal erotism, in J. Strachey (ed.) *The Standard Edition of the Complete Psychological Works of Sigmund Freud* (24 vols), Vol. 17. London: The Hogarth Press.

Freud, S. (1924) The dissolution of the oedipus complex, in A. Richards (ed.) *On Sexuality: Three Essays on the Theory of Sexuality and Other Works by Sigmund Freud*. London: Penguin.

Freud, S. (1931) Female sexuality, in J. Strachey (ed.) *The Standard Edition of the Complete Psychological Works of Sigmund Freud* (24 vols), Vol. 21. London: The Hogarth Press.

Freud, S. (1933) New introductory lectures on psycho-analysis, in J. Strachey (ed.) *The Standard Edition of the Complete Psychological Works of Sigmund Freud* (24 vols), Vol. 22. London: The Hogarth Press.

Hartman, M. (1984) Pronatalist tendencies and religiosity in Israel, *Sociology and Social Research*, 68(2): 247–58.

Heeren, H.J. (1982) Pronatalist population policies in some Western European countries, *Population Research and Policy Review*, 1(2): 137–52.

Horney, K. (1926) The flight from womanhood, *International Journal of Psychoanalyis*, 7: 324–39.

Houseknecht, S.K. (1979) Reference group support for voluntarily childless wives, *Social Biology*, 23: 98–109.

Ireland, M. (1993) *Reconceiving Women: Separating Motherhood from Female Identity.* New York: Guildford Press.

Kestenberg, J.S. (1956) On the development of maternal feelings in early childhood, *The Psychoanalytic Study of the Child*, 11: 257–91.

Kohler Reissman, C. (2000) Stigma and everyday resistance practices: childless women in South India, *Gender and Society*, 14(1): 111–35.

Lacan, J. (1978) Four Fundamental Concepts of Psychoanalysis. New York: Norton.

Lampman, C. and Dowling-Guyer, S. (1995) Attitudes toward voluntary and involuntary childlessness, *Basic and Applied Social Psychology*, 17(1,2): 213–22.

Moroney, H.J. (1992) 'Who has the baby?' Nationalism, pronatalism and the construction of a 'demographic crisis' in Quebec 1960–1988. *Studies in Political Economy*, 32: 7–36.

Morrissette, H. and Spain, A. (1991) Vouloir demeurer sans enfant: recension critique des ecrits, *Canadian Journal of Counselling*, 25(4): 422–32.

Nelson, K.A. (1978) *Toward an analysis of pronatalism as informal social control.* Association for Humanist Sociology.

Parens, H., Pollock, L., Stern, J. and Kramer, S. (1976) On the girls's entry into the Oedipus complex, *Journal of the American Psychoanalytical Association*, 24: 79–107.

Peterson, R.A. (1980) Intended childlessness in late adolescence: personality and psychopathology, *Journal of Youth and Adolescence*, 9(5): 439–47.

Pines, D. (1993) *A Woman's Unconscious Use of Her Body.* London: Virago.

Raphael-Leff, J. (1997) 'The casket and the key': thoughts on creativity, gender and generative identity, in J. Raphael-Leff and R.J. Perelberg (eds) *Female Experience: Three Generations of British Women Psychoanalysts on Work with Women.* London: Routledge.

Sampaio, Y. and Daly, H.E. (1976) The population question in northeast Brazil: its economic and ideological dimensions: comment, *Economic Development and Cultural Change*, 24(2): 413–14.

Schwartz, D. (1995) Current psychoanalytic discourses on sexuality: tripping over the body, in T. Domenici and R. Lesser (eds) *Disorienting Sexuality.* London: Routledge.

Teicholz, J.G. (1977) A preliminary search for psychological correlates of voluntary childlessness in married women, *Dissertation Abstracts International*, 38: 1865-b.

Tyson, P. and Tyson, R.L. (1990) *Psychoanalytic Theories of Development: An Integration.* New Haven, CT: Yale University Press.

Veevers, J.E. (1973) Voluntary childlessness: a neglected area of family study, *Family Coordinator*, 22: 199–205.

Veevers, J.E. (1979) Voluntary childlessness: a review of issues and evidence, *Marriage and Family Review*, 2: 1–26.

Veevers, J.E. (1980) *Childless by Choice.* Toronto: Butterworths.

Winnicott, D.W. (1971) *Playing and Reality.* New York: Basic Books.

Woollett, A. (1991) Having children: accounts of childless women and women with reproductive problems, in Phoenix, A., Woollett, A. and Lloyd, E. (eds) *Motherhood: Meanings, Practices and Ideologies.* London: Sage.

9 Emotional experiences of becoming a mother

Joan Raphael-Leff

Mother *you* made him little
you started him
he was new to you
and you arched
the friendly world
over his new eyes
and shut out
the strange one.

(Rilke [1911] 1978: 37)

Mothers have long been addressed as above, from a child's point of view. In recent years, women speaking out in their own voices have raised awareness that maternity does not simply obey hormonal dictates, nor do women blindly follow unconscious desires or psychosocial interdictions in becoming mothers – there are difficult choices involved.

The need to further realistic understanding of the complexity of women's experiences is exacerbated by an internalized clash between cultural sentimentalization of 'Motherhood' which is in stark contrast to unconscious denigration of mothers. I argue that this denigration, both in society and in dark recesses of male and female psychic reality, is a defence rooted in a fundamentally *asymmetrical* dyadic relationship – not only in terms of a mother's omnipotent power over the child and their divergent needs, but because for him/her the mother is unique, while she may conceive another.

Contradictions and compromises

At the start of a new millennium, the eternal facts of life have altered dramatically. However, despite far-reaching reproductive and political changes, some crucial facts remain unaltered: childbearing still remains sole province – and childrearing mainly that – of women. Nevertheless, the changes that *have* occurred impel us to re-evaluate traditional psychosocial formulations that site maternity at the hub of a woman's identity. Furthermore, I suggest that in the course of the twentieth century, women's increased access to a range of lifestyle choices, to education, professional status and economic resources, have combined to expose some fundamental contradictions:

1 *For the species reproduction is a necessity. For women it is an option.* According to a 1992 survey only 13 per cent of women of childbearing age regard children as a prerequisite to feeling fulfilled (NCW 1992). The average family size in Britain has fallen to 1.73 children (ONS 1998). Studies indicate that some 12–20 per cent of women now choose *not* to reproduce at all (i.e. do not conceive, or to abort if they do) compared to 1 per cent 20 years ago (OPCS 1993). Furthermore, surveys suggest that nearly 50 per cent of conceptions that do occur are unplanned, with one-third of babies born to mothers under 16.

2 *Millennium woman's wishes, ambitions and desires may be discordant with her baby's needs*, which have changed very little over the last million years (as ethological and infant observations and attachment research findings demonstrate).[1] Educational parity encourages women to compete for high powered positions. Effective contraception, safe abortion, gamete transfer and latterly, egg freezing facilitate postponed procreation. Many women delay childbearing until their mid or late 30s when their careers are consolidated; increasingly mothers choose to return to rewarding jobs in the early months of their child's infancy, and a high proportion of babies under one year are in daycare.

3 On the other hand, socioeconomic and scientific advances spawn an *illusion of omnipotent control that may actually hinder choices.* A virtual industry of reproductive technologies has sprung up to counteract both male factors of declining sperm quality (probably due to unknown environmental factors), and purporting to reverse effects of infertility and reduce childbearing risks in older women. However, while fostering hope, these interventions also contribute to unrealistic expectations, dire disappointments and create unprecedented situations such as postmenopausal maternity, multiple births and genetic preselection. New forms of reproduction (such as surrogacy or sperm donation in heterosexual couples or egg swapping between lesbian partners) create *unexplored kinship connections* for parents and their children.

4 Seen from a feminist perspective, although granting choices to individual women, *medicalization of reproduction* introduces yet a further element of centralized (largely male) control over female fertility.

Means-related availability of treatment, preimplantation selection and antenatal screening adds a eugenic dimension. Furthermore, treatment procedures are themselves bizarre, painful, invasive, and expensive and time consuming. Some are potentially physically damaging; others have a poor research record and most an (unpublicized) very low success-rate – for instance only one in 13 cycles of IVF results in a live birth.

5 In non-traditional societies, those women who do go on to mother can no longer rely on unchanging transgenerational guidelines of support but are thrown back on their own *individual resources* – both external (familial and socioeconomic) and internal (conscious/unconscious representations). Finally, I argue that *the insulation and isolation* of ever contracting nuclear families has the paradoxical effect of leaving new mothers *unprepared for mothering* while fostering *an intense dyadic relationship* in which a woman is simultaneously both immensely powerful yet vulnerable to reactivation of her own infantile feelings at the very time of greatest demand on her adult capacities.

So, far from endorsing a view of mothering as 'normal', 'natural' and 'instinctive', I am suggesting here that today each woman's experience of maternity is *a compromise formation* between the many contradictions inherent in the maternal situation itself and the often conflicting facets of her own past, present and future aspirations. Similarly, childbearing revitalizes issues of *'generative identity'* (as I have termed it, Raphael-Leff 1995, 1997) and clashes between its manifestation in actual pro-creativity, as opposed to social, intellectual or artistically creative self-actualization. This aspect of her being too is fuelled by personal wishes, unconscious cross-generational forces and the urgent pull of her (fantasy or real) baby's unmet needs. Needless to say, all these permutations take place in the context of often ill-defined, but powerful sociocultural gender roles and local norms, family pressures, economic realities and the constrictions of her own unconscious defences. The latter largely centre on *regressive forces* which assail her from without in unremitting exposure to her needy infant, and from within, as revitalized pressure to re-enact primitive dynamics.

Generative identity

To begin again . . . As a little girl comes to make sexual distinctions in terms of reproductive capacities, like her male counterpart she has to give up being 'everything' and come to terms with the anatomical restrictions that dictate she can only reproduce in accordance with her sex – in the girl's case, to conceive, carry and breastfeed – but not to impregnate. Similarly, acquiring 'generative identity' means she has to accept that as a child she is incapable of childbearing, although in the future this may be an option. For some, the losses involved in such *differentiation* and *deferment* are richly compensated by a momentous shift – from being a parental 'creation' to seeing oneself as a potential creator – and not only of babies. Some realize that other than reproduction, their capacities need not be linked to anatomy, making the transition from the idea of bodily creations to those of the mind (Raphael-Leff 2000b). For others, mother-hood and creating a baby remains the peak of feminine achievement. For them, infertility feels shattering, preventing fulfilment of a lifelong dream. Pregnancy if it comes, seems a long awaited uniquely female blissful experience in which the woman feels finally able to produce her creation or receive the long awaited 'gift'. For others, for whom mothering is seen as but one role among many, unexpected infertility is a survivable blow, and pregnancy if it occurs, seems a somewhat disconcerting means to the end of having a baby.

Reproductive options

Today women can choose *whether* to reproduce, *when* (earlier menarche and postmenopausal pregnancies extend the span from 11 to 65 years), *how* (natural or assisted conception; gamete donation, surrogacy, etc.), *with whom* (singly, in other or same-sexed relationship), *where* (hospital, clinic, birthing centre, home, ocean-births, etc.) and decide about their own *mothering mode* (exclusive, shared-care, daycare, and so on). These decisions are not easy and while some reflect conscious thoughtfulness others are the result of inadvertent happenings or unconscious motivation.

Unconscious factors, including her internal relationship with her own archaic mother and immediate contingencies such as environmental conditions and local laws, sex, birth order and spacing, offspring quality, paternal commitment, available assistance, and other changeable factors, influence a mother's choices. These determine whether her baby will live or die; whether she will keep this child or have it adopted; whether she will mother exclusively or delegate care; whether she can allow herself to fall in love with her infant, or needs to create conditions to detach herself or even to spurn it.

In a heterosexual relationship pregnancy is a time when even the most egalitarian couple must acknowledge the power of essential differences between their bodies. It is the woman's body who carries the fetus, she who is nauseous, risking her physiological balance in an immunological battle between her own genetic contribution and the foreign half-body of her inseminatory partner. He may participate emotionally or detach himself; he may be kept ignorant of her pregnancy or aware yet excluded or may choose to remove himself from fathering. Ultimately, if the baby comes to be born it is due to the female power of retention, whether she herself is welcoming, ambivalent yet determined to go ahead or powerless to make choices about ending the pregnancy.

For most women, pregnancy revitalizes interchangeable identifications with both the mother of her own gestation and the fetus she is carrying as she herself was carried. Depending on her internal world pregnancy may be conceived of as a positive, even idealized mutual 'communion' or a more persecutory experience in which she feels at the mercy of her parasitic invader or sees him as endangered or deprived by her meagre resources.[2] Both these ideas might make her feel she has to erect emotional barriers between them, to protect herself from her inmate or him from her own inner badness, or that (projected) into the outside world. ('I panicked over the weekend – worried that the hand-cream I'd sampled would contaminate my baby', says an expectant mother).

Conscious expectations, aspirations and fantasy representations of the unborn baby, of the birth and parenting are coloured by these positive and/or negative experiences of *herself* in tandem with the other. A particularly painful experience may be the feeling of mutual incompatibility or even reciprocal destructiveness. Treated overintimately by strangers, one pregnant woman may revel in her luscious appearance; another resents it, feeling fat and ungainly. Anxious about being caught up in the throes of inexorable processes, some women may panic, feeling they lack the courage to proceed and have to take matters under their own control. Such decisions are not easy, however, and conscious ideas may be driven by unconscious forces. A resolution has to be found between current fears and fantasies, and expectations of the future. Some women require therapy to resolve these issues:

> Elizabeth is 40 and pregnant for the third time. On the previous two occasions she was unable to go through with the gestation, feeling invaded and in danger of her identity and life being taken over by the baby. On one level these feelings relate to fears that her highly successful professional career would be overshadowed by motherhood. On a less conscious register, these persecutory anxieties are reminiscent of her emotional experience as a young child; when ousted by two younger sisters in quick succession, she felt murderously jealous of the attention they received at her expense and resentful of her mother for bringing them into the world.
>
> Now she is in therapy and more aware of early sources of her feelings, the idea of the baby she dearly wishes to have acts as a

beacon despite the severe nausea and constant temptation to abort and rid herself of her internal tormentor. Although at times she has to be tethered to an intravenous infusion to counteract her anorexia, she carries to term. To her surprise, assisted by a nanny, she finds mothering a highly rewarding journey, although she is often wracked by thoughts of the other children she might have had and in therapy, pursues the deep antagonism to her mother and sisters which find expression in various ways.

Cathleen has a different experience:

Pregnant for the third time and panic stricken at the thought of having a baby, 40-year-old Cathleen consults me, intent on having an abortion despite being well into the fifth month. In a state of high agitation exacerbated by urgency she fears that if she allows the pregnancy to progress beyond the 24 week point of no return she will feel increasingly trapped and unable to find a way out other than suicide. The delay reflects her ambivalence. Although always hoping to be a mother, she has severe doubts about her own capacities to look after a baby, and worries that she has already damaged the fetus with large doses of antidepressants. Her Irish Catholic upbringing leaves her guilt ridden at the idea of abortion, but she equally believes it is unethical to bring a baby into a war-torn violent world. Needless to say, she herself experienced violence, witnessing through-out her childhood her alcoholic stepfather's physical attacks on her mother who was neither able to defend herself nor leave, given her large brood of kids and financial dependence on her partner as breadwinner. As a child Cathleen took comfort where it was offered, but is now haunted by intrusive thoughts and is anxious that she will pass on to her baby the incestuous sexual involvement she experienced with her brother. As in previous pregnancies, she is tormented by compulsive thoughts about harming the baby or being taken over by it. Sudden images of a little boy's genitalia flash through her mind's eye and knowing her baby is male, she fears she will find him attractive and be unable to bathe the child or change his nappy.

Along with several other women in her advanced condition, she goes through with the private abortion under 'hell-like' conditions, to find she is not relieved of her distress and has the added anguish of having 'killed off' her baby, and probably her last chance of motherhood. However, she feels determined to grasp the dearly bought emotional space to engage in therapy and resolve some of the unconscious factors that for so many years have obstructed her growth.

Maternal 'orientations'

Childbearing thus may be fraught with terrible choices. These are made not only on the basis of external events but dominated by the config-uration of a woman's internal world. Clearly, given the wide range of reactions, we cannot speak of 'women' as a singular category. Maternal aspirations formulated from childhood on manifest during pregnancy as idiosyncratic representations of herself as future mother to her fantasy baby, within the context of her life situation. These representations can be regarded as *the unprocessed unconscious co-product of her imagined or denied babyself with the idealized or denigrated maternal figures occupying her psychic reality*, which come to a head in the actual situation of mothering, influ-enced by many current life-events and circumstances.

When pregnancy proceeds, the idea of an optimal birth too is con-structed according to the internal world scenario: a leisurely 'natural' experience envisaged for a benign baby and trusted self; or a wished-for 'civilized' instrumental birth to control a potentially damaging baby and/or unruly dangerous aspect of the maternal body. Once born, such antenatal configurations may persist. The infant might be deemed a 'familiar' known from communion in the womb or a threatening alien or parasitic invader whose tendencies must be controlled; a caregiving saviour or magical 'reincarnation' of a past figure, or a new stranger that the woman has to come to know over a period of time (Raphael-Leff 1991a, 1991b, 2001).

Over the past few decades, breakdown of traditional childcare guidelines and growing social acceptability of individual choice mean that in the West, each woman/couple is likely to act in accordance with *personal beliefs and internal pressures*, as much as with the dictates of normative practices and demands of the external reality, such as the number and intervals between other children, economic necessity, career status, etc.

In my own research, I have found it possible to delineate three patterns of these chosen 'maternal orientations' in which various factors cluster to produce both distinct styles of mothering, and different precipitants of maternal distress (Raphael-Leff 1985a, 1985b, 1986).

One orientation is that of a Facilitator – the woman for whom mother-ing seems the culmination of her female identity. In her view, she, the biological mother is uniquely privileged, primed during pregnancy and through breastfeeding to intuitively decipher and meet the infant's needs.

Seeing herself as the munificent source necessitates her exclusive care and close proximity to her baby at all times so as to be ready to receive and interpret his communications. Therefore, she adapts her life totally to mothering, utilizing her identificatory capacities to gratify the infant's desires (and by association, vicariously gratifying her own).

This orientation is at variance with that of a Regulator one, where a woman treats mothering as one role among many in her life. She regards her main maternal task as 'socializing' the presocial infant, and therefore getting *him* to adapt to the social order. To this end she establishes a predictable routine which also enables her to share caregiving smoothly. Shared care is possible since in her view mothering is a skill rather than a 'vocation'. As she believes that the young baby does not differentiate between carers, she introduces her co-helpers early, hoping to expose her child to a range of relationships rather than one overweening one. Shared mothering also reduces exposure of the mother to the infant's primitive feelings, decreasing risk of arousal and depletion and the burden of sole accountability. The routine contributes to predictability in a potentially chaotic and disturbing situation. It also relieves the mother from having to identify with the infant to fathom his needs (as does the Facilitator), which alleviates the threat of recognizing aspects of her own infantile needs in the baby.

We can imagine, and indeed, longitudinal studies (Scher 1998) show that babies growing up in these various households have different experiences of negotiating the realms of feeding, sleep, proximity, separations etc. Similarly, for their mothers, the experience of immersion in a world that revolves around infantile needs differs too. Thus, a Facilitator who relishes the timeless time with her infant, may experience demands of a job, high powered or otherwise, to return to, or economic pressures to work, as a gross intrusion into the intimacy of her exclusive time with her baby, whereas a Regulator who lacks such employment, or whose social or economic circumstances do not enable her to share care, feels threatened by the enforced intimacy with a preverbal infant, and lack of adult stimulation. Boredom, alienation and a sense of lessened self-esteem may lead to postnatal distress in a Regulator. Equally, demands of other young children, a busy social schedule, distracting household chores and a non-supportive partner, may all contribute to a Facilitator's depression at not being free to devote herself entirely to her infant according to unconscious dictates of the ideal mother image she wishes to emulate (Raphael-Leff 1985b, 2000a, 2000b).

While these orientations work well for many mothers and babies, it is at their extremes that difficulties may arise. For instance, a facilitating mother may require constant positive affirmation of being the perfect provider to the point where her infant is not allowed to cry, withdraw or complain, or else in her need to indulge the child within her, she misinterprets the needs of her baby. Similarly, to curb frightening forces within herself, a mother may subject her regulated baby to too rigid a regime while treating him as a needy or 'wild' being in need of constant control. Underpinning these is an unconscious ascription to the baby of idealized or repudiated qualities of the woman's babyself and/or those of sibs, and emulation/competition between herself and her idealized or denigrated mother.

A third orientation is that of Reciprocators whereby rather than either mother or baby habitually adapting to the other, each incident is negotiated on its own terms. This complex pattern of interaction is rooted in empathy and mutual recognition of the baby as both similar in having human emotions yet different from herself in being an infant, rather than one based on enacted or denied primary identification. Inevitably, it also involves tolerance of uncertainty and acceptance of ambivalence, both in herself and in the baby.

Finally, a fourth response is a Bi-polar one where conflicting orientations vie with each other in the same mother towards the same baby. These may be unconscious reflections of differences between her own internalized parents, conflicts between stereotypical 'feminine' and 'masculine' facets of herself or more conscious ideological discrepancies, for instance between feminist and childcare ideals.

It is noteworthy that many mothers change their orientations with subsequent babies according to circumstances of conception, experience of pregnancy, labour and birth, and degree of emotional support available. The mother's orientation is also affected by the sex, number, ages of her other children and intervals between them, her experiences of mothering each of them, her own age, career aspirations, occupational status, financial situation and above all, the enduring 'climate' of her internal world and external provisions of emotional support at the time.

Critical reactivations

As each parent engages with unfolding developmental phases in their child's life, they relive the strengths and weaknesses of their own equivalent maturational experiences (Benedek 1959). Thus one mother may sail through breastfeeding while another finds it intensely persecuting. Eating disorders may be passed on down the line when these symbolically represent control over resources and intake. A facilitating parent who relishes the infant's 'symbiotic' connection may herself feel nurturing and well-nurtured while the infant is dependent, but sorely resents the baby's striving towards separateness, experiencing it as rejection. Reliving her own poorly negotiated separation, a woman may experience even his dozing or looking around during a feed as a betrayal. A Regulator mother may find the autonomous toddler more rewarding than the dependent baby, despite the need for vigilance. For yet other parents, one or both may find the critical phase comes with toilet training, as unresolved conflicts from their own childhood battlegrounds resurface. In some, it is the Oedipal period of intense possessiveness and poignant exclusion that retriggers jealousies and incestuous desires in the parent.

In turn through unconscious awareness, or conscious confrontations, these *developmental 'hot spots' are incorporated into each new baby's psychic experience*, to be perpetuated as the weak link in the new developmental chain, unless resolved therapeutically, through parent–infant therapy or later on in child, adolescent or adult work. Some parents find their weak points correspond to later stages of development – boisterous early school days or the taciturn or turbulent behaviours of adolescence, for example. For some, birth of the next child, issues of sibling rivalry, competitiveness and their own difficulties in relating to more than one child in the family may constitute the problematic areas. For those who are unable to tolerate the intensity or to face the mental pain aroused by these repetitions, perinatal, individual or family therapy can prove invaluable, exploring difficulties before these become entrenched in internalized and/or interpersonal patterns.

Despite hard-won achievements, an insecure parent's futility may be tapped during childbearing, endangering their sense of adult competence, thereby contributing to a nihilistic loss of life's rich meaning. This is particularly true of people who have been unable to resolve issues of early deprivation, chronic parental disapproval, emotional absence, childhood abuse or severe neglect. Social adversity, isolation and disempowerment may precipitate depression and low self-esteem, particularly if the new mother lacks an adult confidante who can affirm her worth (Brown *et al.* 1993). This has now been found to be true of fathers as well.

When external circumstances of deprivation, isolation, poverty, inexperience, disenfranchisement and lack of adult gratification are mirrored by a paucity of inner resources, the breakdown of internal structures may result in sadistic control or perverse behaviours ranging from incestuous abuse through subtle manifestations of Munchausen by proxy to overt violence and filicide. Confronted by a baby who represents a repudiated split-off needy or greedy part of her/himself, unless a desperate caregiver can get away from a depleting situation regarded as mutually oppressive, s/he may be tempted to resort to force, to make this 'bad' baby good – or, overcome by guilt at minor incidents of failure or incompetence may even attempt suicide to kill off the internal 'bad' baby-self, or critical parent within.

Other psychopathologies, more subtle in their transmission, are equally dependent on confluence of intrapsychic and interpersonal factors. A forensic expert predicted (on the basis of my model of maternal orientations) that extreme Facilitator mothers who prolong exclusive symbiotic intimacy beyond its adaptive phase would be more prone to bring up transvestite, fetishistic or transsexual boys, whereas Regulator mothers, for whom the baby represents a repudiated 'bad' aspect of the self, would resort to physical battering (Welldon 1988). Another way of looking at this might be a facilitating mother's difficulty in drawing boundaries between herself and the child, who is viewed as an extension of herself (and therefore, her inability to recognize and reflect back the baby as a subject with different perceptions and experiences to her own), and a regulating mother's experience of her child as the embodiment of a split-off aspect of herself she has to negate.

Close encounters

We may wonder at the intensity of feelings in parents. I suggest that in the early postnatal days and weeks, close encounter with a new infant is a highly arousing experience. Rushes of cosy warmth and calm peaceful-ness often oscillate with moments of high anxiety provoked by exposure to wordless distress and acute neediness. Unmediated contact with primal substances such as vernix, amnion, lochia, milk, urine, faeces, mucus and vomit plunge a new parent into inchoate preverbal flashbacks of her own infancy, retriggering early fantasies, poignant yearnings for nurture and merger and/or persecutory experiences of feeling mothered and unmothered.

Although any carer is threatened by the infectiousness of primitive feelings, a newborn does have a particular impact on the biological mother. She feels that in appearance and behaviour, the baby who has come out of her body shows the world what she is capable of producing for better or worse. Conversely, the child who has been inside her may seem to know everything about her, all her hidden resources and vices from the inside out. If she feeds the baby with the fluids of her own body, not only is she on permanent call, leaking milk through her clothes to the tune of his whims, but the quality of her nurturing is starkly evident to everyone, in the baby's weight, complexion and level of contentment. Some women are appalled by the baby's hunger, feeling 'cannibalized' by sucking or disconcerted by the erotic intimacy of breastfeeding; while others welcome the warm sensuality, revelling vicariously in luscious bodily care. A deprived woman may envy her baby the care her partner, or indeed she herself, lavishes upon the child. Another abhors the infant identified with the demanding baby she imagines herself to have been. The child may seem critical of her innermost feelings and resources and every whimper may be interpreted as a complaint or critical accusation of insufficiency.

Whereas positive recognition of the baby forms the basis of compassionate empathy, when repudiated aspects of the mother's own babyhood are denied and invested in the infant, he or she may seem to become dangerous and in need of control. The baby may threaten to expose her neediness or incompetence, or draw her into awareness of her own infantile weaknesses. He is in a powerful position to attack her self-esteem – by making her feel incompetent in meeting his needs, or simply being a bad 'product'. He may show her up in public by being greedy, messy or ferocious or 'prove' her a 'bad' mother by wailing inconsolably when the neighbours can hear or making her scream at him in the supermarket.

Incommunicable distress

These feelings can be disturbing, particularly when there is no one with whom to talk them over. A new mother in the West is often deprived of a community of supportive women. Devoid of practical assistance, female lore, mothering tips and a sense of belonging at this period of her greatest need, a woman may have to resort to hiring someone to provide it. However, for many a mother this is not possible, yet the baby she is handed to take home from hospital as her sole responsibility is the first newborn she has ever seen. Unlike previous generations of large families, or traditional groups of extended kinship where young girls care for siblings or cousins, or the Caribbean-type female camaraderie around a 'yard', most contemporary new mothers have had little direct experience of babycare. I argue that this also means there have been *few opportunities to digest, replay and work through passive infantile feelings as an active agent.*

For inexperienced new parents, as caregiving days blend with disturbed nights, the shapeless round of primary needs with its evocation of archaic physical memories and undigested preverbal feelings may feel overwhelming, even when shared. Many new mothers live some distance from their families. About a third mother without a partner, and those who have one do not necessarily find that joint parenting means shared care, and many, particularly younger women, lack financial savings to pay for additional caregiving help. Increasingly, women face on their own simultaneous emotional demands of maternal responsibility and reactivated infantile cravings.

Most new mothers are unprepared for the helter-skelter world of fluctuating identifications with both infant and her own powerful archaic mother, at times hauntingly revisited by the troubling spectres of 'ghosts in the nursery', as one outreach programme for mothers in distress has called emotional visitations from past experiences (Fraiberg 1980). What are these feelings that return to torment a new parent? I suggest they are *unprocessed residues* of early interaction with their own primary caregivers (and siblings, see Cathleen) in which, through unconscious reception of affective communications, the child's generative identity was formed.

Intersubjective constitution of the self

What enables a parent to dedicate themselves to meeting the needs of their child has been a subject of psychoanalytic debate. Freud (1914) regarded parenting as a function of the mother and father's investment in the child as representative of their own narcissistic desires. Seemingly, identification with the baby grants the parent vicarious satisfaction of their own infantile needs. However a balance must be achieved between indulging these needs and acting as the baby's 'auxiliary ego'. This is epitomized in Bion's (1962) description of the way a mother's 'reverie' enables her to serve as 'container' for the baby's anxieties. Receiving these wordless experiences, if she can thoughtfully metabolize them for the infant and return them in a 'detoxified' form, the child gradually internalizes her capacity to contain and understand his thoughts, thereby creating an internal space in which he can think for himself.

Winnicott elaborated on this theme of formation of the infant's psyche through an intersubjective relationship. He described the mother's face as the baby's mirror, wherein he (or she) reads her love and his own loveability (Winnicott 1971). The sensitive carer's attunement to, and empathetic 'mirroring' of the baby's emotional experiences affirms these, thus sensitizing a preverbal child to his own internal states. However, a mother is not merely a mirror. Thrust into a mothering situation her facial expression also reflects her own internal experiences, her unconscious preoccupations and the expectations through which her responses to the baby's emotions are filtered. The mother's investment of extraneous fantasies may induce the child to develop what Winnicott (1960) called a 'false self'.

Internalizing her ascriptions, the child's psychic configuration and self-image then becomes a co-product of the mother's own unconscious. Her imagined or denied babyself may be projected onto the child, and as well as these wild, hungry, messy or hurt memories in feeling there may be reactions to her own idealized or denigrated internalized imagos, and their imagined reactions to her. In addition she may unconsciously compel the baby to actualize her need for him to be witness, saviour, lover, scapegoat or persecutor, angel or monster, punished substitute for a hated sibling or idealized replacement for a lost love . . . Finally, in her intimate interaction with the infant, she may transmit unbearable scenarios of which she herself is unaware unconsciously absorbed from her own caregivers in the course of her childhood (Balint 1990), now unwittingly passed on to her own infant.

Psychoanalytic theory has largely focused on the effect of the mother on the baby. A mother currently troubled by her own early feelings is to a lesser or greater degree unavailable to be a fully participating companion in the mutual exchange with her baby. Too preoccupied with her own to help her baby 'metabolize' his feelings, she also creates a complex charged atmosphere the preverbal infant is unable to process. I suggest that the child internalizes a transgenerational imago composed of a representation of himself in the mind of the carer, coupled with *her* own unconscious view of herself as both adult of the baby she imagines she was, cared for or deprived by her own archaic mother.

However, the baby also impacts on the mother, revitalizing tender or painful aspects of her own infantile experience and early self-representations. I stress here that *each generation of parents suffers a revival of powerful infantile feelings*. A parent may succumb to deep emotion, or feeling threatened and potentially overwhelmed by depression or rage, may find protection through manic disavowal leading to distortions in the primary interaction. The spectrum of distress is broad and its effects varied. In short, *when early disturbance remains unprocessed into adulthood, it is compelled to be reactivated during early parenthood.*

Clinical experience with sons and daughters shows it is not enough for a carer to 'survive' the child's attacks, anxieties and tantrums. For such survival to be meaningful, it must be conveyed that one has *heard* and *understood* the distress rather than merely tolerated or deflected it. A disturbed parent, whether hypersensitive or insensitive, is unable to grant such understanding. *Lacking this means of processing, the child may repress traumatic events or unresolved chronic issues.* As Attachment theory demonstrates, in a rejecting, dismissive, controlling or inconsistent atmosphere, defensive stances of flight, fight, freeze or confusion reflect habitual patterns of dealing with insecurity within the primal exchange. This is very different from a benign and respectful relationship where a child feels at ease to explore the wider world with confidence, secure in the reliability and protective wisdom of the caregiver.

Gendering the engendered offspring

Despite the power of reproductive control offered by new technology, the human mother lacks the natural power of some rodents to reabsorb an endangered embryo, or activate at will a dormant fertilized egg like the kangaroo. She does not possess the extraordinary ability of wasp mothers, or fish, turtles and alligators, to literally predetermine the sex of each offspring by alteration of sex chromosomes in accordance with environmental conditions. Nor does she usually have the intuitive knowledge of fetal sex and the capacity for spontaneous abortion of wrong sexed litters of some small mammals (like the coypu), or even the capacity for selective gestation of some of our cousin primates (see Hrdy 1999).

However, even in the absence of such drastic measures, the human mother retains a powerful capacity to influence the unconscious gender of their offspring. 'I am talking to a girl' says the psychoanalyst Winnicott to his middle aged male patient, who for 20 years has lain on the couch resisting psychic change 'I know you are a man, but I am talking to a girl . . . I must be mad'. His dramatic interpretation finally reaches the unreachable feminine aspect of this man, the psychic product of his primal mother's powerful projections which hitherto had not been addressed (Winnicott 1966).

In addition to such unconscious mechanisms, a human mother has thinking power to make 'tradeoffs . . . in a world of constantly shifting constraints and options' as Darwinist Hrdy argues (1999: 376). These conscious decisions must juggle socioeconomic subsistence, bodily toll of pregnancy and lactation, emotional requirements of her various loved ones and her own future reproductive prospects.

Today, even before the baby is born a pregnant woman makes crucial decisions in order to ensure her inherent family constellation at the right time for her individual aspirations and demands of her specific sociocultural milieu. Tacitly, routine sonography and antenatal diagnostic tests such as amniocentesis or chorionic villus sampling (CVS) are used to determine not only whether the time is right to reproduce but *which fetus is worth retaining*, raising complex ethical dilemmas. The criteria is usually one of normality but such screening procedures may have other functions; in India, when examined, over 98 per cent of fetuses aborted following ultrasound were found to be female, and in many other places sex-selective abortions are practised despite prohibitions. Political directives and sociocultural expectations interact with individual desires – selective female infanticide in China rose dramatically with the one child per family law. Neonaticide has been made illegal there since a 1991 census found an absence of 1.2 million female babies, presumably aborted, killed or abandoned at birth. Finally, research indicates that maternal interaction differs with male and female babies. Findings differ cross-culturally, but in industrial societies it seems boys are treated more physically, while girls receive more close affectionate contact and talking. The consistent finding is that carers identify more closely with same-sex infants, and since most primary caregivers have been female, daughters have been exposed to greater emotional relatedness than sons (Chodorow 1994).

Clearly, given accessibility of reproductive measures such as effective contraception, safe abortion and new reproductive technologies, each western child is here due to the mercy of a woman – not only the caregiver who accommodated her self-interests to those of the child, but the woman who tolerated that flesh to grow within hers and sustained life rather than abort it from within her fertile womb. These may no longer be one and the same woman. We now distinguish between various facets of maternity – an ovarian mother who provides the egg, a uterine mother who incubates the baby to term, a postnatal mother who may herself suckle and/or care for the baby or appoint someone else to do so on her behalf. Paradoxically, since the 1960s, changes to the eternal reproductive facts – earlier menstruation, readily available contraception, ever younger and socially sanctioned motherhood; donated gametes and postmenopausal conceptions; multiple births due to ovarian hyper-stimulation; same-sex parents; twins born years apart – mean greater complexity of this decision-making process.

Postnatal disturbance

Complexity means that some people grow up to find the challenge of early parenthood too disturbing. According to a variety of surveys and studies, almost half of all new mothers experience some form of postnatal disturbance, with some 13–20 per cent suffering severe depression (O'Hara and Swain 1996). Distress is increased by the sense of responsibility to provide for a needy and vulnerable baby at the very time the mother herself is feeling so incapacitated and needy. I have suggested that for many mothers postnatal distress is further aggravated by awareness of the discrepancy between the intensity of current feelings and the kind of mother she had wanted to be (Raphael-Leff 1985b).

Feeling trapped and devoid of a sense of adult resourcefulness, a troubled parent may feel unable to provide for the baby. Depleted and inadequate to the enormity of the task, a mother may feel displaced and emptied by the loss of her baby from inside her and overwhelmed by flooding with her own baby-like feelings. Unable to even get out of bed, she may succumb to these, becoming baby-like in her own dependence. Others, fathers included, may be up and about, but fearful of using their initiative and drained of agency by investing so much energy into maintaining defences against recognition of their own infantile weaknesses. A parent may resentfully deny the baby love, experiencing the child as source of all their troubles ('Everything was fine; I was so strong until this baby came along'), or if identified with him, may blame parental deficits on the mothering she/he received and failures within the original infantile situation ('I can't give this baby my attention – my mother gave me none because she couldn't think of anyone but herself'). A further twist may be a mother who envies the baby the good nurturing she herself provides.

Manifestation of emotional distress varies according to each person's own internal configurations. Expressions may manifest as *denial*, indifference and/or a defensively detached inability to feel; *idealization* with inevitable disillusionment leading either to *depression* with self-reproaches, guilt and recriminations possibly resulting in suicide ('Poor baby. I wanted it to be so perfect. When he wails I feel so useless he'd be better off without me'); or persistent feelings of disappointment and helpless victimization ('I always imagined I would be transformed by having a baby to love only me but instead she just seems to make demands on ME to give her stuff'). Persistent *persecutory feelings* may lead to phobic flight or aggression as an outlet for frustration (which in extreme cases may lead to violent abuse, or even infanticide). Another may experience disturbing *compulsive thoughts* seemingly coming from 'out of the blue' ('Hard to admit this but I've stopped myself going onto the balcony because I keep getting this mad impulse to drop him over the railings') and/or *obsessional counter-measures* against perceiving one's own ambivalence ('I feel that if I disrupt the routine ever so slightly all hell will break loose').

Working mothers

The conflict between the desire to be the best parent for the baby and to pursue one's own life no doubt further contributes to the high incidence of postnatal depression among western mothers, and in some cases, fathers too (Ballard and Davies 1996) during the first two or three years of a child's life. Nowhere is the discordance of needs between modern mother and 'primitive' baby clearer than in the unavoidable clash experienced by many working mothers juggling requirements of mental concentration, emotional space and/or geographical distance necessary to promote both occupational interests and demands of their maternal ideal. *Raised female hopes of social and economic equality are at variance with unrealistic social and personal expectations of women as primary carers and cultural denigration of motherhood and mothers.* Women today, like their male counterparts, have grown up with educational expectations not only of 'job satisfaction' but a rewarding experience of adult self-expression through work.

Mothers in the workforce clearly demonstrate the gendered nature of the workplace, which expects women in the public sphere to perform their work tasks as efficiently as men, if not more so, with no regard for the fact that many are caught in an ambiguous situation of holding two other jobs, that of supportive partner and mother, simultaneously in the domestic sphere.

However, employment has different meanings. I suggest that distress when it occurs is differentially triggered according to parental orientation. For instance, depression may result from lack of satisfying employment for Regulators, and the necessity to work for Facilitators (Raphael-Leff 1985a). While most Facilitators feel content to spent the first years of each child's life in continuous and exclusive childcare, some are forced by financial or professional circumstances to return to work against their will. Conversely, many Regulators feel the need for adult stimulation and the sense of personal competence provided by their own occupation, but some have no jobs to return to or lack the means to pay for childcare in their absence.

There are few societies that provide for the specifically intensive and varied needs of both infant and parents during this early period. Scandinavian countries are the rare exceptions, going far beyond the token paternity leave provided elsewhere. They offer 18 month fully paid leave which the parents can share between them in any form they see fit. As this personal letter from a mother a small town in Norway reports about life with the 6-month-old baby:

> Vetle has just gone to sleep. He has a slight touch of fever today. Maybe he caught it playing with A [his older cousin]. But he is in very good shape; eating well and seems to be in a good mood. And he is just the sweetest little boy on earth!!!!! I realize now that it is impossible to describe the love you feel for your child to friends without children. I remember my sister tried to explain it for me after A was born, and of course I believed her, but I realize now that you just have to experience it yourself to fully comprehend it. Both my partner and I feel that Vetle has changed our lives completely. And all the warnings about how busy everything is with a child, how limited your life becomes etc., they are not true!!! His big smile in the mornings is better than the freedom to go to the pub whenever you want. And we have discovered that it is easy to bring Vetle, not everywhere, but to a lot of places. So life is really good these days.
>
> Our work arrangement works out very well. I miss him when I go to work, but I also feel that it is nice to be at work and feel that I am still in touch with my profession. Knowing that his father is taking care of Vetle makes it so much easier. And I have my own time with him when his dad is at his work in the evenings. And we

have weekends and holidays together. In fact, our trip to Thailand is booked for the 14th of March and we are very much looking forward to it. We have been allocated seats on the plane and Vetle has been given some kind of a crib to sleep in. Both flights are in the night, so I was very happy to hear that he could sleep in a bed. I would very much like to hear other people's experiences of travelling with children! Now I am going to make myself some food and relax a few hours before bedtime. It's great to read for pleasure again. By the way, my exams went very well, that was a really nice surprise!

In most western societies, a working mother often occupies a no win situation (Forna 1998). Caught between conflicting societal pressures to further her self-fulfilling career and achieve economic independence on the one hand and a guilt-provoking accountability that blames her (not the working father) for all the child's current and future ills on the other, there are few provisions for women to both work and yet feel the emotional needs of her infant are fully met. A high incidence of single and divorced mothers means that many women lacking a co-carer carry this ethical burden on their own.

Discordant needs

The issue itself is not new. Mothers have always worked. However, in the distant past and today in traditional societies, mothers can use their ingenuity to care for their infants while they do routine work, meeting the child's need for close bodily proximity, enjoyable continuity of playful care and accessible breastfeeding. This is possible if the baby is in a sling or loosely strapped to the mother's back as she gathers berries, plants crops, tends cattle, weaves, threshes wheat, washes clothes or does other mundane work. Under less flexible conditions, as in other species as well, when a mother's work necessitates leaving her baby, maternal substitutes, usually another lactating female, care for the young while she is away (Hrdy 1999).

Relegating an infant to the care of another while the mother works is by no means unusual or confined to humans. What is new is that with the invention of pasteurized milk, the feeding bottle and breast pump, wet-nursing, recorded since biblical times, is no longer a necessity. Modern day options eliminate the desperate measures of mothers in fifteenth to nineteenth-century Europe where due to discordant lifestyles, economic necessity or beliefs about the weak quality of urban women's milk, the babies of millions of artisans as well as aristocrats were sent to country wet-nurses or foundling homes, culminating in situations like that of nineteenth-century Paris where only 5 per cent of babies were breastfed by their own mothers (Badinter 1981) and due to shortage of wet-nurses, in some places two-thirds died before their first birthday. Ironically, many of these wet-nurses, like South African nannies under Apartheid, were working mothers themselves, forced to neglect their own infants while using their bodies for profit.

Increasingly, the clash of maternal/offspring interests is not just a feature of the northern hemisphere. In Southern and West Africa over 40 per cent of weaned children are fostered some distance away with relatives who can provide stability and conditions of care working parents cannot. In highly industrialized societies such as Hong Kong, many babies live in residential nurseries during weekdays to accommodate the long hours of working parents. In the absence of close, reliable family networks, despite North American women's reproductive autonomy, in 1995 according to the National Centre for Education Statistics (1998) 45 per cent of infants less than a year old were in some kind of daycare. Similarly, in Britain in 1981 fewer than one in five women with a child under a year old were working; but by 1998 50 per cent of them in the UK were in some form of employment (Browne 1998).

The market laws remain patriarchal and to accommodate their children's needs, the majority of part-time workers are women, and despite equal pay policies, they remain underpaid. In addition, 9 out of 10 lone mothers are on income support or working fewer than 16 hours per week (Utting 1995) meaning they and their babies endure poverty-stricken restrictions. Novel governmental childcare strategies (including paying grandmothers) are insufficient to meet the need, and unless a woman has one-to-one care, nor does the new trend for working at home solve the problem. The more intellectually engaging or economically urgent the task, the more a weary mother torn between job deadlines and a housebound toddler's need to interact and play may spend his precious waking hours willing her lively youngster back to sleep. Taking the baby to her office poses a different set of problems, and particularly in highly competitive male-dominated professions, such as law, the mother may be criticized or even ostracized for her 'unprofessional' stance. It is particularly hurtful when women colleagues appear critical, as female solidarity, empathic companionship and acknowledgement of the juggling feats involved go some way to compensate for hardships. Few workplaces provide crèches and childcare expenses often swallow up any financial gains a woman makes from working. Yet, the work ethos prevails as women strive to meet the demands of their parallel jobs. Working mothers of older children too continue to feel the tug-of-war between their own considerable occupational interests, household maintenance demands and the desire to be emotionally and physically there for their growing children, both to meet increasingly sophisticated ongoing needs related to homework or social processing, and to be available to participate in unscheduled events – whether illness, outings, sports days or concerts.

Power of the past

To conclude, I am suggesting that the complex experience of being a mother is saturated with emotional pitfalls.

> 'I'm ravaged by self-pity', says an insightful woman in therapy 'I must get on with living but am always preoccupied with my old family story. Miraculously, I have this gorgeous baby who seems to enjoy life with such gusto despite my having no direct role model for creating a happy busy childhood. I was bored, always hanging around, waiting for my mother, wanting her to remember me . . . But I'm not ill or poor, not in prison; got a happy marriage and a pleasant home – so why can't I shake off my grievances? I desperately want to be fully here for *my* baby but feel depressed and sluggish, trapped in the past.'

Breakdown of traditional childcare guidelines, medicalization of reproduction, dispersal of family support network, contradictory sentimentalized yet subtly denigrated cultural depictions of mothers and unrealistic socio-economic provisions all create discordant external pressures on a western mother. In addition, under the regressive pull of postnatal interaction with her baby, revitalized infantile forces threaten to overwhelm her internally. In the ensuing struggle conflicts may be *enacted* with the new baby roped into replaying unresolved scenarios with the mother's archaic caregivers and bearing the brunt of her emotional reaction to current stressors. The prime instrument in shaping the new baby's self-image and psychosexual body is thus forged both out of sociocultural forces and of the internalized stuff of a previous generation's unconscious representations.

Finally, I argue that both the power of such transmissions and the wherewithal to break them lies in our human capacity to reflect. By *processing* complex feelings we can digest, modify and utilize past and present experience in a way that allows *new* developments to occur. For many women, the arousing experience of mothering a baby provides a vital momentum to restructure psychic reality and transform restrictive self/other demands. For those unable to do so without help, psychotherapy offers emotional containment and a safe space for thoughtful reflection. Ultimately, the aim is to maximise the capacity to integrate internal and external expectations in a meaningful way. Compassion for her baby, for herself and for her own caregivers fosters the generosity of spirit required to enjoy mothering, enabling a woman to tolerate uncertainty and find creative ways of balancing her own aspirations with those of multiple interdependants.

Notes

1 We may wonder whether even in our distant past, the idealized psychoanalytic view of identity of needs between mother and infant ever was realistic. My own weekly observations of three mother–baby orang-utang pairs over a 30-month period disclosed not only many similarities, but also highlighted the discrepancy between a self-clinging mobile young primate in a close-knit foraging group and the magnitude of dependence of the human infant on the primary caregiver for access to all resources, be they nutritional, stimulatory or comforting.
2 To avoid pronominal confusion with the mother, I refer to the baby as 'he' but unless otherwise specified this applies to both sexes.

References

Badinter, E. (1981) *The Myth of Motherhood: A Historical View of the Maternal Instinct*. London: Souvenir Press.

Balint, E. (1990) Unconscious communication, in J. Mitchell and M. Parsons (eds) *Before I was I – Psychoanalysis and the Imagination*. London: Free Association Press.

Ballard, C. and Davies, R. (1996) Postnatal depression in fathers, *International Review of Psychiatry*, 8: 65–71.

Benedek, T. (1959) Parenthood as a developmental phase, *Journal of the American Psychoanalytical Association*, 7: 379–417.

Bion, W.R. (1962) A theory of thinking, *International Journal of Psycho-Analysis*, 43: 306–10.

Brown, G.W., Harris, T.O. and Eales, M.J. (1993) Aetiology of anxiety and depressive disorders in an inner-city population. 1.Early adversity. *Psychological Medicine*, 23: 143–54.

Browne, A. (1998) A bonnet for the baby: why new mothers are hurrying back into the labourforce, *Observer*, Business Section, 19 July.

Chodorow, N. (1994) *Feminities, Masculinities, Sexualities – Freud and Beyond*. London: Free Association Press.

Forna, A. (1998) *Mother of all Myths – How Society Moulds and Constrains Mothers*. London: Harper Collins.

Fraiberg, S. (1980) *Clinical Studies in Infant Mental Health: The First Year of Life*. London: Tavistock.

Freud, S. (1914) *On Narcissism: an Introduction*, Vol. 14, Standard Edition. London: Hogarth Press.

Hrdy, S.B. (1999) *Mother Nature – Natural Selection and the Female of the Species.* London: Chatto & Windus.

National Center for Education Statistics (1998) *Daycare Statistics 1995.* Washington, DC: National Centre for Education Statistics.

National Council of Women of Great Britain (NCW) (1992) *Superwoman Keeps Going: Understanding the Female Web, a Survey of Women's Lives and Expectations.* London: National Council of Women of Great Britain.

Office for National Statistics (ONS) (1998) *Birth Statistics for 1997 for England and Wales.* London: HMSO.

Office for Population Censuses and Surveys (OPCS) (1993) *Population Trends.* London: Office for Population Censuses and Surveys.

O'Hara, M.W. and Swain, A.M. (1996) Rates and risk of postpartum depression a meta-analysis, *International Review of Psychiatry*, 8: 37–54.

Raphael-Leff, J. (1985a) Facilitators and Regulators: vulnerability to postnatal distress, *Journal of Psychosomatic Obstetrics and Gynaecology*, 4: 151–68.

Raphael-Leff, J. (1985b) Facilitators and Regulators, Participators and Renouncers: mothers' and fathers' orientations towards pregnancy and parenthood, *Journal of Psychosomatic Obstetrics and Gynaecology*, 4: 169–84.

Raphael-Leff, J. (1986) Facilitators and Regulators: conscious and unconscious processes in pregnancy and early motherhood, *British Journal of Medical Psychology*, 59: 43–55.

Raphael-Leff, J. (1991a) *Psychological Processes of Childbearing.* London: Chapman and Hall.

Raphael-Leff, J. (1991b) The mother as container: placental process and inner space, *Feminism and Psychology*, 1: 393–408.

Raphael-Leff, J. (1995) Imaginative bodies of childbearing: visions and revisions, in A. Erskine and D. Judd (eds) *The Imaginative Body – Psychodynamic Therapy in Healthcare.* London: Whurr.

Raphael-Leff, J. (1997) The casket and the key: thoughts on gender and generativity, in J. Raphael-Leff and R. Jozef Perelberg (eds) *Female Experience: Three Generations of British Female Psychoanalysts on Work with Women.* London: Routledge.

Raphael-Leff, J. (2000a) 'Climbing the walls': puerperal disturbance and perinatal therapy, in J. Raphael-Leff (ed.) *Spilt Milk – Perinatal Breakdown and Loss.* London: Institute of Psychoanalysis.

Raphael-Leff, J. (2000b) Behind the shut door: a psychoanalytic perspective, in D. Singer and M. Hunter (eds) *Premature Menopause – A Multidisciplinary Approach.* London: Whurr.

Raphael-Leff, J. (2001) *Pregnancy – The Inside Story.* London: Karnac.

Rilke, R.M. ([1911] 1978) Third elegy, *Duino Elegies*, trans. by D. Young. New York: Norton.

Scher, A. (1998) A longitudinal study of night waking in the first year, *Child: Care, Health and Development*, 17: 295–302.

Utting, D. (1995) *Family and Parenthood: Supporting Families, Preventing Breakdown.* New York: Rowntree Foundation.

Welldon, E. (1988) *Mother, Madonna, Whore: The Idealization and Denigration of Motherhood.* London: Free Association Books.

Winnicott, D.W. (1960) Ego distortion in terms of true and false self, in *Maturational Processes and the Facilitating Environment*. New York: International University Press.
Winnicott, D.W. (1966) Creativity and its origins, in C. Zanardi (ed.) *Essential Papers on the Psychology of Women*. New York: New York University Press.
Winnicott, D.W. (1971) Mirror-role of mother and family in child development, in *Playing and Reality*. London: Basic Books.

10 'An awfully big adventure': ageing, identity and gender[1]

June Blythe Ellis

To think about women and identity in modern British society raises the issue of personal authority. How can a woman find her own authority, be her own 'author', in a patriarchal society? If we go further, and seek to factor in ageing in a culture where to grow old is regarded as a solecism, then it becomes even more problematic. Whatever the difficulties of being a woman in this society, it is harder still to be an older woman; the experience of an ageing body, the devaluation associated with gender, and the stigmatization of age, make a powerful conjunction.

Ageing, identity, and gender can be looked at in a multiplicity of ways that bring with them enhanced possibilities for choice. However, the hierarchical nature of modern British society, with its extreme differences in wealth and opportunity, means that for many women developing a personal identity which involves a sense of agency and goes beyond what is culturally ascribed may seem an impossible luxury, if not a completely irrelevant idea. Nevertheless, choices about personal identity are possible to a greater extent than is recognized, and later life can offer unique opportunities for self-discovery.

We can do no more than sample the range of subtle and intertwining influences at play. While acknowledging and emphasizing the commonalities of women's experience, for instance marginalization and relative lack of power, there are also crucial differences that enter into the shaping of women's social and personal worlds. In writing as I do, inevitably, from a limited viewpoint (white, privileged, heterosexual, Eurocentric) I cannot do justice to the diversity that exists. I can, for instance, do no more than acknowledge the experiences of lesbian women though I suspect there is much to be learnt in relation to the issues we shall be uncovering. This is so in relation to skin colour, ethnicity, sexuality, class, disability, and issues of social exclusion. It would be desirable, though not possible here, to hear the voices of women who can speak from their own lives and, in a brief chapter such as this, there is a danger that differences may be touched on in a way that accords them the status of interesting variations from some central norm and denies their own authenticity.

Ageing

What generally comes to mind with the word 'ageing' is a biological process. To age is to grow older and eventually to grow old. Humans, like other living organisms, show a decline in functional capacity over time, and degenerative processes eventually result in the death of the organism. The importance of this physical substrate to human life will not be underplayed in considering identity, but since human beings are also thinking creatures who inhabit complex social and psychological worlds, the experience of ageing is not, as for animals, determined by physiological processes alone.

Old age as a social category is culturally defined. In British society, signs of ageing are taken as a reference point for a whole range of social ascriptions which not only reflect the intricacies of modern life but carry with them the predominantly negative emotional connotations attached to the shameful state of *not being young*. There is evidence, too, that evaluations of ageing women are more negative than those of ageing men (Itzin 1986).

This stigmatization of older people differs from what tends to be found in less industrialized societies, where increasing limitations of the body are compensated for by greater deference and respect for the status of 'elder' and his or her accrued wisdom. It is an irony that in the West, where ideas of individualism are cherished, the stereotyping of 'the old' is so pronounced. There has been a movement in Britain and in other western countries, in the last hundred years or so, away from regarding ageing as a natural process and towards a perception of it as a specific, age-defined period in life. This is in contrast to less developed countries; for instance, research in Bosnia and Herzegovina has shown that, 'ageing does not commence at a fixed age but is identified by lack of vigour, relating to both physical and mental capacity, and lack of ability to participate in valued activities in the community' (Vincent and Mudrovcic 1993).

The overall neglect of ageing in this society is reflected in psychological theory where the variable of age has been largely ignored for both men and women. What has been amply demonstrated as I have searched for sources for this chapter is the virtual invisibility of ageing as a referenced topic in psychotherapy texts and in developmental psychology – the effect of Freud's emphasis on the primacy of the early years has cast a long shadow. Not only this, Freud's position on later life was unflinch-ingly sombre, with nothing to hope for. Life was a struggle against ever greater odds and all that is left is to meet the end with stoicism, a quality that Freud himself evinced in his later life and painful death.

Despite the failure to accord later life stages a defining logic of their own, there is much that is useful in psychoanalytic thought when we confront ageing. The losses that are an inevitable part of getting older can seem to arise in squadrons to persecute and tip us into the over-whelming anxiety that is at the heart of psychoanalysis. Defensive strat-egies that have been characterized as responses to anxiety can and do come into play: repression, fixation, reaction formation, regression. Denial of mortality tempts us all, and it could be argued that we are in denial as a society; we are caught up in reactions that bypass reflection and keep anxiety momentarily at bay. Defences can and do afford neces-sary protection for an ego threatened by anxiety but they falsify and distort, and to the extent that there is heavy reliance on them in avoid-ance of the separation anxiety that is part of losing a younger, familiar self, they block out what is new and what may be creative.

Like Freud, Melanie Klein emphasizes the early years (indeed she prioritizes the very earliest months). However, as with Freud, there are insights that can further our thinking about ageing. Elliott Jaques, in a classic paper using Kleinian theory, explores the impact of a sense of personal mortality in midlife. He argues that a conscious acknowledgement of one's own death has a creative potential if we can go beyond denial and manic defence to an engagement with the conflict and ambivalencies that are thrown up. Death can be an integral part of life, allowing for 'the enjoyment of mature creativeness and work in full awareness of death which lies beyond – resigned but not defeated' (Jaques 1964). In Kleinian terms, the working through of the depressive position depends upon the capacity to maintain a good internal object. In what we are thinking about here, we could conceive of a developing identity as a 'good object' that has to be held onto, thus mitigating the inevitable pangs of persecutory anxiety that are companions to the grim processes of degeneration.

Erik Erikson engaged with later life issues in a way that other members of the psychoanalytic community did not. He went significantly beyond biology and embraced the notion of a personal identity that took account of social context and cultural variations. He also postulated new challenges and ongoing possibilities for change in later life, with eight major conflicts to be struggled with over the lifecycle. In midlife, the task is to achieve a preponderance of 'generativity' over 'stagnation' and, in the final stage, a ratio of 'integrity' over 'despair'.

While in one sense Erikson was groundbreaking, in another he was still imprisoned in the prevailing *Zeitgeist*. For instance, in his account of the development of ego identity (1973), he fails to take account of gender differences. There is, too, a latent reductionism in a model in which later developments are seemingly predicated on the successful resolution of earlier ones. Adaptation to prevailing social conditions is assumed, and the rather neat delineation of conflicts and tasks in life takes away something from the raw energy and messiness of life as it is. A final stage in which integrity can come to prevail over despair does not do justice to the way in which life throws things at you right until the end.

Identity

A dictionary definition of identity is 'the quality or condition of being a specified person or thing', 'individuality'. Except in situations of extreme pathology, people experience themselves as being different from others and have a sense of their own continuity of being. This is the broad way in which identity is understood here, and it is what we can work with, though not uncritically. For although it is a useful starting point, 'identity' is also limiting. It is often used synonymously with 'ego' and thus carries with it implications of conscious awareness to the exclusion of less conscious influences. Furthermore it can smack of a particular western culture-specific, individualistic self-awareness.

The position I take is of identity as relational in nature. In fact, while a focus on identity is about the inner world, the social is always implicated, for human beings are essentially social creations. This view can be taken further, and a postmodern position goes beyond any particular criticisms, such as those already raised, to question the whole idea that there can be anything like an enduring core of personality, a unified self. Rather it is suggested that there is a multiplicity of selves that we move in and out of. This is a perspective that commends itself to some feminist thinkers because the idea of a unitary self carries within it elements of social control and, in the past, ideas of 'feminine identity' have been limiting and constraining. While integrating concepts such as 'identity' or 'the self' can be useful, the idea of diverse selves is also valuable and relevant and, as already suggested, women have been confined in limiting ways without the opportunity to express the other 'selves' that are there as potential.

Gender

I shall follow the convenient and usual distinction that is made between 'sex' and 'gender'; the former relates to biological states though it is less precise and clear-cut than was once thought. The latter is a sociocultural categorization rather than a 'given' and is subject to immense variation. While gender is often described as 'achieved', there is also a strong element of ascription about it.

It has been noted how the cultural disregard of ageing was echoed in psychology. Not surprisingly, there has been a similar pattern with gender differences; largely ignored in society, they have also been seriously neglected in psychology, where it is definitely a case of 'cherchez la femme'. Prevailing nineteenth and early twentieth-century thought patterns and ideologies coloured the developing discipline; women were largely subsumed under the category 'men' and thus rendered invisible. Strenuous efforts to create a new 'science of the mind' meant there was a fixation on objectivity and the reduction of 'extraneous' variables. Thus context, including gender, could studiously be ignored in the search for a scientific 'neutrality' (Riger 1998). A woman psychologist in midlife recalled that, as a graduate student, she was advised to select only men as participants in an experiment as 'women's responses are "too variable"', making it difficult to obtain significant results! (Clinchy and Norem 1998). In academic psychology, the invisibility of women has extended through the research questions asked, the methods used, and the interpretations of findings, all of which have contributed to a systematic misunderstanding of them. An example of androcentrism was exposed by Carol Gilligan who demonstrated how the failure of women to fit into the prevailing model of 'human' growth and development was presented as evidence of women's inferiority. As in other areas, perceptions of the male are taken to be synonymous with the 'human'.

Gilligan (1982) has mounted a powerful critique of the androcentric nature of the existing body of work on moral development by, for instance, Jean Piaget (1970) and Lawrence Kohlberg (1981). It is male subjects who are regarded as reaching the higher stages of abstract moral judgement, whereas women feature predominantly among those who are regarded as deficient in moral development. In critiquing this work, Gilligan (1982: 19) argues that for women, there is 'a mode of thinking that is contextual and narrative rather than formal and abstract' thus questioning the easy association of difference and inferiority. She claims for women a special significance for attachment and relationships. This view itself is susceptible to criticism as potentially culture-bound but, in her work as a whole, Gilligan alerts us to the way in which women have been systematically devalued in psychology.

Freud can be faulted for his estimation of women as 'incomplete' men and therefore inferior, a view that was robustly countered by the feisty neo-Freudian, Karen Horney, but nevertheless has echoes today.

Growing consciousness-raising among women from the 1960s onwards impacted on psychology, and a feminist voice that is different and not inferior is now being heard. Feminist critiques have gathered force over the years and have enriched the field of psychology by showing different ways of exploring lives and finding meanings. There has been a revalorization of the earlier humanistic roots of psychology.

While recognizing gender as a significant variable, there is a more general point to be made that, whatever approach is adopted, it must be partial. There is no one truth. Whatever perspective or category you use masks others. This is so for gender too. While a focus on gender was a necessary corrective to the 'gender-free' position that prevailed for the first half of the twentieth century, Hare-Mustin and Maracek (1998: 137–8) describe how gender issues have become problematic and divisive in feminist thought:

> Paradoxes arise because every representation conceals at the same time it reveals. For example, focusing on gender differences marginalizes and obscures the interrelatedness of women and men as well as the restricted opportunity of both. It also obscures institutional sexism and the extent of male authority. And this crops up across the whole range of diversity in this society and beyond.

They add, 'Constructing gender is a process not an answer.'

In considering the three elements that are the focus of our concern, it is apparent that women's identity, and the significance of ageing for identity, have been neglected. While the consciousness-raising that has swept across women's experience since the 1950s has profoundly influenced women's sense of themselves, it has had to wait until second wave feminists are themselves entering midlife and later life for feminists to move from an 'ageist' position and begin to take on issues of exclusion and stigmatization.

Women's developing identity

We are embodied creatures, and this is significant for how we define our identities. Within psychodynamic thinking, the physical has always had an important place. For instance, Freud and Klein both emphasize the biological underpinnings of personality. Winnicott (1954), even given his object-relations stance, equates the True Self with the physical self and talks about the 'psyche-indwelling-in-the-soma'. Jung delineates a 'psychoid' region where the physical and the psychological are merged.

The ideas of thinkers such as these were often developed in thoroughly limiting and sexist ways and, given the way in which biological determinism has been used to oppress women and keep them in their place, it is not surprising that in second wave feminist thought biological factors have been seen to be, if not pernicious, then certainly peripheral. Yet it would be surprising if physical experiences such as menstruation, pregnancy and menopause, that are particular to women and so inter-woven with the cycles of our existence, had no effects.

In more recent feminist theory there has been a rediscovery of the body and especially how it is socially constructed. There is a growing canon of work that seeks to distinguish a recognition of the body's significance from an essentialist position. A more discriminating exploration suggests not a simple dualism and opposition between biological and social but rather the possibility of more subtle and flexible relationships (Bell 1999).

In exploring identity issues for older women, it is useful to set them in context, and look more generally at the definition and maintenance of women's identity in this culture. We can then appreciate the nature of the challenges that arise for women in midlife and later life. There are two critical ways in which women's identity is defined in this society. The first of these is woman as 'mother', a role that can be stressed to the exclusion of others, so that women have been defined gynaecologic-ally and their capacity for motherhood regarded as their 'real' destiny. Although the equation of 'true' womanliness with motherhood is now being questioned, those who choose not to be mothers tend to be re-garded as selfish or irresponsible; those who are unable to have children may find it hard to avoid a crippling sense of failure.

A second way in which women can be defined is bound up with their appearance and with their position as objects for men. The frequently quoted words of John Berger come to mind: 'Men look at women. Women watch themselves being looked at' (1988: 47). Or, as Polly Young-Eisendrath puts it, 'Female power is beauty'. She amplifies:

> we become Objects of Desire. Seeking validation primarily through the interest and excitement reflected back at us by others, we gradu-ally lose sight and control of our own needs, wants, wishes. We become objects even to ourselves, constantly surveying our bodies and our psyches as though from an external point of view.
>
> (Young-Eisendrath 2000: 34)

This describes the plight of many women today, who are not valued for what they intrinsically are, or for what they express of themselves. Any power that a woman might feel she does have is doomed anyway because it is ephemeral; beauty fades.

We are, as a society, in the grips of what has been termed the 'beauty myth', a phrase effectively used by Naomi Wolf (1991), whose book of the same name is subtitled '*How Images of Beauty are Used Against Women*'. This new form of bondage for women is part of a long tradition in which women's lives have been confined and rendered contingent; their shapes transmogrified. While for men, clothes have changed around their bodies, for women the body shape itself has been altered in profound and even grotesque ways. Even the broadsheets feature dangerously anorexic, wraithlike models. The cult of skinniness and beauty dooms large swathes of the female population to failure and permanent dissatisfaction with themselves. It represents a kind of extension of adolescent views and aspirations into adult life. The cosmetic surgery industry thrives on this and is appealing to ever younger women and even to some surprising older ones whose feminist stance might seem to have precluded this.

Taking together these two ways of framing women biologically – according to their fertility, and according to standards of youthful beauty – it may readily be appreciated how the physical changes associated with getting older can threaten to derail a sense of identity that has primarily been derived from biological determinism in the service of patriarchy. The loss of uterine function in the menopause has been used as a peg on which to hang many misogynies.

The menopause is undoubtedly a salient feature of midlife for women and, in seeking to think critically about its effects, it is necessary to try and distinguish what is part of a natural process and what constitutes a disease state. It should be noted here that, while recognizing that conclusions from cross-cultural research have to be drawn with great caution, the menopause can be experienced very differently in other cultures from what is taken to be the norm here; there is evidence that women living in non-western societies report fewer menopausal symptoms, and there are examples of how it can represent a positive transition, especially when associated with no loss of status (Arber and Ginn 1991). There has been a longstanding ideology which not only placed limitations and constraints on what women might do but also implied an inherent weakness and inferiority. In the nineteenth century, the menopause was even thought of as a time that threatened insanity: 'The . . . "change of life", as it is commonly called, frequently leads to periods of insanity . . . because certain functions then cease, and the constitution is thereby always more or less deranged' (Ussher 1989). A 30-year-old echoed this:

> I look at every new wrinkle, every grey hair and think of the time when I won't be able to cope with anything: when I'll probably finally go mad. Isn't it true that women who are going through the change are out of their minds for most of the time?
>
> (Melanie, aged 30, in Ussher 1989: 89)

The prevailing bio-medical model is the direct heir to this kind of thought, and the menopause is still commonly regarded as a condition to be treated and 'cured' (new technology making possible ever more in the way of intervention). The medical notion that during the climacteric transition, a woman progresses from 'normal' levels of steroids to significantly decreased levels carries with it the idea that this represents a move to an 'abnormal state'. This is given a very different interpretation by Gannon:

> After approximately 30 years of menstrual cycles, in order to provide transitory fertility, ovarian serenity is restored, estrogen once again becomes stable and levels return to normal, menstruation ceases. The woman experiences release from reproductive pressures and is able to participate fully in her career, social, and family activities as she need no longer be concerned about the problems associated with menstruation, birth control and pregnancy and is no longer at a heightened risk for endometriosis, uterine fibroids, and breast cancer.
>
> (1999: 243)

Gannon further argues that the prominence given to the menopause as a disease state in women's lives obscures what might be thought of as normal ageing processes and creates an inferior position vis-à-vis men, whose ageing is seen as 'determined by their life experience and their accumulated wisdom, not by their biology'. She also points out that the heightening of the significance of the menopause as the central factor in the ageing of women by the introduction of the terms 'premenopausal' and 'postmenopausal' is 'yet one more way to essentialize women as reproductive beings'.

While some women pass through the menopause hardly noticing it, others feel depressed or panicky or have other symptoms, and may need help to ease them through difficult times. However, the widespread use of the prescription pad can mean that control of their bodies is wrested from women. Complicit in this is the widespread use of hormone replacement therapy which, as well as carrying certain medical risks that have not yet been fully investigated, is a function of the medicalized approach and exemplifies the current 'stay young at all costs' philosophy (it was even dubbed 'the youth drug'). This is not to deny that there are levels of physical and emotional distress that do indicate a need for whatever medical and psychological help may be available. Rather, it is seriously to question the wholesale medicalization of a natural state that threatens to deny women the opportunity of finding meaning in an experience which should be a significant part of personal development.

A definition of 'illness' inevitably brings a negative cast and, if the menopause is regarded as synonymous with loss and decline, then this in itself could lead to the depression that is often seen as a symptom of it. A linking of 'loss of libido' with the menopause (a connection that seems to have little empirical justification) is yet another way in which 'a woman's sexuality is embedded within her reproductive status' and contributes to a view of older women as neither being worthy of the sexual interest of others nor subjects of their own sexual desire. The 'stereotype of the asexual, incompetent, depressed and ridiculous older woman is both pervasive and powerful' (Ussher 1989: 110). This has been a very obvious factor in the promotion of HRT where 'youth images of attractive women are commonly used, often embracing a male partner' (Hunter and O'Dea 1997: 201). The following extract conveys the despair of a woman caught up in these negatives and pressured into feeling redundant as a human being and allowing herself to be defined by all that is lost.

> What, fat, forty-three, and I dare to think I'm still a person? No, I am an invisible lump. I belong to a category labelled a priori without interest to anyone . . . the mass media tell us . . . that we are inadequate, mindless, ugly . . . are obsolete. Think what it is like to feel attraction, desire, affection towards others . . . and to be told every day that you are not a woman but a tired object that should disappear.
>
> (Itzin 1986: 129)

The dearth of positive images for women at this time of life appears to suggest a severe limitation of options: perhaps to give up and become invisible, colluding with society's verdict that one is no longer a fully paid up member of the club; alternatively, one might deny one's age with a manic defence and so risk becoming a sad and slightly embarrassing object.

In fact, attitudes towards the menopause are very varied and are linked with other life experiences. The menopause can be a time of anguish for a woman who has wished for a child and for whom this has not been possible. For childfree women who have never wanted to be mothers there may be the prospect of relief from the relentless tyranny of periods. And for women who have never bought into the prevailing limiting definitions of women, the menopause may be no big deal. It is likely that lesbian women who are not part of the heterosexist model of relationships have a more spirited capacity to be themselves and there is some evidence that women of colour have more positive attitudes to the menopause. It has also been found that those women who have passed through the menopause tend to express more positive attitudes than those who are younger – perhaps the reality may not be as grim as the fantasy!

So, there are alternatives. It is possible not to be a victim – to get beyond a response to the images of midlife and menopause that are commonly projected. Germaine Greer (1992) has argued in her lively polemic *The Change* (an expression that has often been used perjoratively), that this can also have a very different meaning and can be about a change to a greater freedom. The menopause can become a journey into a different kind of consciousness.

As well as an experience in and of itself, midlife is also a transitional stage with all the uncertainties and ambiguities that this involves; it contains within it signs and premonitions of what is to come. The awareness of one's mortality (we are, after all, the 'mortals') has an edge to it that is new, and the heightened consciousness of death is a powerful, organizing principle. Tom Stoppard's (1968: 51) words acquire a new and compelling force:

> We must be born with an intuition of mortality before we know the words for it, before we know that there are words, out we come bloodied and squalling with the knowledge that for all the compasses in the world, there's only one direction and time is its only measure.

A sense of mortality presents itself with increasing frequency and in different guises. The robust parents of our memories become frail; their deaths leave us in the front line, with nothing between us and . . . ? Yesterday, the children were playing on the beach with buckets and spades; today they are young adults, vibrant and sexual. Perhaps the most daunting experience of all is the way in which our peers, and even those who are younger, start to die in numbers. There is a sense of life rushing by, propelling us along with gathering speed. These indications of mortality change our perception of life; it takes on a darker, elegiac quality. There is the inescapable recognition that old age, which we thought would never happen, has caught up with us, and perhaps we feel that sense of distaste that Simone de Beavoir describes: 'every society . . . extols the strength and the fecundity that are so closely linked with youth and it dreads the worn-out sterility, the decrepitude of age' (1977: 46).

With changes in health care and general prosperity, people are living longer than ever before and there are more of them. Words like 'burden', even 'threat', are applied to older people and these negativities are internalized. This all gives the tag 'senior citizen' a hollow ring. It is wryly interesting that The Who's song, *My Generation*, with its line 'Hope I die before I get old' has caught them out in a kind of apostasy: they are all 'old' now – and still rocking!

We are faced with ageism, 'the process of systematic stereotyping of and discrimination against people because they are old' (Arber and Ginn 1991: 34), which is so rife in western society at an institutional as well as an individual level. 'The old' are objectified, subject to social control and pejoratively stereotyped in ways that allow younger members of society to repress their own feelings and remain moderately comfortable in themselves.

Disinformation abounds. Ageing is all too readily equated with a disease-state to be treated so that the person can be returned to a kind of 'normality' (reminiscent of attitudes to the menopause). There is a marked tendency to assume that the process of ageing is relentlessly grim for all, but if we look more closely at the actuality it is apparent that it is by no means a uniform process. Organs and systems age at variable rates in different people and there is an enormous difference between 'active' old age and 'deep ageing' where dependency, indignity, and degeneration really takes hold. Despite this, the stereotypical overall view of ageing is of something more akin to the latter.

Similarly, there are mistaken fears about psychological decline. Although 20 per cent of people over 80 show signs of mental impairment (Briggs 1990), it is necessarily the case that 80 per cent do not. A research focus on 'intelligence' testing and tasks that require speed of response has tended to obscure areas of functioning that remain stable or even improve with age. It is possible for some to 'excel in many fields of life, such as politics and art, late in life' (Briggs 1990: 95). There is typically very little fall-off in mental capacity before the age of 70. So it is by no means a flat and pessimistic picture. In fact the irony is that later life can be a time of increasing diversity. The 'old', in our present society, have ages spread over about 30 years. They have had very varied life experiences and, for instance, those who lived through the second world war will have markedly different attitudes from those who were born later. It will be unimaginably changed again when individuals who have been bathed in postmodernism themselves come to be old.

All of these influences affect both men and women, but not equally, as women are faced with the combined forces of ageism and sexism. Susan Sontag has detailed the double standard at work in ageing which grossly disadvantages women, 'for most women, aging means a humiliating process of gradual sexual disqualification' (1997: 20), much earlier than for men. While men are 'allowed' to age in a natural way that is socially acceptable, women incur powerful social penalties. 'Nothing more clearly demonstrates the vulnerability of women than the special pain, confusion, and bad faith with which they experience getting older' (Sontag 1997: 24).

The deprecation of older women is rooted in mythology and in fairy tales. While younger goddesses were valued because their sexual energy could be drawn on by men, the goddess who was old, a crone, was thought of as sucking energy from men. There is a deep male fear of women and their power, and the projections that fuelled these beliefs are still rampant in jokes about mothers-in-law and wicked stepmothers. They are to be found too in the words that are used to describe old women: hag, harridan, old bag, old biddy, witch.

There are certain systematic differences if we compare men and women. Although women live longer than men, they are more susceptible to debilitating illnesses that mean they need to be cared for, thus raising the possibility of changes in gender relationships. The double standard in ageing operates at a material level, and the increasing divorce rate means that there is a rise in the number of women struggling to support themselves on incomes that compare unfavourably with those of men. Women are more likely to be widowed but less likely to remarry than men. Arber and Ginn take the view that, 'Despite the combined effects of ageism and sexism towards older women . . . [they] may be developing a more authentic identity and orientation, especially following widowhood, when they are no longer constrained to fulfil gendered role obligations expected within marriage' (1995: 174).

We can find some of the most potent expressions of what old age is like in literature. First, the possibility of a woman choosing to be different, to branch out for herself, is nicely caught in *All Passion Spent* by Vita Sackville West (1931), a book that makes one want to stand up and cheer. It tells of how a woman in her 80s, widowed after a lifetime of duty and self-abnegation, cuts across the deliberations of her children who are reluctantly facing the burden of 'what to do with mother'. She astonishes them by creating an independent life for herself. Even under the dead weight of a lifetime of cultural expectations, and in advanced old age, there was a creative self, waiting to be out.

Equally heartwarming is May Sarton's story of Caro Spencer, a 76-year-old former teacher, sent to an old people's home. She begins, 'I am not mad, only old. I make this statement to give me courage. To give you an idea what I mean by courage, suffice to say that it has taken two weeks for me to obtain this notebook and a pen. I am in a concentration camp for the old' (1983: 9). The book is a celebration of the human spirit, of how a woman, abandoned to a place of indifference and brutality, holds on to her own integrity and with determination, courage and love, triumphs. Some of the quality of this book is shown by the author, May Sarton, reflecting on her own old age:

> one is able to live more intensely in the present as one grows old . . . death . . . is never far from my mind . . . possessions become less important: time to think, time to be becomes more important . . . so that the essential person may be alive and well at the end . . . the greatest joy is that one can be absolutely open, say outrageous

things . . . the old are permitted to be eccentric . . . in old age we have greater freedom than ever before to be our true selves.

(1997: 230)

Claiming identity

It is instructive to compare the relative positions taken by Freud and Jung on later life. Freud (1905) took the view that working with older people in analysis was unlikely to bring about much change for there was not enough libido for a strong transference: 'near or about fifty the elasticity of the mental processes, on which treatment depends, is as a rule lacking – old people are no longer educable' (1905: 264). Such a mindset would not be conducive to working creatively with an older patient. If one includes the remainder of the sentence: 'and on the other hand, the mass of material to be dealt with would prolong the duration of treatment indefinitely' (1905: 264), there is a kind of 'why bother?' defeatist quality that, incidentally, fits in well with current resource-driven thinking; a sense that nothing new is likely to happen, it is simply a matter of working with the same issues rather less effectively.

A review by Rechtschaffen (1959: 82), a later Freudian, of factors likely to be contra-indications for therapy in older people include:

reduced ego strength; defences that cannot take the strain; that the older person is thereby too open to self-examination; the undesirability of looking back on the whole of one's life as neurotic and maladjusted; that induced change may not fit with possibilities extant in a patient's life situation.

This displays a continuing pessimism about older people and even a sense of danger in exploring within.

An exploration of mature expressions of women's identity requires a challenge to a Freudian orthodoxy that paints such a bleak picture. Jungian theory (while neglecting very early experiences) gives weight to the possibility of developments in later life and I shall draw on his work in thinking further about women's identity in later life. This may appear a strange, even perverse, choice. Jung is both androcentric and often misogynist, and some find his gender bias so unacceptable that they are completely deterred from any engagement with his ideas. Nevertheless, it is possible, though not without tension and a substantial reworking of the theory, to call oneself both a Jungian and a feminist. His work provides a starting point for an exploration of older women's identity and, divested of its sexism, can be a source of liberation for women, and indeed, men.

Jung's contribution

Jung's theory of individuation, the concept at the heart of his approach, analytical psychology, is about becoming what one uniquely can be, free 'from inner compulsions and voices that operate on one unconsciously' (Wehr 1988: 49). What sometimes gets overlooked is that individuation also involves relationships with others: 'As the individual is not just a single separate being, but by his very existence presupposes a collective relationship, it follows that the process of individuation must lead to more intense and broader collective relationships and not to isolation' (Jung 1991: 448). Jung distinguishes this idea of selves-in-relation from what he terms the 'collectivity' (society's norms and values). The more individuated we become, the more we are able to stand aside from the battery of societal demands that exert a compelling pressure to conform in an unreflective way. He uses the term 'mob psychology' which, although crude, is quite an accurate description of people who are caught up and carried along on a social tide (see, for example, earlier comments on the 'beauty myth').

Implicit in analytical psychology is a teleological perspective – an emphasis on purposes rather than causes. This opens up possibilities for growth and change and, in contrast to the modernist cast of psycho-analysis, is more consonant with postmodernism, and the idea of making 'lifestyle' choices. This concern with ends and objectives, his own midlife traumas, and his clinical work with older patients, led Jung to accord a pivotal place to midlife in his theory of development. He suggested that you cannot live the second half of life in the way you live the first. His rather oversimplified picture was that the tasks earlier in life are to do with gaining ego strength and making a mark in the world but, in the second half, the responsibility is more about getting into a relationship with inner processes. 'For a young person it is almost a sin . . . to be too preoccupied with oneself; but for the ageing person it is a duty and a necessity to devote serious attention to oneself' (Jung 1960: 399). It is interesting to note that support for this position is found in more recent psychological work:

> Stability in outer attitudes and interests appears to characterize most people as they grow old. There does, however, appear to be a shift towards an increasing focus on inner thoughts and feelings, already evident in mid-life, consistent with the ideas of developmental theorists such as Jung and Erikson.
>
> (Coleman 1990: 96)

This inward journey can be a painful process. For women in this society, the physical ageing which leads to the withdrawal of society's imprimatur, allied for many with the departure of children who have been life's focus, midlife can be a time of despondency. Dante's lines starkly depict the way in which what one has known and relied on has lost its savour:

Midway this way of life we're bound upon,
I wake to find myself in a dark wood,
Where the right road was wholly lost and gone.

(Dante Alighieri 1949: 71)

All is not lost, however. Jung regards midlife as a time of psychic movement that does not entirely depend on conscious effort on the part of the individual. He has a model of psyche that is ultimately on the side of the person who wants to grow. He outlines a function of the self that is at work psychologically 'adjusting, supplementing', and regards this 'compensatory activity of the unconscious as balancing any tendency towards one-sidedness on the part of consciousness' (Samuels *et al.* 1986: 32). Compensation can be a powerful feature of midlife; Jung does not regard unconscious processes as simply in opposition to more conscious elements of life, and sees midlife as providing a crucial opportunity to get into a closer relationship with unconscious parts of the self.

In thinking about women's development, Jung's concept of the shadow is a powerful aid. It is to be distinguished from the 'persona' that faces the world, and it incorporates all we do not wish to be, or are afraid to own. Jung explains, 'By shadow I mean the "negative" side of the personality, the sum of all those unpleasant qualities we like to hide, together with the insufficiently developed functions and the contents of the personal unconscious' (1966: 66).

Jung clearly indicates that the shadow contains potential for development as well as what we may be ashamed of. Elsewhere, he describes it as containing pure gold. It is also important to note that the qualities we split off may include those regarded as culturally inadmissible.

In western society, the persona for women is coloured by social pressures and fuelled by their wishes to be pleasing and nice. The shadow, in stark contrast, comprises qualities that are 'other', shameful, and which have been repressed because of their threatening nature. In midlife, the dynamic of compensation may mean that contents that have previously been split off make their presence felt in ways that are alarming. It is in the nature of shadow qualities, buried since early days, that they are raw and unprocessed; anger can rip situations apart, greed and envy take hold with unwonted ferocity, delight can astound, and the wish to play the fool overwhelm. These may seem to be pretty dysfunctional responses, and it is true that the shadow is full of dark and difficult experiences but, in relation to the honed, groomed and denatured images of women that abound, they are undoubtedly real. For women whose guiding principles have been to subordinate themselves and think of others, to bite back their anger, and to be eminently sensible, to become authentic requires an acknowledgement and connection with less acceptable parts of the self. The very unruliness of the shadow is its great gift, for it has the potential to overthrow a neat, well-crafted persona.

Seeking to relate to the shadow parts of the self is a lengthy process that is not accomplished in an entire lifetime but, in so far as women can begin to connect with repressed qualities and own them, not only will the energy that previously was invested in keeping them at bay become available, but the whole personality is set to be enlivened and enriched. To the extent that shadow elements are accorded a rightful place and consciously related to, so they can be used; no longer saboteurs, draining energy, but part of a person who is increasingly living from her centre and to her limits.

A Jungian psychotherapist, Pearson, has written of her experiences at the time of the menopause in a way that epitomizes psychological change in midlife, and which she sees as a possibility for all. It involves actively claiming something for oneself rather than going along with 'the collectivity'. In her view, heroes do not only belong to history, 'we are all heroes and we are all on a journey', and for each of us, she maintains, there is the need (very Jungian) to make the journey, 'slay the dragon, find the treasure, and then return to transform the kingdom' (Pearson 1996: 8). Symbolically, we each need to find our treasure, but this will involve going into dangerous, unknown places and will require courage. For her, at this time (and it is true of midlife in a wider sense as well as during the menopause), there is 'a call toward autonomy, toward being self-defined as opposed to reactive' (1996: 10):

> lately I feel less inclined to do things just because other people want me to do them, and I no longer feel like I have to prove myself to anyone or to the world . . . it is easier to be true to myself. I also see a desire to simplify . . . and to focus more on what really matters. On the other hand, while menopause feels like a journey into autonomy, I've noticed that relationships with my children, husband, and friends have become more important. I'm also experiencing an impatience with dependency. For me this is new. I simply don't want to be close with people who expect me to take care of them or rescue them. So it's a turn away from a more motherly stance in the world. I'm not talking about codependence. I'm talking about . . . completing my work [as] the loving parent, the nurturer . . . at least for the time being.

(Pearson 1996: 11–12)

There is a decisiveness about this, a quiet ruthlessness. There is, too, a sense of discovery; of getting into a relationship with the self which exemplifies the twin ideas of individuation: the clearer delineation of separateness and, at the same time, a sense of connection with others that has a new-minted quality. It is reminiscent, too, of Erikson's thinking: that the alternative to stagnation is generativity which is about wanting to create something new.

Pearson sees being a lover as 'very much a menopausal experience' and not something that is left behind at that time: 'I've observed women actually finding their sexuality in a new way. They are claiming it as not being about reproduction, not being about making somebody else happy or calling somebody to them, but as a kind of joy for its own sake' (1996: 12–13). It has to be said that women can vary in their responses to sexuality and the menopause and, in contrast to Pearson, may choose to opt for a life that is not complicated with sex. The possibilities of a life of serenity and potency that is not defined by regular sexual activity is persuasively explored by Germaine Greer (1992). And a well-known cookery writer, now in midlife, said that she now prefers a good meal to sex any day! The point is that women can choose what is right and meaningful for themselves; it is a time when creative differences can emerge.

Pearson also describes how, earlier in life, she eschewed traditional female roles: 'Now, in midlife, I'm reclaiming the feminine, but in a way that has nothing to do with stereotypical definitions of femininity. It is more about a quality of being – of spirit embodied in loving connection with other people, society, the earth' (1996: 13).

What Pearson is also talking about is about the ability to be free from any ideology, including feminism, 'about being able to be with . . . your own process in a more patient, conscious way . . . about creating a new life for yourself that fits the new transformed you.' What is important is the tone, the overall direction, which is about a woman taking charge of her life.

A critical look at Jung's work

Although Jung is often thought of as being sympathetic to women (more so, on the face of it, than Freud) his conception of the 'feminine' comes dangerously close to validating the prejudices of a patriarchal society. For instance, in developing his key process of individuation, he seems blind to the possibility that there may be differences according to gender in the way that greater wholeness is reached.

For individuation, Jung saw it as necessary that the person 'dies to the ego' as a defining principle. This change in emphasis is part of relating to a wider concept of self which includes unconscious forces (collective and personal) as well as that which is conscious. For the person who has been defined in ego terms, it means becoming open to new qualities of feeling and imagination. Such compensation has a clear relevance for men who have been programmed into developing ego qualities to the exclusion of others; it also has force if it is thought of as referring, at a wider social level, to the need to honour those imaginative and feeling qualities that have little place in this society's prevailing logico-rational discourse. Where it makes much less sense is for women whose formative experiences have been in a milieu where social forces are unsympathetic to the development of a strong ego in the first place. Rather than any weakening of ego qualities, individuation for such women would seem to require the opposite, a strengthening of ego – more autonomy – in the interests of greater wholeness.

'Anima' and 'animus', while useful concepts for indicating a potential for further self-development in both men and women, are also illustrative of Jung's limitations, of his failure to acknowledge the role of social structure. The anima refers to the inner representation of the feminine in a man, and the animus is a comparable inner representation of the masculine in a woman. This sounds very even-handed, but Jung's androcentrism is unmistakable: 'Since the anima is an archetype that is found in men, it is reasonable to suppose that an equivalent archetype must be present in women' (Wehr 1988: 64). Thus, women's position is merely deduced from that of men.

These contrasexual images operate unconsciously, and individuation requires that persons become more aware of, and begin to own consciously those elements that are psychologically regarded as 'other'; thus men will increasingly take on Eros qualities of love, life, and relatedness; and women, Logos qualities of reason, knowledge and truth. However, Jung's essentialist position fails to take into account the influence of social context in constructing what belongs to whom, and it is at least arguable that what is psychologically regarded as feminine and masculine would be equally susceptible to explanation in terms of cultural conditioning.

Jung's writings on anima and animus are riddled with sexism. For instance, he takes the view that while men can understand what is meant by the anima, 'I have, as a rule, found it very difficult to make a woman understand what the animus is' (Wehr 1988: 65), and he sees a woman's development of animus qualities as a potential threat to her femininity. In discussing 'animus-ridden' women, those said to be unconsciously in the grip of their negative animus, he falls into a kind of patronizing diatribe: 'the animus encourages a critical disputatiousness and would-be highbrowism . . . a perfectly lucid discussion gets tangled up in the most maddening way through the introduction of a quite different and if possible, perverse point of view' (Wehr 1988: 120). Carl Jung's projections are blatant, but are nicely balanced by his wife Emma Jung's cool and reasoned comments, rooted in her own experience, of the way that women can experience the negative animus as a kind of inner saboteur: 'First we hear from it a critical, usually negative comment on . . . all motives and intentions, which . . . cause feelings of inferiority, and tend[s] to nip in the bud all initiative and every wish for self-expression' (Wehr 1988: 123). As well as being seen as a comment on patriarchy (a connection that she herself does not make) this observation of Emma Jung's, which has a heartfelt quality, may also, one is tempted to think, say something about the marital relationship?

In fairness to Jung, he does have an awareness of sexism while still being in its grip. 'Most of what men say about feminine eroticism, and particularly about the emotional life of women, is derived from their own anima projections and distorted accordingly' (Wehr 1988: 97). As we have seen, there are strong elements of conservatism in Jungian thought. For instance, the emphasis, which we have not been able to explore, given to the 'goddesses' in understanding women has sometimes been used to underpin a restricted, essentialist view. However, there are indications, especially towards the end of his life, of a move towards a more constructivist position (Young-Eisendrath and Hall 1991), and his discussion of multiple subjectivities, as part of individuation, is exciting. In being prepared to ask the hard questions, and to move in search of meaning beyond the existing limited psychological prescriptions, he offers much to the understanding of ourselves and the world. Notwithstanding its bias, analytical psychology represents an imaginative attempt to confront crucial issues of meaning and value that have been ignored in the broad sweep of western psychological thought, rooted in logical materialism. It offers continuing choices in life. To this extent, it is consonant with a postmodern perspective and challenges the assumptions about later life that are widespread in this society.

Some thoughts on implications for counselling and therapy

Attention has been drawn to a particularly hard-line Freudian position that analysis in later life is fruitless. Scepticism remains: I heard recently the view expressed that, since a patient was in her late 40s, one could not expect much change. But over the years there have been a few therapists who have written about their work with older patients who have achieved a degree of resolution of earlier conflicts (for example Segal 1958; Coltart

1991). King, a Freudian with a strong interest in the potential for change in later years, describes colleagues as confessing, almost apologetically, to working with patients in the second half of life. She herself is un-apologetic and argues from her clinical experience that, in middle-aged patients, there is:

> a new dynamic and sense of urgency [in] their analyses, thus facilit-ating a more productive therapeutic alliance than one manages to establish with similar young adult patients . . . the lessening of the intensity of instinctual impulses . . . reduces the need for the main-tenance of the rigidity of their defence systems . . . they are able to assimilate new objects into their psychic structure, thus facilitating new ego growth . . . the feeling of alienation from themselves and others decreases . . . and they begin to experience a new sense of their own identity . . . and worth . . . it is as if the centre of their gravity moves from the edge of themselves to their own inner centre . . . I find that they are then often able to get access to new forms of creativeness within themselves, which result in experi-ences of satisfaction quite different from any experiences during the first half of their lives.
>
> (King 1974: 33–4)

This is very close to Jungian thought (and King was obliged to read her first paper to the Society of Analytical Psychology as it was unacceptable within the Freudian culture).

Jung took the view that older patients (and two-thirds of his patients were over 40) were ripe for therapy, the more worldly preoccupations of earlier life giving way to existential questions. The work was far away from illness and cure. He engaged with these older patients in their search for meaning, and was thereby challenged to devise innovative ways of working. For instance, he developed ways of dialoguing with the variety of inner selves that are available to us all and which are an enrichment if we can communicate with them. He introduced the tech-nique of 'active imagination', described as *'the* most powerful tool in Jungian psychology for achieving wholeness' by Marie Louise von Franz (in Introduction to Hannah 1981, original emphasis), and going further than dream work. These are significant techniques in Jungian work today with patients of all ages (Hannah 1981; Redfearn 1985).

A picture has been painted of how women in this society have to contend with forces that weaken and, in some cases, undermine a sense of personal agency. So subtle and pervasive are the influences at work that, without realizing it, women can become social artefacts. Some do see that there could be options but may find the risk of stepping aside from the collectivity too risky. Others have lives where hope and expectation are snuffed out. A minority have developed strong egos and can therefore fit quite comfortably into a male paradigm. Yet others, apparently strong, lead lives that are split and confused. The psycho-therapist, Young-Eisendrath (2000: 4–5), writes of working with such women:

> Yet as successful as many of these women have become, they often feel 'out of control' in their personal lives. Although they can speak openly and passionately about the values and principles they believe in, and defend others' rights, they still resist claiming and asserting personal needs and desires, especially when these are in conflict with others'. They fear being seen as too bossy or too self-absorbed.

For all women, however, ageing is likely to threaten earlier adjustments, celebration of youth and beauty giving way to denigration. While the asymmetry between the sexes continues into old age however (the craggy appearance of the mature man is more socially acceptable than the stigma of ageing in women) to the extent that women can free themselves from a self-definition that depends on what is externally validated, then they may have enhanced opportunities for development when compared with men, whose identities have been more narrowly work-based. The emphasis on the freedom to be what we want, notwithstanding declining physical vigour, extends an invitation to women to kick over the traces and to claim their own authority.

An 80-year-old woman has the last word: 'Age puzzles me. I thought it was a quiet time. My seventies were interesting and fairly serene, but my eighties are passionate. I grow more intense as I age' (Sarton 1997: 230).

Note

1 This phrase comes from J.M. Barrie's *Peter Pan*: 'To live would be an awfully big adventure' at the end of Peter Pan in Barrie, J.M. (1928: 576) *The Plays of J.M. Barrie* (ed. A.E. Wilson) London: Hodder & Stoughton. This mirrors the more familiar 'To die will be an awfully big adventure', page 545 (end of Act 3).

References

Arber, S. and Ginn, J. (1991) *Gender and Later Life*. London: Sage.

Arber, S. and Ginn, J. (1995) Connecting gender and ageing: a new beginning?, in S. Arber and J. Ginn (eds) *Connecting Ageing and Gender*. Buckingham: Open University Press.

de Beauvoir, S. (1977) *The Coming of Age*. New York: G.P. Putnam.

Bell, V. (1999) *Feminist Imagination*. London: Sage Publications.

Berger, J. (1988) *Ways of Seeing*. London: Penguin Books.

Briggs, R. (1990) Biological ageing, in J. Bond, P. Coleman, and S. Peace (eds) *Ageing in Society*. London: Sage Publications.

Clinchy, B.M. and Norem, J.T. (eds) (1998) *The Gender and Psychology Reader*. New York: New York University Press.

Coleman, P. (1990) Psychological ageing, in J. Bond, P. Coleman, and S. Peace (eds) *Ageing in Society*. London: Sage Publications.

Colthart, N. (1991) The analysis of an elderly patient, *International Journal of Psychoanalysis*, 72(2): 209–19.

Dante, A. (1949) *The Divine Comedy*, Cantica 1: Hell, trans by D.L. Sayers. Harmondsworth: Penguin Books.

Erikson, E. (1973) *Childhood and Society*. London: Penguin.

Freud, S. (1905) On psychotherapy, in J. Strachey (ed.) *The Standard Edition of The Complete Works of Sigmund Freud*, Vol. 7. London: Hogarth Press.

Gannon, L.R. (1999) *Women and Ageing – Transcending the Myths*. London: Routledge.

Gilligan, C. (1982) *In a Different Voice*. Cambridge, MA: Harvard University Press.

Greer, G. (1992) *The Change: Women, Ageing and the Menopause*. London: Penguin Books.

Hannah, B. (1981) *Active Imagination: Encounters with the Soul*. Santa Monica, CA: Sigo Press.

Hare-Mustin, R.T. and Marecek, J. (1998) The meaning of difference: gender, postmodernism and psychology, in B.M. Clinchy and J.T. Norem (eds) *The Gender and Psychology Reader*. New York: New York University Press.

Hunter, M.S. and O'Dea, I. (1997) Menopause: bodily changes and multiple meanings, in J.M. Ussher (ed.) *Body Talk*. London: Routledge.

Itzin, C. (1986) Media images of women: the social construction of ageism and sexism, in S. Wilkinson (ed.) *Feminist Social Psychology*. Milton Keynes: Open University Press.

Jaques, E. (1964) Death and the mid-life crisis, *International Journal of Psychoanalysis*, 46(4): 502–14.

Jung, C.G. (1960) *The Structure and the Dynamics of the Psyche*, Collected Works Vol. 8, 2nd edn. London: Routledge & Kegan Paul.

Jung, C.G. (1966) *Two Essays on Analytical Psychology*, 2nd edn. London: Routledge.

Jung, C.G. (1991) *Psychological Types*, Collected Works Vol. 6. London: Routledge.

King, P. (1974) Notes on the psychoanalysis of older patients, *Journal of Analytical Psychology*, 19: 22–37.

Kohlberg, L. (1981) *The Philosophy of Moral Development*. San Fransisco: Harper and Row.

Pearson, C.S. (1996) The new hero's Journey, in B.J. Horrigan (ed.) *Red Moon Passage*. London: Thorsons.

Piaget, J. (1970) *Structuralism*. New York: Basic Books.

Rechtschaffen, A. (1959) Psychotherapy with geriatric patients, *Journal of Gerontology*, 14: 33–84.

Redfearn, J.W.T. (1985) *My Self, My Many Selves*. London: Karnac Books.

Riger, S. (1998) Epistemological debates, feminist voices – science, social values, and the study of women, in B.M. Clinchy and J.T. Norem (eds) *The Gender and Psychology Reader*. New York: New York University Press.

Sackville West, V. (1931) *All Passion Spent*. London: Hogarth Press.

Samuels, A., Shorter, B. and Plant, F. (1986) *A Critical Dictionary of Jungian Analysis*. London: Routledge.

Sarton, M. (1983) *As We Are Now*. London: The Women's Press.

Sarton, M. (1997) Toward another dimension, in M. Pearsall (ed.) *The Other Within Us*. Boulder, CO: Harper Collins/Westview Press.

Segal, H. (1958) Fear of death: notes on the analysis of an old man, *International Journal of Psychoanalysis*, 39(1): 178–81.

Sontag, S. (1997) The double standard of ageing, in M. Pearsall (ed.) *The Other Within Us*. Boulder, CO: Harper Collins/Westview Press.

Stoppard, T. (1968) *Rosencrantz and Guildenstern are Dead*. London: Faber and Faber.

Ussher, J.M. (1989) *The Psychology of the Female Body*. London: Routledge.

Vincent, J. and Mudrovcic, Z. (1993) Lifestyles and perceptions of elderly people and old age in Bosnia and Hercegovina, in S. Arber and M. Evandrou (eds) *Ageing, Independence and the Life Course*. London: Jessica Kingsley.

Wehr, D.S. (1988) *Jung and Feminism – Liberating Archetypes*. London: Routledge.

Winnicott, D.W. (1954) Mind and its relation to the psyche-soma, *British Journal of Medical Psychology*, 27: 243–54.

Wolf, N. (1991) *The Beauty Myth: How Images of Beauty Are Used Against Women*. Vintage.

Young-Eisendrath, P. (2000) *Women and Desire – Beyond Wanting to Be Wanted*. London: Judy Piatkus.

Young-Eisendrath, P. and Hall, J. (1991) *Jung's Self Psychology: A Constructivist Perspective*. New York: The Guildford Press.

Afterword

Nicola Barden and
Susannah Izzard

This is not a book about how to work with women; that would assume a homogeneity about the sex that belies the enormous variety of female experience, attested to in these chapters. If one thing comes through the various contributions to this book, it is that there is no such thing as a woman – a reified unit that can be generalized. There can only be an infinite number of ways of being a woman, and each woman must find her own path. So we cannot speak of 'mothers', 'female friends', 'working women', but must allow for diversity of experience, and allow our female clients to speak for themselves. While not a 'how to' book, it has been written in the hope that those working with women might be informed as to the various factors which might shape her way of being in the world – not simply internal factors but those arising from the context in which she lives.

Despite the continuing advances in analytic and sociological thought about gender, it can seem as if the doors of the consulting room remain closed to these developments. The necessary emphasis on the intrapersonal world of the psyche with its elements of phantasy, defence, collective and personal unconscious, and the deeply personal nature of the therapeutic relationship that engages with this internal world, can make the external world seem like an irrelevant intrusion.

Yet the contributors to this book have, each in their own way, demonstrated the indissolubility of the very public from the very private, and the falsity of creating absolute separations between the two. Recognition of this was crucial in feminist thinking in the second half of the twentieth century, where the phrase 'the personal is political' was coined to combat the assumption that only the political really mattered in the struggle for equality. Women then were trying to express what perhaps they were in the best position to know – that the life of the individual was the clearest reflector of the effectiveness of social change, and that the concerns of the individual should shape the essential concerns of social movements. This standpoint led to the thinking that therapy was itself a potentially radical movement, as it developed the capacity for a true self that could exist in relation to others.

The individual lives of women and men are deeply affected by the external structures of gender which their internal selves must inhabit. Even women who successfully occupy gender roles outside of those structures have no choice but to stand out as 'different', and thus to have an experience of their lives as 'other', whether or not that would have been their intention or their pathology. In order to truly meet the client, therefore, the therapist must begin to bring conscious awareness of their own and their environments' gender constructions into the consulting room, and begin to understand the role these things play in the countertransference, neurotic or otherwise, to the client. This is a difficult task, as it requires taking a position separate to one's own norms, which often reside in a place of unconscious awareness. Impossible to engage with in a deliberate way, nevertheless the work can be done by an open engagement with the clients' material in which the therapist sifts the countertransference of difference with attention paid to the possibility of external as well as internal engagement. For example, a client talking about her experience at work, or her difficulties in intimate relationships has, we suggest, a right to her therapist giving consideration to structural and social forces that may be impacting on the client's experience, as well as the more traditionally considered forces of early life and internal dynamics, and also to the therapist's own response to and interaction with these forces.

This book has not explicitly addressed the implications of the recognition of gender constructs on analytic technique, although an awareness of this has been strongly present, particularly in the accounts of clinical work. The emphasis has rather been on recognizing that psychoanalytic theory and sociological analysis are both essential to an understanding of gender development in the individual, and the critique of analyses is that it has rested too much within its own field. There is no doubt that this is at last changing, and the thinking of the contributors to this volume attests to that.

Perhaps the other significant factor, implicit in the conception of the book, is the idea that the sense of gender identity is continually acquired throughout life, continually moulded and changed by the engagement with the attachment world. From the limitations of the infant's sense of her own gender, to the experience of women engaged in the final stages of life, being female matters, makes things different, is reacted to differently and creates different reactions in turn. It may be that an initial sense of identity as female is part of early life (though it may vary in its relationship with the biological sex of the individual), although even at anything like a 'beginning' it is clearly an internally–externally affected identification. This is a place to start from rather than somewhere to finish however, and the unfolding of that gender identity will continue throughout the whole of life.

Part of the wonder of living in the twenty-first century is the myriad possibilities that people now live with in many aspects of their life. Choice, and plenty of it, has become a key characteristic of this time. While internal identity is not simply a matter of choice, it is now possible to live out externally a life that previously could only have been a part of conscious or unconscious fantasy. This makes it more feasible to distinguish between the literal and the symbolic, and challenges psycho-therapy to reassess its interpretative stance on some matters of gender identity. Psychoanalytic thought has, with its roots in nineteenth-century Vienna, been slow to catch up with the movement into post-modernist deconstruction. What faces women today is a gender identity that has the potential to offer diverse expression. It is our hope that analytic work can assist women to greater freedoms and more authentic self-recognition, and if this book facilitates that in any way, it will have been worth writing.

Index

abuse, 157
   sexual, 69–71, 72
active imagination, 224
activity, 8, 39, 80–1
administrative staff, 114, 115
adolescence, 51–74
advertising, 155
affect, 40, 40–2
affective self, 37
Africa, 199
ageing, 205–25
ageism, 214, 215
aggression, 90, 111
alcohol, 68
All Passion Spent: Vita Sackville West,
   216
analytic theory, 6, 7, 21, 26, 223
anatomy, 8
anatomy as destiny, 167
Ancient Greece, 17
androcentrism, 208, 217, 222
anima, 13–14, 222, 223
animus, 13–14, 222
anorexia, 71, 72, 73, 156, 157
anxiety, 206
As We Are Now: May Sarton, 216
assertion, 90
attachment theory, 86, 193
attachment world, 27, 33–6, 38,
   42

Australian study, 163
autonomy, 9

beauty, 210
binary gender divide, 13–14, 16, 19,
   24, 26
biology, 11, 37–8, 159, 167, 209
black communities, 10
black women, 62
body, 25, 26, 159
   see also female body
Bosnia, 205
boundaries, 61, 96, 119
boys, 37, 44, 46
brain, 40–2, 46–7
Brazil, 163
breast, 149
bulimia, 71, 156, 157

Caribbean, 191
central nervous system (CNS), 42
The Change: Germaine Greer, 214
chaos, 27
child development, 56
child labour, 53
childbirth, 21, 167
childhood, 55, 73
childlessness
   and pronatalism, 162–9
   by choice, 172–5

inability to bear, 169–71
  postponers, 171–2
China, 194
choices, 15, 172–5, 223, 230
Clare, A.: *On Men: Masculinity in Crisis*,
  11–12
closeness, *see* postnatal closeness
Cognitive Analytic Theory (CAT), 79
cognitive analytic therapy, 89, 91, 94
cognitive behavioural therapy, 78, 88,
  89
compensation, 219
competition/competitiveness, 99
  in the workplace, 107, 110–13
conflict, 111, 188, 198–200
connectedness, 113
consumerism, 144
control, 72
cosmetic surgery, 152, 153, 211
counselling, 223–5
cross-gender identity, 13
cross-sex relationships, 82
cultural conditioning, 36, 222
cultural stereotyping, 35, 62
culture
  and adolescence, 53
  and friendships, 85, 89, 98, 99
  and Cognitive Analytic Therapy, 91
  and intimacy, 120, 122

daughters, *see* mother-daughter
  relationship
deconstruction, 19
depression, 66, 82–3, 129
desire, 145
despair, 206, 207
destructive instinct, 146
destructiveness, 156–7
developmental theory, 26, 54–7, 205
difference, 20, 21
dimorphism, 15, 19, 34
discordant needs, 198–200
discordant needs, *see* conflict
distress, *see* postnatal distress
diversity, 228
dyadic relationships, 41, 81, 92–5, 99,
  174

eating disorders, 68, 71–4
economic necessity, 54
ego, 25, 27, 153, 207, 222
ego psychologists, 121, 123
egocentricity, 54
embodiment, 143–5, 159
emotional deprivation, 128
emotional development, 42, 43
emotional experiences (motherhood),
  180–201
endocrine system, 37
enhancement, 24
envy, 99, 107, 112
equality, 104
Erikson, E.H., 56, 57
Eros, 14, 146, 222
erotic-maternal split, 173
ethnicity, 62
ethnographic studies, 20
Europe, 10
exploitation, 53

facilitators, 186, 187, 188, 189, 197
failure, 110
fantasy
  adult world, 48
  child's world, 129, 145, 146
  and female sexual expression,
    148–51
  and men, 130
father-centred theory, 123, 124
fathering, 119
fathers, 136, 137
feelings, 46
fellatio, 155
female body, 141–60, 157–8
female development, 55
femaleness, *see* femininity
feminine/female identity, 8–16,
  209–17
  and ageing, 217
  and mothering, 107
  development, 13, 14, 209–17
  Freud, 122–3
  generative, 182–3, 192
  Lacan, 123–4
  rethinking, 175–7

sexuality, 121–2
theories, 120–1
see also gender identity
femininity, 8, 12, 16, 119, 168
feminist movement, *see* women's
  movement
feminist thought, 209, 228
feminization, 108
fetishism, 19
Freud
  and biology, 37
  on childlessness, 170
  and female identity, 122–3
  and gender identity, 7, 8, 13, 15,
    21, 25
  on later life, 206, 217
  on adolescence, 55, 57
  on infantile sexuality, 145
  on sexual instincts, 146
  Outline of Psychoanalysis, 146
  on parenting, 192
  penis envy theory, 120–1, 123,
    126, 166
  on women, 208
friendship
  definition, 79
  importance of, 82
  psychotherapeutic perspectives,
    83–91
  sociological perspectives, 80–2
  theory of, 91–7

gay gene, 18
gender, 24–6, 39, 45–6, 229
  and ageing, 207–9
gender awareness, 30–48
gender behaviour, 44
gender bias, 63
gender confusion, 23, 25
gender dynamics, 114
gender expectations, 44
gender identity, 7–8
  and childlessness, 170
  and infancy, 39, 167, 193–5
  and attachment world, 27
  cross-gender, 13
  masculine, 8–16

sexual, 16–23
  transsexual, 24–6
  transgender, 24–6
  see also Freud, homosexuality
gender identity disorder, 22
gender power, 120
gender stereotyping, 22
gendering, 193–5
generative identity, 182–3, 192
generativity, 206, 221
genitalia, 45, 46, 47
girl power, 67
girls, 37, 44, 46
good-enough concept, 108, 109
Greer, Germaine: *The Change*, 214
groups, 81

harassment, 62, 63
hedonism, 144
hegemonic paradigm, 9
helplessness, 151–2
heterosexuality, 11, 12, 26
higher education, 66
home-work split, 105–6
homosexuality, 11–12, 16, 17, 21, 22
Hong Kong, 199
Horney, Karen, 120–1
hostility, 107, 156
Hughes, Ted: *Tales from Ovid*, 141
human development, 40
hysteria, 158

I am/Me, *see* self
ideal love, 137
idealization, 107, 129
identification, 128, 149
identificatory love, 15
identity, 32, 207
  see also feminine/female identity,
    gender identity
incest, 185
independence, 52, 68, 72
India, 163, 194
individualism, 68
individuation, 43–5, 56, 218–23
infant development, 30–48, 167,
  193–5

infant-caregiver dyad, 41
infantile experience, 31, 193
infantile sexuality, 47, 145
inferiority, 128
infertility, 165, 183
instability, 168
integrity, 206, 207
intersubjectivity, 192–3
intimacy, 56, 118–39
    friendship, 81, 84, 87
    lesbians, 131–5
    and mother-daughter relationship,
        119, 120, 127–31, 136
    working relationships, 114
Israel, 163

jealousy, 112
journals, 78
Jung, Carl, 7
    on ageing, 218–23, 224
    on the binary gender divide, 13–14

Kinsey, A.C., 19, 20
kinship, 93, 181, 191
Klein, Melanie, 15, 148–51, 206

Lacan, Jacques, 122–4, 131, 152
Lady Macbeth, 15
language, 62, 168, 216
leadership, 113
lesbians
    and friendship, 95–7
    and childlessness, 171
    and gender identity, 21
    and intimacy, 118–19, 131–5
    and marginalization, 63
    and menopause, 213
listening, 9–10
Logos, 14, 222
loss, 59
love, 128

male bias, 9, 55, 56, 121
maleness, *see* masculinity
management, 104, 108, 114
marginalization, 63–5, 166, 204
masculine identity, 8–16

masculinity, 8, 11, 12, 119, 168
masochism, 150
maternal figure, 118
maternal function, 114, 115
maternal orientations, 186–8
maternity, 181
maturity, 57
Me/I am, *see* self
media, 58, 60
medicalization, 17, 181, 212
men, 11
menarche, 58
menopause, 211–14, 220, 221
menstruation, 58, 150
mental health, 82, 83, 98
Metamorpheses: Ovid, 141
methodology, 80
midlife, *see* ageing
mob psychology, 218
Moir, A. and Moir, B.: *Why Men Don't
    Iron*, 11
Mormon communities, 99
mortality, 206, 214
mother-centred theories, 121, 129
mother-daughter relationship
    and fantasy, 149
    and intimacy, 119, 120, 127–31, 136
    and women's friendships, 84–5, 92
mother-infant relationship, 123, 157
motherhood
    and adolescence, 52, 59, 60
    and childlessness, 165, 166, 170,
        171, 173
    emotional experiences, 180–201
    Lady Macbeth, 15
    and psychoanalysis, 165, 172
    role, 41, 119, 121
    and women's identity, 210
    and work, 103, 107, 110, 119
mourning, 169
Munchausen by proxy, 189

nature, 18
nature/nurture debate, 9, 12
need, 88
negative attitudes, 163–4, 165, 166
neonatal unit observations, 35–6

neutrality, 172, 173, 174
nuns, 95

object love, 15, 21
object relations, 120, 121, 123, 131, 138
objectified social forms, 6, 91–2, 93, 97
objects of desire, 210
occupations, 104
Oedipal stage, 26, 189
Oedipal theory, 6, 8, 16, 21
Oedipus complex, 8, 14, 26, 166–7
On Men: Masculinity in Crisis: A. Clare, 11–12
orgasm, 154
Orlan, 142, 153
othermother tradition, 10
otherness
    and gender, 20–1, 26, 229
    and individuation, 222
    Jung, 13–14
    and the workplace, 113
Outline of Psychoanalysis: Freud, 146
Ovid: *Metamorphoses*, 141

pair-bonds, *see* dyadic relationships
parenthood, *see* pronatalism
parenting, 119, 192
partners, 124–7
passivity, 8
past experience, 200–1
paternal function, 114, 115
penis-envy, 120–1, 123, 126, 149, 166
perversion, 1, 17, 156
phantasy, *see* fantasy
phenomenology, 159
polymorphism, 15
Portman Clinic, 156
postmodernism, 223, 230
postnatal closeness, 190–1
postnatal distress, 191–2, 193, 195–6
postnatal learning experience, 36
postponers, 171–2
power, 7, 10, 72, 116, 143
power analysis approach, 158
pregnancy, 157, 172, 183–5, 186

primary caretaking, 38, 42, 44
privacy, 94, 95, 116, 158
projection, 60
pronatalism, 162–9
prostitutes, 53
psyche, 122, 128, 209, 228
psychoanalysis, 12, 158
    and infantile experience, 31, 193
    and motherhood, 165, 172
    and sexuality, 145–6
    theory, 121, 129, 229
    see also psychotherapy
psychological approaches, 80, 82, 83, 98, 208
psychopathologies, 188–90
psychosocial development, 55
psychotherapy, 124, 200, 205
    and friendships, 83–91
public domain, 116

qualifications, 66

race, 10, 17, 62
race laws, 26
racism, 10, 62, 63
rape, 61
rapprochement crisis, 44
reactivations, 188–90
reciprocal roles, 90, 91, 94, 96, 97
reciprocators, 188
regulators, 187, 188, 190, 197
religious orders, 95
reparation, 106–7
reproduction, 181, 183–5
roles, *see* reciprocal roles

Sackville West, Vita: *All Passion Spent*, 216
Sarton, May: *As We Are Now*, 216
Scandinavia, 197
schemas, 88–9
secretaries, *see* administrative staff
secularization, 17
security, 34
self
    adolescence, 51, 60
    affective, 37

and the body, 25, 26
definition, 32
development in early infancy, 30–48
and identity, 207
intersubjectivity, 192–3
race, 10
stages of emergence, 38
self-harm, 70
self-mutilation, 156
sensuality, 152–6
separateness, 113, 168
separation, 9, 52, 56
separation-individuation process, 43, 45
sex, 32, 207
sex roles, 22
sex steroids, 47
sexism, 215, 222
sexologists, 17
sexual abuse, 69–71, 72
sexual assaults, 61
sexual dimorphism, 34
sexual double standard, 55, 62
sexual expression, 141–60
sexual identity, 16–23, 25, 97, 120
sexual inequality, 120
sexual instincts, 146–7
sexual orientation, 19, 124
sexual practice, 156–7
sexual unhappiness, 135–8, 155
sexuality, 121–2, 143, 158, 159
  and psychoanalysis, 145–6
  female, 147–8
shadow, 219, 220
shame, 51
sister relationships, 94
skin-ego, 153
social development, 43
social networks, 82–3
socialization, 36
sociology, 79, 98, 229
soma, 122, 145
space, 162–7
speaking, *see* talk
splitting, 60
stagnation, 206

stereotyping
  ageist, 205
  cultural, 35, 62
  gender, 22, 34, 46
  workplace, 114
stress, 68
suicide, 68
symbolic thinking, 48
symbolization, 169

Tales from Ovid: Ted Hughes, 141
talk, 9–10, 80, 81
tension, 15, 16
therapists, 229
therapy, 223–5, 228
Tiresias, 142, 154, 159–60
toddler stage, 32, 47
tomboys, 13
toys, 39
transgender identity, 24–6
transsexual identity, 24–6
transition, 176

underachievement, 65
unhappiness, *see* sexual unhappiness
urbanization, 17
US Department of Labour, 53
US studies, 9, 163, 165

value systems, 7, 14
vegetarianism, 11
victimization, 63, 64
violence, 157–8
vulnerability, 57, 58

weight, 60
wholeness, 14, 16, 19
Why Men Don't Iron: Moir, A. and Moir, B., 11
womb-envy, 121
women-only organizations, 113
women's movement, 83–4, 103
Women's Therapy Centre, 113
work, 103–16, 119
working mothers, 196–200

youth, 54